George Wither

The Psalms of David

Translated into Lyrick-Verse (Part I.)

George Wither

The Psalms of David
Translated into Lyrick-Verse (Part I.)

ISBN/EAN: 9783744798037

Printed in Europe, USA, Canada, Australia, Japan

Cover: Foto ©Lupo / pixelio.de

More available books at **www.hansebooks.com**

THE

PSALMS OF DAVID

TRANSLATED INTO LYRICK-VERSE.

BY

GEORGE WITHER.

PART I.

PRINTED FOR THE SPENSER SOCIETY.

1881.

CONTENTS.

THE PSALMS of DAVID *Tranſlated* Into LYRICK-VERSE, according to the ſcope, of the ORIGINAL. And *Illuſtrated, with a Short* Argument, *and a breiſe* Prayer, *or* Meditation; *before, & after, every* Pſalme.

By GEORGE WITHER.

Imprinted *In the Neatherlands* By Cornelius Gerrits van Breughel. M. DC. XXXII.

(*Lowndes*, p. 3966; *Hazlitt*, No. 17.)

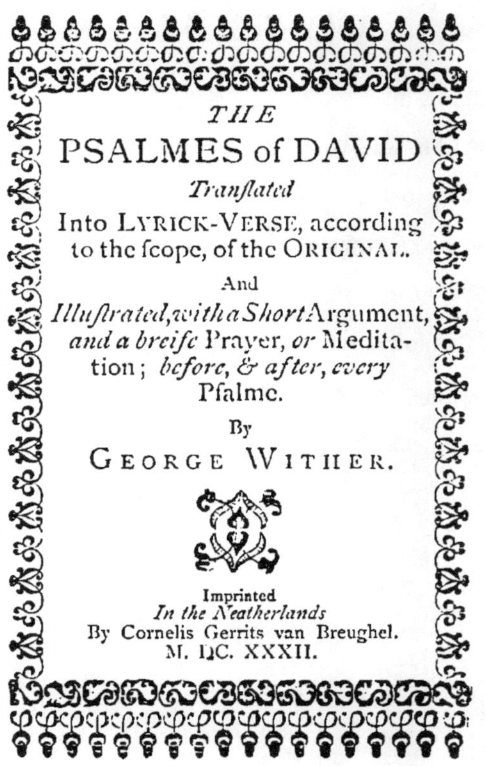

THE

PSALMES of DAVID

Tranſlated

Into LYRICK-VERSE, according to the ſcope, of the ORIGINAL.

And

Illuſtrated, with a Short Argument, *and a breiſe* Prayer, *or* Meditation; *before, & after, every* Pſalme.

By

GEORGE WITHER.

Imprinted
In the Neatherlands
By Cornelis Gerrits van Breughel.
M. DC. XXXII.

To the MAIESTIE of the most Virtuous and high-borne Princesse

ELIZABETH

PRINCESSE *of* Great Britaine, QVEENE *of* Bohemia, COVNTESSE *of the* Palatinate *of the* Rhyne &c.

Most excellent Princesse.

May faile in Vulger Titles; *But, in my valuation of your heroïcal Virtues, I cannot be deceaved. Therfor, I am the less curious in common* Attributes. *For, those* Accōplishments, *which in my repute, are your greatest glorie, are well manifest in that, which is the greatest temporall honour*; *even in those* Virtues, *which have conquered a Kingdome for you, in the harts of many millions of people*: *And procured you thousands of affectionate servants (who never sawe your Majestie) Not only in your owne Territories, and in the Dominions of your Freinds*; *But, in the Citties*

& Kingdomes of your Enimies also: And, they who are vnwilling to confesse this, to give you honour; have honored you, in discovering it by their envy.

Among those, who are in Affection, your Ma.ties *loyall servants, I am one: and, in my owne Country, great multitudes have tooke notise of a speciall* Obligation, *which I had, above many others, to honor & serve you. For, I do hereby most humbly, & thanckfully acknowledge; that, when my over-forward* Muse *first flutterd out of her neast, Shee obtained the preservation of her endangered* Libertie, *by your gratious favour: and perhaps, escaped also, thereby, that Pinioninge, which would have marred her flieng forth, for ever after.*

Which extraordinary Clemencie (in so great a Princesse, *to a person so vndeservinge) did not only much magnify your noblenes, in the opinion of others; but so chayned my hart also to the love of your princely Goodnes; that (allthough I was hitherto compelled to smother my vnprofitable thanckfulnes in my breast, because I wanted meanes to discover it according to my desires) I have ever since, bene spiritually present with your* Ma.tie *(& with God, for you,*

you, by my Prayers) in all your Afflictions, *&* Exaltations. *And, faine I would have effected ſomething, which might have witneſſed, that I had a* Hart, *though not a* Fortune, *to be ſerviceable in the beſt manner.*

My Muſe, *was the hopefulleſt meanes I had of this ambition; & by her, I, awhile promiſed myſelf, ſome healp. But (after I came to better vnderſtanding) I preceaved, her over-early* Flights *into the world, had (in her prime growth) ſo ſpent thoſe tymes of opportunity whereby she should have enabled her ſelf, for brave Attempts; that shee could never be ſtrong enough, to make wing halfe ſo high as my* Deſires.

Yet, by your Ma.ties *royall* Father, *of bleſsed Memorie (who, a litle befor his death, was pleaſed to honour mee with his gratious reſpect) I was commanded to perfect a* Tranſlation *of the* Pſalmes, *which he vnderſtood I had begunn; & by his encouragment, I finished the ſame about the tyme of his* Tranſlation *to a better Kingdome. Wherein, God ſoe enabled mee, that many have well approoved thereof; and, I, latelie reſolving to make it publike (wanting other Teſtimonie of my thanckfulnes (conceived it would be no dishonour to your* Ma.tie *if before the ſame, I conveyed your beloved* Name *to that Nation, who ſo dearlie affect you.*

But, when I had well conſidered thereon I thought it would be a very pertinent complement, ſo to doe. For, they were Afflictions *or* Deliverances *from* Afflictions, *which were occaſions of every* Pſalme: *Therfore, none but they who have bene afflicted, cann relish the ſweetnes, or vnderſtand, the depth of theſe* Raptures ; *And therfore alſo, they who come nearest in their Chriſtian ſuffrings to thoſe whome they perſonated, shall beſt feel, & vnderſtand their meaning. In which (if I be not more a ſtranger to your* Highneſſe, *then I thinck I am) you have bene honored aboue all the kings & princes of the world: &, in my opinion you have had more occaſion to make perſonall Application of theſe* Hymnes *vnto your ſelfe, then any of them.*

And, there is no shame (moſt excellent Princeſſe) *in the* Croſſe *of* Chriſt. *For, the higheſt honor cōſiſteth not in wearing a* crown; *but, in a Crowne that hath many* Thornes *in it ; & the more* Thornes *the more honorable. Though the ſonns of men, do skoffingly turne this* glory into shame, & ſeek after Vani-
ties ;

ties; *yet, they who shall sitt nearest unto* Christ Iesus *in his* Kingdome, *must drinck deepest of his* Cupp: *And, your* Highnes *hath (in my Observation) more largly, pledged him, then many other. For, in all these* Hymns (*all which, are prophecies of such things as pertaine to* Christ, *& his* Mysticall body) *there are fewe passages, communicable to his* Members, *but (even in my owne knowledge) your* Ma. *may apply them unto your self, as a dependant on him. And, God let mee not live, if I do not thinck, that more honours you, then to be* Empresse *of the world.*

And, because it is the greatest honour to come so near, both to the Type *& the* Prototype, *of our suffrings, as your* Ma. *hath done, &,* to beare so many marks of the Lord Iesus. *Because also, some skoffing* Ismaelites *have mentioned these* Glories *to your* Dishonour; *I wil to your Praise, repeat some few, out of those many which are appliable to your* Ma. *&, they shal be such, that most will confesse, they are the very same Afflictions, whereof (as a type of* Christ) *king* David *complained.*

He, was exalted by *God*; &, yet, cast downe. He was annonited *king*, & yet enioyed not the *Kingdome*. He was driven from his owne possessions, & compelled to soiourne in a forraigne Land. *Kings* & *Rulers,* were confederated against him. He, was remooved from his *Kindred*; & his *Acquaintance* were sett far off. His enimies were powrefull, & too strong for him. His adversaries were multiplied: *Yea,* they insulted over his calamities; *& many judged his cause so bad, that they pronounced him* forsaken of God. The *proud,* forged lies against him. False witnesses layd things to his Charge which he knew not. *Princes,* sate & spake against him. *The* mighty, persecuted him without a Cause. They had almost consumed him vpon earth. They waited to destroy him. The *Bands* of the wicked robbed him. They spake of peace vnto him when they purposd warr. Trouble, & anguish, tooke holde vpon him: &, he was persecuted, when God had smitten him. The Vngodly reioiced in his Adversity; & cryed *There, there, so wee would have it.* He was reproched of his Neighbours. He was the scorne of fooles. The Dranckerds made songs of him. They said he was cast downe, & should never rise againe: *And many*

many other suchlike passages, there are, which my memory confusedly retaines. In all which, (together with your Roiall Consort,) *you have beene a partaker, in such measure, as Christians of inferior* Degree, *cannot communicate in the like Suffrings, in the same sense.*

Nor are these things, only, Appliable vnto your Highnesse *in an extraordinary manner; But, all those* consolations, Hopes, Deliverances, *promises of* Mercye, Favours *enioyed, Resolutions of* Praise, & Thanksgiving, *with others of this nature, throughout the* Psalms; *are in a singuler manner, pertinēt also to you : & (no doubt) so applied, by your* Ma: *in your owne hart, as occasion is offred.*

Which, when I had considered (for, your Highnes, *as a glorious Member of* Christ Iesus, *is often in my serious & retired thoughts) And, I, remembring also, that, long since, I vowed a Pilgrimage to your* Ma.tie *(so soone as I could be furnished with some* Presēt) *I thought this my endevour would not be impertinētly presented: therefore, I thus prepared the same; &, am now come, to accomplish my* Vowe, *Which I humbly desire, may be acceptable to your* Matie *I doubt not, but you often peruse this* Booke *in other* Translations. *Yet, these* Meditations,

A 5 *may,*

may, perhaps, occaſion (either now, or hereafter) ſome vſe or application of them, to your extraordinary comfort. Howſoever; It is, in my owne eſteeme, the beſt Iewel, *that I have: and, if it were anſwerable to my humble Affections, it would be the richeſt that ever was preſented to a* Princeſſe.

But, leſt my over-long Epiſtle *become tedious, I will* thinck, *by my ſelfe, what, I have more to* Say; *craving pardon for thus preſuminge, vpon my hopes of your Acceptation; and, for my conceiving it poſſible, that (after ſo many yeares) the memory of his* Name *should be retained, with your* Highneſſe; *who hath, in all this time, produced vnto your veiwe, no Teſtimony that he retaines any Memoriall of the benifites, which he long agoe receaved, by your favour I diſtruſt not, the obtaining of that which I deſire; for, my hart tells mee I am thanckfull; Some live, who have heard mee profeſſe it; God, is witneſſe of it, every time I come vnto him for my owne Soul; And I am, in all that I am.*

Your MAIESTIES

Moſt humble

and

Long-profeſſed ſervant

GEORGE WITHER.

A Preface to the Reader.

T*His* Tranſlation, *long ſince, finished in blurred papers (and often called for) I, lately, made legible to others: & it had my leave, to ſeek a publike* Paſſe *into the world: which if it merrit to obtaine; Be the fault theirs who shall oppoſe it. I waited long, to ſee a more exact* performance: *But, none appearing, anſwerable to the dignitie of our* Engliſh-Muſes, *I have ſent forth my* Eſſay, *to provoke others, to diſcover their endeavours, on this* ſubject; *that, choice being had, the beſt might receive the beſt Approbation.*

I have had more care, to ſuite the Capacitie of the Vulger, *then to obſerve thoſe* Critiſciſmes *which arride the* Learned: *yet, I hope, with ſo much deſcretion, that the beſt* Iudgments *shall have no cauſe to deſpiſe it. For, though the Language be plaine, it is ſignificant; & ſuch a Dialect as is likely to continue vnchanged, when fantaſticall expreſſions will growe as vnfashionable as our clothes. It is alſo breifer, by above a fourth Part, then the* Tranſlations *which I have yet ſeene, in any language of* Europe*: and preſerves, likewiſe, the words of the* Proſe; *the fulnes of the* Sence, *& the relish of the* Scripture phraſe, *as well as any of them. VVhich, conſidering how much other vulger Tongues have ignorantly bene preferred before ours, (how difficultly the* Hebrewiſmes *are contracted; how much the often* Tranſition *from one* Matter, *& from one* Perſon *to another, interrupts breiſe knitting of things together; & how much the frequent* Rimes, *& other things conſiderable in* Lyrick Tranſlations, *interrupt ſuch Breiſnes) is a great honour to our* Language: *Eſpecially, ſeeing my Brevitie, hath made no Pſalme obſcurer; But rather, ſo eaſie to be vnderſtood, that ſome* Readers *have confeſſed, it hath bene inſteed of a* Comment *vnto them, in ſundry hard places.*

If

If you expect such elegant-seeming Paraphrases, *as are composed by those, who selecting easy and Passionate* Psalmes, *have trimmed them vp with Rhetoricall Illustrations, (sutable to their fancies, & the changable garbe of Affected* Language) *I shall deceave your expectation: For, I have purposely avoyded those Descants, & confined my self to the grave, & simple* Language *of the* Text: *And I was thereby the better kept from wandring after mine owne sense, as in their* Circumlocutions *they have done. Beside; their* Versions *are fitted rather to be* Read, *then* Sung: *which giveth a greater Libertie to the* Translator. *For, though it be most gracefull in a reading*-Poeme, *when the Period is cast, sometime into one parte of the* Line *or* Stanza, *and sometime into another: Yet, in a Lyrick Composition, where the same* Staff *is often reiterated to one* Tune; *the* Periods, *and words of the same* Quantity, *must be alwaies observed in the same Places. For, if there be not allwaies a decent pawse in the Matter, when the Tune is ended; or, if in the singing, the naturall quantity of the word be adulterated; or, if wee be not carefull, that a* full-point *fall not, where the Tune is in the height of a continueng straine; It will sound verie absurdly to a indítious eare: as may appear, by offring to sing some of those Composures, which are plausible in Reading.*

I have vsed some, varietie of Verse; Because. Prayers, Praises, Lamentations, Tryumphs, *and subiects which are* Pastoral, Heroical, Elegiacall, *and* mixt *(all which are found in the* Psalmes) *are not properly exprest in one sort of* Measure. *Yet, respecting thē who cannot attaine to many* Tunes, *I confined my selfe to such kinds of Verse as I found in the old* Psalmebooke; *fitting them in such manner, that every* Psalme *in this* Booke, *may sung to some* Tune *formerly in vse, either in the single, or in one of the double* Translations.

And

And, becauſe ſome will thinck to examine my Verſion *by the Proſe* Tranſlations, *I doe here inform them; that the* Language *of the* Muſes, *in which the* Pſalmes *were Originally written, is not ſo properly expreſt in the proſe dialect as in verſe: &, that there is a poeticall emphaſis, in many places, which requires ſuch an alteration in the* Grammaticall *expreſsiō, as will ſeeme to make ſome difference in the iudgment of the Common Reader; whereas, it giveth beſt life to the* Author's *intention; & makes that perſpicuous, which was made obſcure, by thoſe meer* Grammaticall Interpreters, *who were not acquainted with the proprieties, & Liberties, of this kinde of writing.*

I do likewiſe inform them, that I have not alwaies vſed the Metaphor *which is in the* Original; *but, otherwhile (tendring the vulger capacity) do expreſſe it, by what it ſignifies. For, the* Hebrewiſmes, *being in ſome places obſcure (as where the* Tongue *is interpreted,* Glorie; *and in many other ſuchlike perticulers) I do vſe, expreſſions beſt agreeable with our* Engliſh *Dialect, & the vulger Capacity.*

Moreover, when the Repetition of the ſame word *or* Clauſe; *Or when two or three* Synonama's *togither in one ſentence as* (Heare, give ear, attend) *or, where either a* Periphraſis, *or a* tranſpoſition *of ſome words, ſeemes not ſoe gracefull in* Engliſh, *as in the* Hebrewe; *nor ſo powrfully to expreſſe the meaning of the* Holy-Gheſt, *by the ſame* Idioms *of ſpeach: I have not ſuperſtitiouſly tied my ſelfe to the* Hebrewe *phraſe, nor to any ſtrict Order, or number of words (except ſome* Myſtery *ſeemed thereby touched vpon) but, vſing rather brevitie where* Circumlocution *appeared needles, & affecting the Dialect moſt proper to our owne* Tongue; *I labored to deliver the meaning of the* Originall Text, *as powrefully, as plainly, & as breefly, as I could,*

For

For that Cause, I have not everie where observed the same Tense; *But, vsed the* pretertense, *the* Present-tense, *& the* Future-tense, *indifferently, one for the other, in some Actions attributed to God. For, most things, which God is said in this booke, to* have done *for his people, or against his enimies*; *he* now doth, & will doe hereafter. *That, also, which he* will doe, *he may be said to* do now, *& to* have done heretofore; *because, all time is* present *with God. Nevertheles, I have herein taken such care; That I confounded not* Historie & Prophecie; *But, in those places, have religiously observed the proper* Tenses; *& wheresoever els, I found it material, so to do.*

And, whereas, I perceaved that this particle FOR, is not alwayes, a Causual; *Nor this particle BUT, an* exceptive, *in every place*; *But (as YEA, NAY, & other such like words in our* English*) sometime rather inserted as* supplements, *only, becomming the Dialect, (or meerly customary) without any material significancy, according to their ordinary vse; And, finding that those* Particles, *in the* English, *did in some places, either obscure the sense, or make lesse powrefull the expression thereof, by interrupting a natural connextion of the sentenses; I have there, waved or quallyfied, the vse of those words.*

For like Reasons, I have in some places, kept the Person *vnchanged, throughout the* Psalme, *which is sometime varyed in the* Hebrewe *(as in the* 13 & 104 *Psalmes) But, with such heed, that where any worke (according to the* Schoole *distinction* Ad intra, *or* ad Extra*) seemes more proper to one distinct* Persō *of the* Trinity, *thē to the other (or where els it is Materiall) I have retained the* Person *according to the* Originall.

And, in regard some abuse the propheticall Imprecations, *as if* David *had given exemplary warrant of Cur-*

ſing their enimies, I have (to prevent that prophanation) otherwhile expreſſed that by the Future tenſe, *which many do trāſlate by the* imparative moode; *whereby, thoſe paſſages, the more planely appear, prophetically intended. In all which, let what I have done, be duely weighed, (not rashlie condemned) by thoſe who shall by ſome proſe* Tranſlations, *examine my* Paraphraſe. *For, I hope I have preſerved the lawful freedomes of an* Interpreter, *in all theſe things: Seeing, I have not therein followed my owne opinion only; but the warrāt of beſt* Hebrew Grammarians, *the Authoritie of the* Septuagint, *&* Chaldeā paraphraſe, *the example of the auntient & of the beſt moderne proſe* Trāſlators, *togither with the generall practiſe & allowance, of all orthodoxe* Expoſitors.

Before every Pſalme *I prefixe a ſhort* Preface, *partly declaring the* Scope *&* vſe *thereof; not thereby limiting either their* Scope *or* vſe. *For, every* Pſalme *is divers waies vſefull, according to the ſeverall parts it hath; or according to the many Ages, Eſtates, & neceſsities of the* Church; *or her particuler members. But, that, which I have intended in my breef Prefaces, & in thoſe Meditations after the* Pſalmes; *is, to shew the vnlearned, how to make ſome good* vſes, *of thoſe many, to which they ſerve.*

Much more might be ſaid as conſiderable (if it would not make this Preface overlarge) for, ſo it fares with ſome of us, that when wee have taken much paines to doe well, wee muſt take as much more to prevent miſconſtructions; & thinck our double paines, well rewarded, if at laſt, wee may eſcape without a miſcheef. But (how ever I shall be cenſured) I cann be well pleaſed when I have recollected my ſelfe: &, though I ſeeke to avoide Rubbs *that are caſt into my way; Yet, I can skip over them, or contemn them, if I find it more troubleſome, then profitable, to remove them.*

Though others may performe this, more exactly; yet,

Goodmen

A Preface to the Reader.

Goodmen will confesse, I have bene honestly employed herein, & attempted an honorable work. *But, if I have soe endeavoured; That it manifestly appeareth to be better, then, what the partialitie of this Age will accept, (and that* Mumpsimus, *must still be preferred before* Sumpsimus*) Then, this* Worke, *shall become the* Iudge *of those partiall Iudges; And, to their disgrace, gaine esteeme, hereafter, in despight of their envy.*

I regard the Censorious approbation of none, but such, as are (in their vnderstanding, at least) both Divines *and* Poets: *For, they, only, are competent Iudges, who knowe how much the* Phrases *or* Mysteries *confine the* Translator; *what* Proprieties *are to be observed in both* Languages; *& what Liberties, & restraints, belong to a* Lyrick-poem.

And, ———— but, I will now say no more save this; If I have pleased my Readers, *I am glad: if not; Yet, I am glad, I have honestly endeavored it. And, (being assured my labour shal not all be lost) I will sing, & be Merry, by my* selfe, *in the Vse of this* Translation, *vntill others please to sing it with mee; or, vntill a more exact* Version, *shall be produced, & allowed.*

Fare well.

THE

The Psalmes of David.

Psalme. I.

It shewes wherein Happines *consisteth ; Illustrates the present and future estate both of the* Iust *&* vniust *; and comforts the* Righteous *both by declaring Gods approbation of their* Way. It may be sung for an incoragment in the right Path. &c.

THe man is blest, who neither straies,
Where Godles counsellers haue gone,
Nor standeth in the Sinners waies,
Nor sitteth on the Scorners throne.
For, in Gods Lawe his pleasures be ;
Theron, he day & night bestowes.
And, therfore shal be like a tree
Which near vnto the riuer growes.
2. His fruites, in season, he doth give,
Green leaues he shal for euer wear :
All things he takes in hand shall thrive
But, thus the Sinner doth not fare.
For, Wicked men with e'vry winde,
Like dust or chaff, are blown aside,
And therfor shall no standing finde,
When they their Judgment must abide,
3. Nor place, nor fellowship haue they,
Among those men that are vpright :
For, God approoves the Just-mans way
But, Sinners path-waies perish quite.

Grant oh mercifull God, that shunning all the paths *&* seats *of impietie, we may exercize & rest our selves in the true love & practise of thy* Law, *& that (being planted in thy* Church, *& refreshed by the living waters of thy* Word) *we may florish to our comfort & in due time, so*
B *fru-*

fructifie to thy glorie, that we may be numbred among thine Elect; *be iuſtified in the general* judgment; *& become partakers of eternal bleſſednes in the kingdome of heaven, through* Iesus Chriſt *our lord*, Amen.

Another of the ſame.

BLeſt is he, who neither ſtraies
Where the Godles man miſguideth,
Neither ſtands in ſinners waies,
Nor in Scorners chair abideth:
But, in Gods pure Lawe delights,
Thereon muzing, daies & nights.
2 Like a tree ſett near the ſprings,
He doth alway freshlie floriſh,
Still, his fruits he timely brings,
And his leaf shall neuer periſh:
Ev'rie thing shall proſper to,
Which he vndertakes to do.
3 Thus, the wicked shall not fare,
But, be like ſuch duſtie matter,
As the whirl-winde here & there,
On the ſpacious earth doth ſcatter:
Nor shall they withſtand their doomes,
When the day of Judgment comes.
4 Neither haue they place, or ſtay,
In the righteous congregation:
For, God knowes the Juſt-mans waie,
With a gratious approbation:
But, thoſe paths that Sinners tread,
To aſſured ruine lead.

Pſa. 2.

It is a prophecie *of* Chriſt *& his kingdom, Act. 4. declaring the vaine furie of his* Oppoſers, *the wrath of God againſt them; his eternall* Decree *concerning that* King; *& the powre & extent of his kingdom. &c. it* *ex-*

exhorts Kings, & ſubiects alſo, to fear and ſerue him. It may be ſung to encreaſe Faith amid the Churches perſecutions *&c.*

WHat mooves the Gentiles to repine?
  What makes the people foolish growe,
That Earthlie Kings do thus combine,
  And Rulers meet in Counſell ſo?
The Lord, & his beloved *Chriſt*,
Rebelliouſly they diſobay:
His powre (ſay theſe) let vs reſiſt
  And break, & caſt their cords away.
2 But, God who ſitts in heav'n aboue,
Their foolish purpoſe will deride:
His anger shall their torment proue,
  And, them, in wrath he then shall chide,
Ev'n I' *(ſaith God)* my King did place
Vpon my holy *Syon* hill.
And, by the *Lord*, what vttred was
  To me (ſaith *Chriſt*) now ſing I will.
3 Thou art my Sonn begot by me
This day; and (if thou make demande)
The gentiles I will give to thee,
  And make thee King of e'vry land.
An yron ſcepter thou shalt ſway,
And (if thy Lore they followe not)
Thou shalt compel them to obay
  Or break them like an earthen pott.
4 Then Kings be wiſe; & Rulers lerne
To ſerue the Lord, with awfull joy:
Yea, kiſſe the *Sonn*, leſt wroth he turne
  And ouerthrow you in your way.
For, when his wrath inflamed growes,
(Though but a little moou'd he ſeem)
Then bleſt are all who shall repoſe

Their constant hopes, & faith in him.

, *Blessed* Sonn of God, *begotten before all time (and by thy* Father, *appointed to be* King *over the whole world) let thy* Kingdom *come, & all the oppositions of thy adversaries be turned to thy glorie, let thy grace enable vs to pluck downe that* Antichrist, *which the* world, *the* flesh *or the* Devil *shal seek to set vp against thee in the* Tēple *of our harts; that wee yealding due obedience to thee & thy commands, may escape thy burning indignation, sincerely embrace* thy Gospell, *& with awful ioy persevere in the way leading to that felicity which is prepared for those who put their trust in thee. Amen.*

Another of the same.

SUch uproars mad, why do the Gentiles make?
What follies do the people doate upon?
Earths Kings conspire, & Rulers counsel take,
Against the *Lord*, & his *Anointed-one.*
Oh come! & let us break their bands (they say)
Come, let vs cast from vs, their cords away.
2 But God in heav'n deriding their designe
Shall (vexing them) his minde in wrath declare:
Who e're (saies he) repines this King of mine
On *Syon* sitts; 'twas I that plac'd him there.
And, what the Lord himself, to me hath told,
(Concerning him) I purpose to vnfold.
3 Thou art my sonn, this day begot I thee;
Demand therfore (he said) & I will giue
The Gentiles, thine inheritance to be;
And rule of all the world thou shalt receiue.
An iron mace, thou shalt vpon them lay;
And break them like a sherd of potters clay.
4 Therfore yee Kings & Rulers be more wise:
Come serve the *Lord* your God, with awfull ioy.

And

And kisse the *Sonn* ; lest, if his wrath arise,
You be destroid, & perish from the way.
For, when inflam'd his burning anger growes,
Right blest are all who trust in him repose.

Psa. 3.

A psalm of David when he fled from Absolom his Son. *It mystically Phrophecied the multitude of* Christs *foes; their bitter censures; the great love of God; the effects of* Prayer ; Christ *his* Death; & Resurrection ; *the confusion of his* Adversaries, *& the safety of his* Elect. *&c.* It is vsefull to strengthen faith in our temptations *&c.*

MY foes, how many Lord are they !
  What swarmes of them there be !
And of my soul, how many say,
  In God no part hath he !
Yet thou art, Lord, my praise, my gard ;
  Thou didst my head vprear :
And from thy holy-hill, hast heard,
  What my entreaties were.
2 I lay & slept, & safe arose ;
  Because thou brought'st me ayd :
And though tenn thousands me enclose,
  I will not be afraid.
Rise, Lord my God ; & from all foes
  Me safe, now also, make :
Their Jaw-bone smite, & let thy blows
  The teeth of Sinners breake.
3 For, saving health, alone to thee,
  To thee, oh Lord, pertaines :
And whosoe're thy people be,
  Thy peace on them remaines.

Sweet Iesu *who being caustesly compassed about with all those innumerable enmities & persecutions which wee de-*

serued, didst neverthelcs (trusting in the powre of thy God head) *ly down without fear, sleeping (as it were) in the midst of them by a voluntary* Death, *& wake againe the* third day, *by the same powre, to the confusion of thy foes: Grant we pray thee, that the multitude of our corporall & spirituall enimies never make vs despaire of thy mercy; but that in all troubles & temptations, we reioicing & trusting in thy love, may be kept harmles; & confesse that our* salvation, *is by thee only, who livest and raignest world without end.* Amen.

Psa. 4.

To the cheese musician on Neginoth a Psalm of David. *It vpraides those who deride the* Truth, *& exhorts to* faith *&* Repentance. *The common wish of* world-lings, *& the desire also of a* faithful-soul, *is here expressed.* It serves to confirme vs against the scornes of Atheists, & meer carnal men. *&c.*

OH God my Righteousnes, give ear ;
  Enlargd I was by thee :
My humble suite, now also, heare,
  And pitty take on me.
Vaine Sonns of men, how long will yee
  My glorie thus abuse ?
Though lies you seek, assured be
  That God the just will chuse.
2 Yea God will hear me when I cry,
  Fear therfore to offend ;
And, on your bedd serch privatly
  Your thinckings, & amend.
Make Righteousnes your sacrifize,
  On God, assurance place.
For worldly Goods, the world-ling cries,
  But grant me, Lord, thy grace.

3 For,

3 For, thou my hart haſt joyed more
Then corne & wine's encreaſe :
Thou mak'ſt me ſafe, & I, therefore,
In thee will ſleep in peace.

Oh thou fountaine *of all righteouſnes, & free* juſtifier *of thine* Elect, *ſeeing, by thy* common grace *we are ſome-what enlarged from our natural bondage; grant a full deliverance from all our corruptions, by thy ſpeciall favour. Let neither frailties, diſcouragments, nor alurements, incline vs to* vanitie: *But, ſo cauſe vs to conſider whome thou* chuſeſt, *that with a filial fear we may refrain from ſinn ; & having our inward man renewed, as well as our outward actions reformed, we may offer the true* ſacrifize *of* righteouſnes, *Encourage vs alſo through, aſſurance of thy favour, that contemning the deſire of* world-lings, *& reioicing more in thy gratious aſpect, then in al temporal advantages, we may ly downe to ſleep our laſt* ſleep *without horror ; & reſt in the firme hope of a glorious Reſurrection.* Amen.

Pſa. *5*.

To the cheef muſician on Neginoth a Pſalm of David. *It beſeecheth audience of God, for ſundry reſpects; & prayeth that he would ſubvert his* Adverſaries, *& be mercifull to his* Church. It may be vſefull when we are oppreſſed by the enimies of Chriſt, for his Cauſe *&c*.

LOrd, weigh my thoughts, my words attend,
My King, my God, encline thine ear :
My ſuites I will to thee commend,
And thou my voice betime shalt hear.
I will, oh Lord, betimes ariſe,
And pray, & wait for thy ſupplies.
2 For, thou in ſinn haſt no delight,

No evills, in thy dwellings be;
The foole abides not in thy sight,
The wicked are abhord of thee.
  Thou root'st out all who falsehoods prate,
  And bloud, & guile, in man, dost hate.
3 But, I, in thy abounding grace,
Thy house will visite in thy fear,
And worship in thy holy-place;
Oh teach me, Lord, thy Justice there:
  Unto my vewe, thy way disclose,
  Because of them, that are my foes.
4 Their words & thoughts are false & naught:
Their throte is like a gaping graue:
Therfore, oh God, let them be caught
And fall by what they plotted haue,
  Yea, seeing they thy foes haue binn,
  Expose them to their swarmes of sinn.
5 But, chear vp those who trust in thee,
That such as well thy name affect,
May, still, therin triumphant be,
And joy that thou dost them protect.
  For Lord, the just thou shalt reward;
  And, sheild-like, make thy grace their gard.

Oh, soveraigne Lord God, *make vs both timely & diligent seekers of thy grace. Let the due consideration of thy* perfections, *& of our natural* unworthines *cause vs humbly to attend on thee; vnfainedly frequenting thy* Congregation; *& there, truly serving thee according to thine owne* ordinance. *Instruct vs fully in thy* way, *lest our spirituall adversaries drawe vs into error: Let our experience of their malice & subtility, keep vs the more cautious: Let them be taken in their owne* snares *to thy glorie, & let the* faithfull *alwaies reioice in thy protection, through* Iesus Christ, *our* Lord. Amen.

Pſa. 6.

To the cheef muſitian on Neginoth vpon Sheminith a Pſalm of David. *It bewailes the miſeries & corruptions of the humane nature, & with penetential expreſsions emplores Gods mercy &c.* It may be ſung when oppreſſed by our ſinns & infirmities, we haue invoked God, & received comforts:

LOrd, in thy rage correct me not;
To me, oh! do not roughly ſpeake,
Nor chide me when thy wrath is hott
But, pitty me, for I am weake.
Oh Lord, vouchſafe to cure my paines;
For, through my bones, the torments goe:
My hart is vext, & much complaines,
Good God! how long shal this be ſoe?
2 Returne, & help my ſoul oh Lord;
Mee, let thy meer compaſſion ſaue:
For, who in death shall thee record,
Or give thee praiſes in the grave?
With groanes I tire; & in the nights
My bedd in flouds of teares doth ſwim;
Through in-ward greefs, & foes deſpights,
Mine eies decay, my ſight growes dimm,
3 But, Sinners, now depart fro mee:
God heares my ſuite, my plaint, my crie;
Which let my foes with blushing ſee,
And vext, & greeu'd, my preſence fly.

Moſt awfull God, *ſpeake favourably to vs, in this day of thy offered* grace, *leſt in the day of thy wrathfull* indignation *we be caſt into hell fire. Behold our* frailties, *our* torments, *& our horrible* diſtempers: *Obſerve into how great perills our deſperation may caſt vs, & have mercy (oh lord) have mercy vpon us miſerable offenders. Purify* *our poluted* flesh ; *enlighten our bleared* eyes ; *cure our wounded* harts ; *chear our afflicted* fpirits ; *revive our fainting* foules, *& chafe away all our malitious* accufers ; *that we (efcaping the* dungeon *in which thy praife is forgotten) may magnify thy mercies in the* land of the living ; *to the vexation of malignant fpirits, & to the honor of thy* name, *for euer & euer.* Amen.

Pfa. 7.

Shiggaijon of David which he fung to the Lord, concerninge the words of Chush the Benjamite. *It is the Complaint of an* innocent, *vniuftly accufed, & referring himfelf to be iudged according to his innocency.* It may be vfed, when the true Church or any members thereof, are flandered by their foes &c.

LOrd God, on thee I do depend,
  Me, from the fpoiler fave :
Left Lion-like my foule he rend
  When I no helper have.
For, if oh Lord my God, in this,
  My hands found guiltie be ;
If I rewarded him amiffe
  That was at peace with me.
2 Nay, I to him did mercy shewe
  Who fought my caufeles blame ;
Els, let my foe my foule purfue
  And ouertake the fame.
Yea, let him tread (when down I fall)
  My life into the clay ;
And, in a duft-heap, there-withall.
  Mine honor let him lay.
3 Oh Lord ! thy felfe, in wrath advance,
  For, wroth my fpoilers be :
According to thine ordinance,

Arife

Ariſe, & judge thou me.
That multitudes to thee may come,
(For their ſakes) great appear:
Yea judge them Lord, & giue me doome
As iuſt, ag I am clear.
4 Confounde the ſinners wickednes;
But, ſtill, the juſt maintaine:
For, thou (oh God of righteouſnes)
Canſt ſerch both Hart & Reine.
God is my sheild, & he protects
The Godly from decay.
His doomes are juſt, & he corrects
The wicked ev'ry day,
5 Except they turne, his blade he whetts,
A bowe, ſtill bent, he hath:
He, shafts for perſecutors getts,
And inſtruments of death.
For, lo; with miſcheeues being bigg,
They firſt conceive a ſinn;
Next, bring forth lies; then pitt-falls digg,
Where, they themſelues fal in.
6 Thus, on their heads, their miſcheeus all
Do iuſtly tumble downe;
And wicked mens deviſes fall
On their devizers crowne.
For which, the juſtice of the Lord,
I'le ſtrive to glorify;
And, will, in ſongs of praiſe, record
The name of God, moſt high.

Eternal God, *defend us from ſlanderous accuſations, & from that roaring* Lion *who is alway ready to devour vs: And, though our accuſers are often ſo malitious, that in reſpect of them we may have ſome appearance of innocency; yet, cauſe vs ſo to acknowledg our ſelves guiltie in thy ſight, that*

that we may be Iustifed by the righteousnes, *which we have by imputation from thy dear* sonn ; *for, we have no* Innocency *but his* ; *No* Saviour *but he* ; *nor dare we (in our greatest puritie) appeare any where, but at the* Throne *of thy* mercy, *which let us, who seek the same, alwaies obtain; & let the severitie of thy iustice, fall only on our Adversaries who despise thy grace; that both in* mercy *&* iustice, *thou maist be magnifyed for ever & ever.* Amen.

Psa. 8.

To the cheef Musitian vpon Gittith a Psalm of David. *It sings the glory, powre, and dominion of* Christ ; *& magnifies the love of God in the admirable exaltation of the humane nature, by the incarnation of his Sonn &c.* It may be vsed, to praise God for the great priveledges which we haue receaved thereby.

HOw famous, Lord, our God, appears
Throughout, the world, thy glorious Name?
Above the height of all the Sphears,
Thou spreadst the splendor of thy fame.
The mouths of babes, thy powr to show ;
And sucklings tongues, thou didst ordaine :
To stopp the mouth of ev'ry foe ;
And, their avengings to restraine.
2 When on the heav'ns I fixe mine eye,
And moone & starrs (thy creatures) heed ;
Why careth God for man (think I)
Or why regardeth he his seed !
He was below thine Angells plac'd,
And, higher, now advanc'd is he :
To rule thy works, him raisd thou hast,
And, at his feet, all creatures be.
3 O're heards & flocks, in stall & folde,
O're cattell which at randome goe,

The

The ſov'raigne place he now doth holde
And, over foules & fishes, to.
Yea, rule throughout the ſea, he bears,
And over all within the ſame ;
How famous, Lord our God, appears
Throughout the world, thy glorious Name !

Moſt glorious Lord God, *thou ſo lovedſt the humane nature, that it pleaſed thee to be made man ; by the mouths of babes & ſucklings magnifienge thy great powre ; & by humbling (as it were) of the* Deitie *for a tyme, to exalt the* Manhood *for euer. For this thy vnexpreſsible humiliation, & incomprehenſible favour, we ſubmiſsively proſtrat our ſoules, and bend the knees of our bodyes to the honor of thy* Name ; *beſeeching thee, that as all other creatures are obediently ſubiected to thy* Sonns *Dominion, ſo wee may truly ſubmit our wills to his good pleaſure ; & in* Act, word & thought, *be thanckful for our many priveledges, by his bleſſed* Incarnation, Reſurrection, & Aſcention, *now & for euer,* Amen.

Pſa. 9.

To the cheef Muſitian vpon Muth-labben a pſalm of David. *Herein, the faithfull praiſe God, for many good cauſes, & exhort others to do the ſame.* It may be vſed, to praiſe the Lord, for his manyfold mercies vouchſafed to his Church ; &, for his juſt judgments on their foes. &c.

NOw, Lord, with all my hart, & voice,
Thy wondrous works I,le magnify :
Of thee, I'le ſing ; Of thee, reioice ;
And praiſe thy name (oh God moſt high)
For, thou didſt put my foes to flight ;
They fell, & fled out of thy ſight.
2 My lawfull cauſe thou doſt vpholde ;

Thou

Thou ſit'ſt enthron'd, thou judgeſt right;
The Gentiles, are by thee contrould;
The wicked, thou deſtroieſt quite:
  And, thou their names away doſt blot,
  For evermore, to be forgot.
3 Thy ſlaughters, now, thou cruel Foe,
Are to an end, for ever, brought;
Thoſe Townes which thou did'ſt overthrowe,
Are nameles now, & out of thought:
  But, God ſtill ſitteth on his throne,
  Preparing judgment thervpon.
4 The world, he shall vprightly doome;
And, juſtly judge the nations all.
The pore, when times of trouble come,
He gardeth, like a caſtle wall.
  And, they who ſeek & know his name,
  Are ſafe, by truſting in the ſame.
5 To God, therfore, in *Syon* ſing;
To nations all, make known his deeds:
For, when to light, he blood will bring,
He poremens wrongs, & criengs, heeds.
  Now alſo, Lord, thy grace I crave:
  Oh! mark what woes, & foes I have.
6 Thou ſav'ſt me from the gates of hell
That I thy praiſe, with chearfull voice,
  To *Syon's* daughters may reveal,
And in thy ſaving-health rejoice.
  The Gentiles, had a pitt-fall wrought;
  But, they themſelves therin were caught.
7 Their Nets haue their owne feet en-ſnar'de,
And, God is by his iudgments knowne;
The Sinners hands have trapps preparde,
Whereby themſelves were ouerthrowne. Shiggaijon. Selah.
  Thus, downe to hell the wicked goe,

As

As, all who feare not God shall doe.
8 There is a time to minde the pore,
Their hope shall not, for ever, faile ;
To judge the Gentiles Lord, therfore,
Arise, and let no man prevaile.
The Nations fright, vntill they see,
That they are men as others be. *Selah.*

WVe haue often experience, oh God, *that by thy favour all oppressions, insultings, & secret cruelties, shall come to an end; and that thy* Mercies, *& thy* Justice, *shall everlastingly continue, both for the savegard of thy servants, & to reward the wicked, according to their deserts. Let this experience, therfor, be alwaies remembred when we are persecuted or afflicted, & let our confidence be ever so fixed vpon thee, that we may neither be discouraged in* Adversitie, *nor forgetfull in* prosperitie, *to magnifie thy mercies ; but, be readie vpon all occasions, to glorifie thee, both for the suppression of our foes, & for all our other deliverances, through* Iesus Christ *our Lord. Amen.*

Psa. 10.

The Pride, Crueltie, Prophanesse, & fraude of Antichrist, Atheists, & Hipocrites *is described: God is invoked to redresse it: his Dominion acknowledged, & his mercifull regard of the afflicted is, confessed.* It may be vsed, when we are oppressed by temporall or Spirituall Oppressors.

THy face, oh Lord, why dost thou hide,
And stand aloofe, so farr?
Lo, Sinners, meerely out of pride,
The Spoile of poremen are.
Insnare them, by their owne devise,
For, of their Lust they boast
And praise those Freindes to Avarice,

Who-

VVhome God abborreth most.
2 Their scornefull eies regard not thee,
Their hartes do thee denay.
Too high for them thy judgments be ;
Stil greeuous is their way.
They snuff, & sleight their greatest Foes,
And (come what mischeeves will)
Within their hartes, they doe suppose,
That they shal prosper still.
3 Their mouthes, with cursings overflowe ;
Their tongues, lie, swear, & vaunt :
The pore to catch & overthrowe,
Obscured paths they haunt.
They watch, unseene, for simple-men,
To ceaze them vn-aware.
They lurck like Lions in their denn,
And slielie them insnare.
4 To catch the pore, by lowlie shewes,
Their strength, doth help them on,
They think in hart, that God nor vewes,
Nor careth what is done.
But, rise oh Lord, thy powre to showe,
Leaue not the pore forgot.
For, why should Sinners sleight thee soe
And think, thou mind'st them not ?
5 Thou see'st, yea see'st their wickednes,
That punishd it may be :
And loe, the pore & Fatherles,
Commit their Cause to thee.
Lord God (their helper) break the strength
Of ev'ry wicked-one ;
Serch out their sinnes, & thou (at length)
Shalt cause them to have none.
6 Our everlasting king thou art,

Thou,

Thou, from the Realme likewife,
Haft forc'd the Gentiles to depart,
And heard the poremans cries.
Their harts thou fhalt eftablish to,
And hear & judge, the pore;
That, earth-bred man, the Orphanes foe,
May them oppreffe no more.

Almighty God, *feeing our fafetie confifteth in thy loving prefence, be thou near at hand, to defend & affift in all extremities. Abate the malice & wickednes of our foes, & let their pride, fraude, & crueltie, make vs the more heedfull that we depart not willingly out of thy* protection. *Vouchfafe alfo, fo to raigne in our foules, to the fuppresfion of all intrufions, that (our affections being ordered by illuminated* Reafon, *& fanctified by* Grace) Chrift *may have the fole* dominion *there; &, that we may fincerely embrace him with our whole* harts; *honor him with all our* faculties; *confeffe him with our* tongues; *& glorify him by our* works, *together with thee, oh* father, *& the bleffed* Spirit, *now & for ever.* Amen.

Another of the fame.

LOrd, why ftandeth thou fo farr?
Why at need, am I forfaken?
Poremen, wrondg'd by Tirauts are;
Let them in thofe guiles, be taken,
Which by them contrived were.
2 For, in boaft, the Sinner fayes;
That, his longings he poffeffeth:
He, the Covetuous doth praife,
(And their practifes he bleffeth)
Though the Lord abhors their waies.
3 Proud & loftie lookes, hath he,
God, nor feeking, nor beleeving:

C Al

All his Courſes greevous be ;
And thy judgments *(paſt conceivinge)*
Are too high for him to ſee.
4 With contempt he ſleights his foes,
Fearing neither falls nor ſliding :
From his mouth much curſing flowes,
Vnderneath his tongue, ſtill hiding,
Miſcheef, ſinn, & guileſull showes.
5 In blinde paths, he lurks & pries,
Harmles men to ſpoile & murther :
At the pore he darts his eyes,
And (unſeene) his driſts to further,
Like the denned lion, lies.
6 He doth watch the pore to ſpoile,
Whome he ſnares & ouerthroweth :
For, to take him in his toyle,
He with humble crowchings boweth,
Ceazing him by force, the while.
7 Then, in hart, thus muzeth he ;
God shall ſleightly paſſe it over :
Hide his face, & never ſee :
But, riſe Lord, thy ſtrength diſcover,
That the meek aven'gd may be.
8 Let not Sinners mock thee ſoe,
As if thou didſt nought regard it :
Lo ; thou ſee'ſt, yea ſee'ſt them do
Spightfull wrong ; &, to reward it,
Thou shalt ſet thy hand there-to.
9 Thou, art poremens hopefull ſtay,
Orphanes helper, in oppreſſion :
Break the Sinners armes I pray,
Serch thou after his tranſgreſſion,
And, then, purg it all away.
10 God who reignes for evermore,

From

From his land, the Gentiles driueth;
Hears, & chears, & helps the pore;
And, the Orphane ſo reviveth,
  That, he feares not, as before.

Pſa. 11.

To the cheef Muſitian a Pſalm of David. *The faithful ſoule (being tempted to deſpaire) makes faſt the Anchor of his Hope by conſidering Gods powre, his love to ſuch as truſt in him, & his hatred to their vnfaithful adverſaries &c.* It may be vſed, to comfort vs in deſperate temptations, & imminent perills.

IN God, my truſt is placed ſtill;
  Then, wherefor do you ſay,
That, as a bird vnto the hill,
  My ſoul ſhould fly away?
For, loe, their bow the wicked bend,
  And arrowes they prepare,
That they, vnſeene, their ſhafts may ſend,
  At ſuch as needie are.
2 If overthrowne the Ground-works lie,
  What cann the beſt men do?
Gods holy ſeat, is heav'n on high,
  And he muſt look therto.
Man-kinde, with cloſd, & open eyes,
  (Ev'n righteous men) God prooues;
And, him he doth, in ſoul, deſpize,
  That wicked Courſes loves.
3 For wicked men, the Lord prepares,
  (And raines into thir cupp)
A ſtorme of brimſtone, fire, & ſnares,
  Which they muſt ſwallow up.
But, being in himſelf vpright,
  He, juſtice doth affect;

And, godly men, have in his fight,
 A looke of good refpect.

Permit not oh God! *the accufings of our* confciences, *nor the bitter cenfures of others, (whether iuftly or vniuftly pronounced) to overthrow our hopes of thy* Mercy. *Let not the* groundworks *of our faith be vndermined by any* Temptation; *but, feeing thou fercheft the fecrets of our harts, & findeft that (raked vp among our many frailties & corruptions) there are yet vnquenched in our foules, the* fmokings *of that* fire, *which was firft kindled by thy* grace; *Re-inflame, we pray thee, our fpiritual affections to* thee *& thy lawe. That, when malitious offenders receive the bitter* draught *prepared for them, we may thanckfully take the* Cupp of Salvation, *& reioice in thy gratious favours, through* Iefus Chrift *our Lord.* Amen.

Pfa. 12.

To the cheef Mufitian vpon Sheminith, A Pfalme of David. *The elect are prayd for; The circumvention & infultings of the wicked are mentioned, with a promife of redreffe; & the ftabilitie of Gods word is declared.* It may be vfed when herefie, or prophaneffe beginnes to fpread. *&c.*

HElp Lord; for, no Good man is left:
 All faithfulnes is quite bereft,
 And from the race of men departs:
They, lies vnto their neighbours, tell;
Vpon their lippes, faire fpeaches, dwell.
 When falfhood lurketh in their hearts.
2 But, God fhall cut their lipps that gloze,
And, pluck away the tongues of thofe
 Who proudly make their vauntings, thus:
Wee of our tongues will mafters be;
Our lipps are ours, & who is he

That

That ſhall have Lord-ſhip over vs ?
3 But, I (ſaith God) will now ariſe,
Ev'n for the ſighengs & the cries
Of thoſe that wrong'd or greeved are :
And, I will them in ſaftie ſett,
Beyond their powre, who in their nett,
The poremans footſteps would enſnare,
4 Gods wordes refinde, the Teſt will bide,
Like ſilver ſeav'n tymes purifide ;
And, God will keep them ever true :
Though, for a while, men lewd & baſe,
Do ſitt in honors higeſt place,
And, ev'ry where their folly ſhewe.

Conſider (oh Lord*) the general vnfaithfulnes which now overpreads the whole earth ; Obſerve the falshood, pride, hypocriſie, & inſolences of the* Adverſaris *of Truth; Behold the ſuffrings of thy ſmall* flock; *Convert or confound their oppreſſors ; fulfill thy gratious promiſes made to the* pore in Spirit ; *preſerve thy* word *from being made fruſtrate or perverted, by thoſe wicked-ones, who are now exalted, both in* church *& commonwealth, to thy dishonor ; and (when they have acted their follies, during the tyme which thou shalt permit) let thy purified* word *prevaile to the purging of this corrupt world, & to the encreaſing of the number of thy* elect, *through* Ieſus Chriſt *our Lord.* Amen.

Pſa. 13.

To the Cheef Muſitian a Pſalm of David. *It expreſſeth hartie longinges after ſpirituall Conſolations, & shews the perplexties of a ſoule, ſeeking reſt in her owne Counſells &c.* It may be ſung, when feeling our natural defects, & the malice of our foes, we deſire the comforts of the Holy-gloſt &c.

C 3 How

Pſalme XIII.

HOw long forgetſt thou mee!
Shall thus obſcured be
Thy cheerful face, oh Lord, for aye?
Still, in my ſoul, ſhal I
Perplext, & muzing lie,
With hart oppreſſed all the day?
2 My God! ſhall ſtill my foe,
Inſult vpon me ſoe?
Hear, & mine eyes enlighten thou:
Els, death wil me ſurprize;
And then mine enimies,
Will ſay; we have prevailed, now.
3 For, they who malice mee,
Will Ioy my fall to ſee:
But, Lord, thy mercies I will minde,
I'le in thine ayde rejoice,
And praiſe thee, with my voice;
Becauſe, to me thou haſt bene kinde.

Dear God; *vnſufferable is a* troubled ſpirit *ſeeking reſt in it ſelfe. Or in any thinge without thee. when thou art abſent, the preſence of all temporall conſolations doe but encreaſe torment; & vnles thou ſpeake peace to our ſoules all thy creatures help to aggravate our* afflictions. *Revive therfor our hartes by thy ſweet preſence; Enlighten the* eyes *of our mindes that we* ſleep *not in ſinn, & ſo chear vs by the light of thy* Countenance *that our foes inſult not over vs: but grant rather, that we reioicing in thy* Saluation, *may both live & dy with Comfort, to the honor of thy bleſſed* Name. Amen.

Another of the ſame.

OH Lord, how long wilt thou drawe back,
And hide thy face fro me?
How long ſhal I ſelfe-Counſell take

And,

And, greev'd in ſpirit be?
How long ſhal my oppreſſors thrive,
And, I their ſcornings beare?
Leſt, of my life, it me deprive,
Behold, oh Lord, & heare.
2 For, els my foes will ſay, in boaſt,
That I the ſoile have had,
And, they who now afflict me moſt,
Will of my fall be gladd.
But, in my hart, are hopes of thee
Which health & joy will bringe;
And, thou haſt dealt ſo wel with mee
That I thy praiſe will ſing.

Pſal. 14.

To the cheef Muſitian a Pſalme of David. *It ſheweth mans general corruption, & our natural eſtate before we become regenerated by Gods eſpeciall Grace &c.* We ſhould ſing it to minde vs, what we are of our ſelves, & how much we ſhould deſire a Renovation.

THe foole, his God in hart denayes;
And, quite corrupt mankinde is growne:
Their walkings are in hatefull waies;
Vpright, or good, there is not one.
The Lord, from heav'n declinde his eye,
And, all the ſonns of men he ſcannd!
That he from thence might ſerch & trie,
Who did him ſeek, or vnderſtand.
2 But, all of them corrupted were,
All men beſide the way are gone;
He ſaw not one deal juſtlie there,
Not one man good; oh no, not one.
So bruitiſh are Tranſgreſſors all,

That they like bread my people eat:
On God, (likewiſe) they never call;
  And, therefor is their terror great.
3 For, God preſerves the faithfull ſeed,
Ev'n them who righteous waies affect;
And, though his Counſel none doth heed,
Yet, God, the poreman will protect.
Would we Gods ayde from *Syon* had,
Which muſt his folke, from thraldome bringe!
For, *iacob* would therof be glad,
  And Iſr'el ſhould rejoice & ſing.

Acknowledginge (oh! moſt gratious Redeemer*) our generall corruption, & that in vs there is no goodnes; we humbly beſeech thee (by the* Salvation *promiſed out of* Syon*) to deliver us from our ſpirituall* captivitie; *& ſo to ſanctify our poluted* nature, *that our* terrors *may be removed*; *our* lives *amended*; *thy evangelical* counſells *hartelie embraced*; *and that we (becomming true* Iſraelites *in whome there is no guile) may at laſt be ſaved by thy* Mercie, *& reioice among the faithfull in thy new* Jeruſalem, *for ever & ever.* Amen.

Pſa. *15*.

A Pſalm of David. *It queſtions & anſweres, who shal be admitted into Gods famelie (to wit) ſuch as are ſanctified in thought, word, & deed, &c.* It is vſefull to inform vs, what our Converſations ought to be, who profeſſe our ſelues to be of God's houſhold.

LOrd, who ſhall reſt within thy tent,
  Or on thy holy hill?
But, he that's trulie innocent,
  And ſheweth mercy, ſtill.
Whoſe hart emploies a truth-full tongue;
  And none by ſlander greeves:

Who

Who neither doth his neighbours wronge;
  Nor lies of them beleeves.
2 Who favours thoſe that feare the Lord,
  And, ſinners doth abhor:
Who ſhifts not from his promiſ'd word,
  Though to his loſſe he ſwore.
Who putts not coine to griping loane,
  Nor takes a wicked fee,
He, doubtles, is a bleſſed one,
  And, ſhall vnmooved be?

Fleſh & bloud, *oh* God, *is neither able to fulfill thy lawe, nor to enter into the kingdome of heaven before it be purged & ſanctified by the pretious* body & bloud *of thy dear* Sonn. *Seeing, therfor, thou requireſt that both our* outward & inward *man ſhould be conformable to that example of perfect* Righteouſnes *which he hath left who is gone up, before (into thy holy* Tabernacles, *to prepare manſions for all who deſire to be followers of him) make vs we beſeech thee, ſo obedient to the diſcipline of the* Catholick Church *(his dwelling place on earth) that we may have his* righteoſnes *imputed; & be kept immovable in thy favour, vntill we ſhalbe tranſlated to thoſe heavenly* habitations, *where thou liveſt & raigneſt world without end.* Amen.

Pſa. 16.

Michtam of David. *It is a literal prophecie of* Chriſt. Act. 2. 25. *& it hath relation to the communion of ſaints, The ſole mediatorſhip of* Chriſt, *his reſurrection, & his ſitting at the right hand of God, &c.* It is uſefull to confirm vs in theſe articles of our faith afore mentioned, *&c.*

SAve me, oh Lord; for, I haue laid
My truſtfull hope, alone, on thee:

And, to thy ſelf, my Soul hath ſaid,
That thou (oh Lord) her Lord ſhalt be.
My goods, to thee are nothing worth :
But, in their vſe I will declare,
That I affect thy Saints on earth ;
And, ſuch as well-deſervers are.
2 All they who ſerve another God,
Shall gaine encreaſe of greefs & blame ;
Their drinck-oblation ſtaind with bloud,
I'le nor prefer, nor ſpeake their Name.
God is my birth-right, & my ſhare ;
He fills my Cupp ; maintaines my Lot ;
Faire portions, my diviſions are,
And pleaſant places I have gott.
3 The Lord be praiſd, who wrought it ſo :
For, he in this, did me advize.
My Reines, by night, inform'd me to ;
And, God I place before mine eies.
Who ſtands at my right-hand ſo near,
That, me no fears of chaing moleſt :
It both my heart & voice, doth cheare :
My fleſh likewiſe, in hope doth reſt.
4 For, Lord, thou neither wilt permit
That left in hell my ſoul ſhould lie ;
Nor wilt thou ſuffer in the Pitt,
Thy holy-one to putrifie.
But (through lifes path-way) me ſhalt bring,
Where, in thy ſight (at thy right hand)
All Ioyes, and each delightfull thinge
For ever, & for ever, ſtand.

Grant, oh Lord, *our ſoules may ſo truly affect thee, that thy pore* members *may reap the fruites of our charitable affections. Let vs continue ſo conſtant alſo, in thy true worship, that all our offrings maybe made acceptable by the mediation*

mediation of Chriſt Ieſus, *and that we may inherit our* portion *with him* : *So, his bleſſed* Soul *&* body *(againſt which nor* hell *nor* corruption *could prevaile) shall drawe after him, our* ſoules, *out of the* hell *of an* afflicted conſcience, *& our* bodies *from the graves of* ſinn, *&* mortalitie, *to enioy with him, a ioyfull reſurrection at his* right-hand; *& the fullnes of all pleaſures, in thy glorious preſence, for evermore.* Amen.

Another of the ſame.

PReſerve me Lord; for, I on thee depend;
And, for her Lord, my ſoul profeſſes thee.
Though to thy ſelf, my wealth no profit lend,
Thy Saints on earth, my love ſhall therby ſee.
But, they ſhall feel their ſorrow ſtill encreaſed,
Whoſe offrings are to other Gods addreſſed.
2 Their bloudie-drinck-oblation to preſent,
Or, with my lipps ſo name them I diſdaine:
Thou art my Lott, where with I am content;
Thou art my cupp, a portion ſhalt maintaine.
To me, the Lines a goodly ſhare divided;
And praiſd be God, that me ſo well hath guided.
3 My reines likewiſe, inſtruct me in the night:
Before mine eyes, the Lord ſtill ſeemes to ſtand;
And, ſure, I ſhall preſerved be vpright,
Becauſe, the Lord remaines at my right-hand.
It glads my hart; with joy my tongue now ſingeth;
And, hopeſull reſt, vnto my fleaſh it bringeth.
4 For why; my ſoul thou ſhalt not leave in hell,
Nor let thy holy-one corruption ſee:
But, vnto me, thy path of life reveal,
Which thither tends, wher joies perfections be;
Ev'n thither, where at thy right hand attending,
Thoſe plæſures are, which never shall haue ending.

Psa. 17.

A prayer of David. *It personates* Christs *members in persecution desiring succour, & comforting thẽselves in hope of the blessed vision of God, after their Resurrection ; &c.* It is vsefull, when we have cõsidered the quality of our foes, & by faith applyed vnto our selves, the innocency of Christ, with an affection therevnto.

LOrd, hear my cause, my suites, my cries,
Which from vnfained lipps doe flowe ;
To rightfull things decline thine eyes,
And, from thy self, let sentence goe.
My secret thoughts are in thy sight ;
Thou vew'st them, in the darkest night.
2 Thou trid'st my fault, & foundst it none ;
For, from offence I kept my tongue :
And (as for things by others done)
My words preserved me from wrong.
Oh ! be thou pleasd my course to guide ;
And stay my feet, lest els they slide.
3 On thee I call ; for thou wilt hear :
Lord, hear, & my complaint attend.
Let thy great love to me appeare,
And thy right-hand my life defend ;
Ev'n that right-hand which from their foes,
Gards them, who trust in thee repose :
4 From Tiraunts, me beseiging round,
From Sinners, who my harme assay,
Lord, as thine eye-ball keep me sound ;
And, over me, thy wings display.
For, they with fatt, quite round are clad ;
And, haughtie braggs, their mouths have made.
5 Me, in my waies, they have withstood,
And sought about with downe-cast eyes,

Like

Like lions (when they hunt for food)
Or lions whelp, which lurking lies.
  But, riſe, reſiſt ; and foile them Lord :
  From Sinners, gard me, by thy ſword.
6 Lord, from thoſe world-lings gard thou me,
Who in this life, their lot receive ;
Who full of wealth, and children be,
And for their babes large portions leave.
  To wake from ſinn, & looke on thee,
  In thine owne forme, contenteth mee.

Accept oh Lord, *our weak endeavours, & ſo teach us to moderate our* thoughts, *to govern our* tongues, *& to order our* converſations ; *that no temporal or ſpirituall adverſarie, may inſtiy accuſe or harm vs. Take us into thy ſpeciall* protection ; *becauſe, our foes are powerfull, cruel, & deligent in ſeeking our deſtruction : but, above all, keep vs from the poluted converſations & affections, of thoſe whoſe belly is their God, and whoſe portion of happines, is in this life ; that when we shal awake out of our* graves, *we may appear in thy* righteouſnes ; *reioice in our happy* lot ; *& be fully ſatified in the fruition of thee, who liveſt & raigneſt world without end.* Amen.

Pſa 18.

A Pſalm of David the ſervant of the Lord, who ſung vnto the Lord, the words of this ſong, when the Lord delivered him from the hand of al his foes, and from the hand of Saul. *It myſticallie declareth Gods maieſtical proeeding in the work of our redēption.* And it may be vſed to praiſe God for our deliverances, by the Incarnation, reſurrection, & exaltation of Chriſt ; & for the benifits which we receive thereby.

I Love the Lord ; for, my ſupport,
  My horne of health, is he :

My

My Rock, my trust, my Sheild, my fort,
And, oft hath helped me.
He merrits praise; for, when I cry
Me, from all foes he saves;
Though wrapt in pangs of death, I lie
And plung'd in sorrowes waves?
2 Yea, when by death & hell en-snar'd,
I sought the Lord, in fear;
My God, within his Temple heard,
And my complaints did hear:
Earths ground-work shook to feel his yre;
The trembling hills, did quake:
His nostrills fum'de, his mouth breath'd fire,
Which burning-coales did make.
3 Then, downe he came, & heavn he bow'd
His feet thick darknes hid.
A flieng Cherube he bestrode;
The winged windes, he ridd.
A duskie fogg, his Cov'ring was;
Dark waters were his tent;
Before the brightnes of his face,
Clouds, fire, & hayle, he sent.
4 The Lord, from heav'n did also make
His thunders to be heard:
Yea, when that great Almighty Spake,
Both fire & haile appear'd:
His darts, on ev'ry side he threwe,
Till they dispersed were:
His burning Lightninghs, flashing flewe,
And caused them to fear.
5 When he did frown, a dreadfull blast
He from his nostrills blow'd,
Which, vp the seas lowe Depths did cast,
And, Earths foundations show'd.

Then

Then downe he ſent, & from among
 Great floudS, advanced me;
And from thoſe foes that were too ſtrong;
 He likewiſe garded me.
6 They in my Cares did me prevent;
 But, ſtill, God was my hope:
He, for his love-ſake, ſuccour ſent,
 And gave me larger ſcope.
The Lord, my Righteouſnes obſerv'd.
 His favour he beſtow'd;
And, as mine innocence deſerv'd,
 So, he his mercy ſhow'd.
7 For, in Gods wayes my walkings were,
 From him I have not ſtept;
Still in my ſight, his iudgments are,
 And I his lawes haue kept.
In him, I iuſtifide became;
 For, I did leave my ſinn:
And, as I iuſt & righteous am,
 Rewarded I haue binn.
8 As he my hands did guiltles finde,
 He, ſo did me requite:
For, to the meek the Lord is kinde,
 To righteous men vpright.
Among the pure, he will be pure,
 And, on the froward frowne.
The poreman he will make ſecure,
 And, pluck the proud-man downe.
9 My Darknes, God ſhall brightnes make;
 My Lampe, enlight he ſhall.
By him, I through an Army brake,
 And overleap'd a wall,
Gods way is right, pure is his word;
 He ſaves if ſought he be:

For

For, who is God, except the Lord,
  Or who cann fave but he?
10 About my Loines, he ftrength did binde,
  He, fett my path-way ftreight:
He, made my feet out runn the Hinde,
  And rais'd me to this height.
My hands to fight, my Armes to bend
  A bowe of fteel, he taught;
His Buckler, he to me did lend,
  And, faving-health it brought.
11 His right-hand hath fupported me,
  His love hath made me great;
My ftepps, by him enlarged be,
  And, fafe my feet are fett.
I did perfue (yea tooke) my Foes,
  And flewe til all were flaine.
They fell downe wounded by my blowes,
  And could not rife againe.
12 For, he (to fitt me for the war)
  With powre, did me indue,
And, thofe who my oppofers are,
  Beneath my feet he threwe.
To conquer them, who mee envide,
  Me, ftrong enough, he made.
They cride, and (though to God they cride)
  Replies, nor helps, they had.
13 Then, as the duft which whirl-windes toffe,
  So fmall I them did beat;
And threw them forth as myrie-droffe,
  Which lies about the ftreat.
Thus, from the peoples vp-roares freed,
  I (through his grace) became:
And, now to be the Gentiles *Head*;
  By him, advanc'd I am.

14 A-

14 A nation ſhall my Servants be,
which knowes me not as yet :
Aſſoone as they have heard of me,
Themſelves they ſhall ſubmit.
The ſtranger ſhall ſtand out no more ;
But, in his Bullworks ſeare :
Oh praiſe the living Lord, therfore ;
Aloud, Gods praiſe declare.
15 Let God, my ſaving-health, be praiſd,
By whome to paſſe it came,
That, I above the people raiſd,
And thus avenged am.
Above all them that me oppoſe,
He doth exalt my throne ;
And, ſaveth me from all my foes,
Ev'n from the Cruel-one.
16 Among the gentiles, now, therfore
I'le thanck him for the ſame ;
My ſong ſhall be for evermore,
In honor of his Name.
His king, & his anointed-one
He gloriouſly hath freed ;
And, everlaſting mercie ſhown
To David & his ſeed.

Vouchſafe, moſt gratious Lord, according to thy accuſtomed mercie, to be ſtill our Protector ; *& let thy* Name *be alwaies glorified for the miraculous deliverances of thy* Church, *now & in al Ages ; eſpecially from the great worke of mans generall* redemption. *Inſtruct vs in the ſpiritual* warfar ; *enable vs againſt all our viſible & inviſible* foes ; *ſubdue vnto vs all our owne rebellious* Affections ; *deliver vs out of all our* ſuffrings ; *Give vs victorie over everie* temptation : *Encreaſe thy kingdome by the calling of thoſe, who are not yet thy* People ; *And make vs vnfainedlie* *thanckful vnto thee for theſe, & all the reſt of thy mercies through* Ieſus Chriſt, *our Lord,* Amen.

Pſal. 19.

To the cheef Muſition a Pſalme of David. *It declares the vniverſal preaching of Gods* Divinity *by the* book *of his* Creatures, *& it is a* prophecie *of the generall publication of the* Goſpel, *Rom.* 10. *It ſheweth alſo the properties, of the divine* word. *It* may be uſed to praiſe God for the priveledges which we have by his word; &, as a prayer for ſanctification. *&c.*

GOds glorie, ſhines among the Spheares;
The heav'ns, his handie-works diſcloſe;
Their daylie ſpeach, his powre declares;
And e'vry night, his wiſedome ſhowes.
Their language, in al tongues is found;
Their Line, about Earths globe, doth runn:
Through-out the world their words do ſound;
And, there's the Pallace of the Sunn.
2 He Bride-groome-like, refreſh'd appears,
When he forgoes his lodging place;
Or gyant-like, when vp he rears
And chears himſelf, to runn a Race.
His Iorneies, are from thence begun,
Ev'n where, the bounds of heav'n are ſett;
And, he quite round the world doth runn,
Refreſhing all things with his heat.
3 God's Rule is plaine, & ſoules convarts;
His witnes firme, & maketh wiſe:
His lawes are juſt, & glad our hearts;
His Precepts pure, & clear our eyes.
His blameles Feare is vn-confin'de,
Both true & right, are all his doomes,
More worth then gold (ev'n gold refin'de)

More

More ſweet, then hony in the combes.
4 Moreover, they thy ſervant warne,
By keeping them, he profit winns :
But, Lord, his guilt who cann diſcerne?
Oh ! therfor purge my ſecreat ſinns.
From daring Crimes, thy ſarvant ſave,
And, let them bear no ſway in me :
So, I the leſſe rebuke ſhall have,
  And, from the great-offence, be free.
5 Oh ! when I ſpeake, let ev'ry word,
And ev'rie muzing of my hart,
Be pleaſing in thy ſight, oh Lord,
  For, though my ſtrength, & ſaviour art.

No excuſe is left, oh mercifull Father, *if we be ignorant of thee, or vnconformable to thy* will : *for, by the* book of thy Creatures, *it was long-ſince declared vnto the whole* world, *which* Text, *being corrupted by humane* Inventions, *thou didſt explaine it againe in the volumes of the* Prophets ; *Since then, it was more illuſtrated by the writings of the* Apoſtles ; *And the prime ſcope of all theſe* Bookes, *thy bleſſed* Spirit *daylie preacheth & interpreteth throughout the world, by ordinarie or extraordinarie meanes. The powre, truth, puritie, ſweetnes, & profitabelnes of this* divine word *wee do, or muſt, confeſſe alſo, to be evident, Nevertheles (becauſe wee have much wilful ignorance, & many ſecret corruptions, we humbly pray thee, ſo extraordinarilie to enlighten our* darknes, *& to purge our concealed* polutions, *that (we being illuminated & ſanctified by the* holie-ghoſt*) the* vnpardonable Sinn *may be avoided, & we made acceptable to thee in* Chriſt Ieſus. *Amen.*

Pſa. 20.

To the cheef Muſitian a Pſalme of David. *It is*

a prayer for ſpirituall graces, with a proteſtation of affiance in God; & it miſtically toucheth the Preſt-hood & royal dignity of Chriſt &c. It may be vſed to deſire Gods acceptance of vs in his Sonn; & may ſerve, in ſome caſes, as a prayer for chriſtian princes and paſtors. *&c.*

THe Lord, at need, vouchſafe thee grace,
Let Jacobs God, thy cauſe defend,
Protect thee from his holy-place,
And, ſtrength to thee from Syon ſend.
Thy guiſts, let him remember, ſtill,
Let him accept thy Sacrifize, *Selah.*
Thy harts requeſt, let him fulfill,
And, proſper all thou ſhalt deviſe.
2 We wil reioice thy peace to ſee,
And in Gods name our Enſignes wave,
When al thy ſuites are granted thee:
For, God (I know) his Chriſt will ſave.
By his right-hand's almightie force,
God hears vs from his holy-hill.
Some truſt in charrets, or in horſe,
But, we Gods Name remember, ſtill.
3 In that regard, we raiſed are,
And ſtand upright, when they do fal.
Oh! let the king, our prayers hear,
And ſave vs, Lord, when we do call.

Aſsiſt vs mercifully oh God, *in all our* Aflictions; *Accept the* Sacrifiſe *offred for vs by* Chriſt Ieſus, *the* high-preiſt *of our ſoules; & in his* Mediations, *graunt vnto vs, all our faithful petitions; That ſo (renouncing al temporall Aſſurances, & truſtinge only in thy defence) we may ariſe from thoſe ſinns, into which many fail without repentance; and that we may be made partakers of thy* Salvation, *with our kinglie* Mediatour, *who liveſt & raighneth*

raighneth with thee oh father, *&* *thy* holy-spirit, *world without end.* Amen.

Psa. 21.

To the cheef Musitian a Psalm of David. *It is a literal prophecie of the kingly dignitie of* Christ, *mentioninge some of his royall prerogatives, &c.* It may be vsed as a thanckfull commemoration of the preheminence of our spirituall king. *&c.*

LOrd, in thy strength, how joies the king?
And, of thine aide, how glad is he?
His harts desires, in ev'rie thing,
Have bene bestow'd on him, by thee *Selah.*
With blessings, thou didst him prevent,
With purest gold, thou cowud'st his head,
To ask for life, was his intent;
And, he of endles life, hath sped.
2 Through thy defence he famous growes,
And, is to high preferment reard;
On him, thy blisse-evernal flowes,
Thy gratious lookes his hart have chear'd.
Through thy meer love, the king shal stand
Still firme, if he on thee repose.
And, Lord, thy hand (ev'n thy right-hand)
Shall serch, & finde out all thy foes.
3 As ovens, hot with flames, will do,
So, thou shalt scorch them in thyne yre:
And, in thy wrath consume them so,
As if they burned in the fire.
Yea, thou shalt from the race of man,
Root out their fruite, & pluck their seed;
Because, to wrong thee, they begann,
Although they could not act the deed.
4 Thou shalt expose them (as it were)

A Marke, within thy shooting place ;
Thy stringed shafts thou shalt prepare
And, Stick thine Arrowes in their face.
Thus, be thou still exalted, Lord,
By thine owne powre, thy trophies raise :
And then, with joye wee will record
  Thy Matchles might, in songs of praise.

Blessed be thy Name, oh God, *for that high preferment which thou hast vouchsafed the* Manhood, *by assuming the same to thy* Deitie, *& by bestowing theron a* soveraigntie, *over al the rest of thy Creatures. Give vs* humility *to ascribe al the glorie therof to* Christ Iesus ; *Hear all our petitions in him; Teach vs by his example, so to trust in thee, that we may obtaine the* priveledges *of his glorious* kingdome, *& become partakers of that Life-eternal to which he ascended. So ; escaping those terrible Iudgments which thou inflictest on thy malitious foes, we shall behold their confusion, to the exaltation of thy* powre, *to whome be all* honor *&* glorie, *now & for evermore.* Amen.

Psa. 22.

To the cheef Musitian vpon Aijleth Shahar A Psalm of David. *It is a prophecie of Christ his passion, vnfolding divers passages thereof, & mentioning alsothe calling of the Gentiles, &c.* It may be sung to commemorate the Passion, & some other misteries of our Redemption, *&c.*

WHy hast thou, oh my God, my God,
  Why hast thou me forgone?
Why, nearer is not thy abode ;
  To hear & help my mone?
Vnheard of thee, I cry whole daies ;
  Whole nights the same I doe ;
Yet, thou art Isr'els cheefest praise,

And

And, thou art holy to.
2 Our fathers did on thee depend,
And, thou didſt them ſecure :
They cride, & thou didſt them defend ;
Their faith did them aſſure.
But, I, pore worme, an Abiect am,
No man, but one forlorne :
The people make of me their game,
Their proverb, and their ſcorne.
3 When me they vewe, their heads they nod,
Make mouths, & jeering, ſay ;
God was his hope, now then, if God
Him loves, him ſave him may.
But, thou didſt gard me in the wombe,
Thou didſt convay me thence :
At nurſe, my hope thou didſt become,
And, keptſt me everſince.
4 Er'e-ſince my birth, my God thou art ;
My truſt is all in thee :
Oh ! do not far fro me depart,
For, perills compaſſe mee.
Strong Bulls (ev'n herds of Baſhan race)
Beſet me round about :
They ſtand wide-gaping in my face ;
Like Lions, roaring-out.
5 Like water, I am pour'de aſide ;
My bones are ſtrain'd apart :
Ev'n potſherd-like, my ſtrength is dride ;
Like wax, diſſolues my hart.
Vnto my Iawes, my tongue is glew'd ;
For, thou didſt me confound,
With cruel doggs I am perſu'de ;
By Sinners, cloſed round.
6 My hands & feet, they nailed faſt ;

D 4 My

My bones apparant were :
Vpon my vefture, lots they caft,
My garments they did fhare.
Thine ayde, therfore, no more delay,
But, Lord my ftrength, draw near,
Caufe not the fword, my foul to flay,
Nor doggs to rend my dear.
7 Me, from the mouthes of Lions, garde,
As I, in former daies,
From hornes of vnicornes was heard :
So, I will fing thy praife.
Thy fame, I'le in thy church record,
My brethren being there.
Oh ! praife him yee that fear the Lord,
And Jacobs offpring are.
8 Him, oh yee feed of Ifr'el, fear ;
For, he doth nor defpize
Afflicted foules, nor ftop his eare,
Nor turne from them his eyes.
But, when thy crie, their cries are heard ;
For which, his praife I fing :
And, in great throngs, where God is feard,
My vowes to him I'le bring.
9 The meek fhal feed till they are full,
And praife the Lord therfore.
All yee, who feek him in your foul,
Shal live for evermore.
The worlds far ends, to minde fhall call
Their dutie to the Lord :
And, he of heathen kingdomes, all,
Shall fee him felf ador'de.
10 For, his the kingdome is, indeed,
All nations, ruleth he.
Earths fatlings on his bread fhal feed,

And

And, thanckful they ſhalbe.
Yea, they ſhall all before him bowe
Whoſe lodging is the grave,
For, none but he hath powre enough,
The ſoul from death to ſave.
11 A ſeed, whome he ſhall count his owne,
Shal then, to God returne;
And, make his Acts of Juſtice known
To people yet vnborn.

Oh! thou glorie of Iſrael, *& the hope of all who truſt in thee; ſeeing by a* voluntarie humiliation, *thou haſt in thine own perſon felt the bitternes of* reproches, *the crueltie of* perſecuters, *the sharpnes of* povertie; *the extream torments of the* fleſh, *the ſtrongeſt Agonies of the* ſoul, *and every* horror *which may affright vs, (when in our greateſt* tryalls *&* temptations *we ſeem (as it were) vtterly forſaken both* of God *&* man*) remember (oh remember) thine owne* paſſion, *& have mercie vpon vs.* Hear *vs, when we crie*: help *vs, when we can crie no longer: And when all our ſtrength faileth, let thy powre pluck vs out of our tormenters Iawes; that we & they whom thou haſt promiſed to collect from al* places *&* Ages *of the world, may meet in thy heavenly* kingdome, *to glorify thee, for ever & ever.* Amen.

Pſa. 23.

A Pſalm of David. *The Chriſtian ſoul acknowledgeth Chriſt her paſtor enritching, feedinge, reioicinge, reforming, beautifieng her, & providing for her an eternall habitation, in his owne preſence &c.* It may be ſung to praiſe God for the beniſits herein mentioned, &c.

THe Lord my Paſtor daignes to be,
I nothing, now, ſhall need:
To drinck ſweet ſprings he bringeth mee,

And on green Meads to feed.
For his Name-ſake, my hart he glads,
He makes my wayes vpright :
And, I, the vale of deaths black ſhades,
Cann paſſe, without affright.
2 Thy ſtaffe, thy preſence, & thy rodd,
My joyfull comforts are,
And, thou before my foes (oh God)
My Table ſhalt prepare.
Oyle on my head, pour'd out thou haſt,
My Cupp doth over-flowe,
And thou, on me, whilſt life doth laſt,
Thy favours wilt beſtowe.
3 Yea, Lord, thy goodnes & thy grace,
Shall alwayes follow me :
And, in thy houſe, my dwelling place
For evermore ſhall be.

Keep vs, oh thou faithfull Sheapherd of our ſoules, *that the* Devil *take vs not out of thy* ſolde, *nor entiſe vs from thy* paſtures *by faire alurements. Setle vs in thy* Church, *Refreſh vs by thy* Spirit, *Inſtruct us by thy* Sacraments, *Guide vs by thy* example, *reforme vs by thy fatherly* correction, *& ſo comfort vs by thy* preſence ; *that we may acknowledge, there is no need of thoſe beggerly aſsiſtances whereon* worldlings *depend* ; *and, that we may walke without repininge, through the aflictions of this* life ; *& without fear, through the ſhaddowes of* Death, *to thoſe manſions, which thou haſt appointed for thy choſen* flock; *in the kingdome of heaven.* Amen.

Pſa 24.

A pſalme of David. *It deſcribes the largnes of Chriſts inheritance, & shewes who are members of his* Church. *Then, by a poetical* proſopopeia, *the everlaſting Gates are*

are ſummoned to give paſſage for the Aſcention *of that glorious* King, It is vſed, in commemoration of the Aſcention.

THe Earth's the Lords, with her encreaſe;
  The world, & all her goods:
He founded it vpon the ſeas,
  And layd it on the Flouds.
What man is he that ſhal have grace
  To climbe the hill of God?
Or Who ſhall in his holy-place,
  Obtaine their free abode?
2 Sure, they whoſe hands are innocent,
  Whoſe meanings are vpright.
Whoſe harts to folly are not bent,
  Who ſwear, without deceit.
Such, gaine from God, a bleſſed meed,
  And, from their ſaviour grace:
And, ſuch (oh Iacob) are their ſeed
  Who truly ſeek thy face.
3 Yee Gates, liſt vp your heades on high,
  (Yee dores which laſt for aye)
The king of glory paſſeth-by,
  Vncloſe, & give him way.
Who is the king of glorie? tell,
  Oh tell! who might he be?
The Lord, who doth in ſtrength excell,
  That glorious king, is he.
4 Yee Gates, aloſt your Arches heave,
  (Yee dores that have no ende)
Vnto the king of glorie, give,
  Free paſſage to aſcend.
Who is the king of glorie? ſay'
  Oh ſay! who might he be?
The Lord of Armies in aray,

That

That glorious king is he.

Seeing thou hast evidently declared, oh Christ the Kinge of glorie, *who they are whome thou wilt admit into that* kingdome *whither thou art ascended; and who are truly of that* spirituall seed, *to whome thy promises appertaine. Grant, we beseech thee, that we may make our* Election *sure, by the workes of* regeneration, *& not be deluded by the false perswasions of a fruitles* faith. *So, all thy Creatures, shall give both way, and assistance, to our* Ascention *after thee; to whome with the* father *&* holy spirit, *be ascribed all praise, powre, & glorie, now & for evermore.* Amen.

Psa. 25.

A Psalme of David. *It containeth many petitions of an afflicted penitent Soul; declares the excellence of the Lawe of Grace, & the priveledges of the regenerate &c.* It may be vsed when we are dejected by the sight of our guiltines, & are truly penitent, *&c.*

I Lift my soul to thee;
  My trust in thee is plac'd:
Oh let me, Lord, nor scorned be,
  Nor by my foe disgrac'd.
  But, keep reproches all
  From those who thee attend,
And, let on them Confusion fall
  That without Cause offend.
  2 Thy waies to me me impart,
  Let me thy Truth be taught;
For, thou, oh God, my Saviour art:
  Whome I have alway sought.
  Be still, to me as kinde
  As thou of old hast binn;
And, bear thou not those faults in minde,

Which

which I have erred in.
3 But, grace to me afford,
Ev'n for thy goodnes ſake ;
As thou art good, & gratious, Lord,
On me compaſſion take.
Direct al thoſe that ſtray,
In iudgment, guide the meek,
And, them informe thou in thy way,
That humbly, thee de ſeeke.
4 For, Truth & Mercie, Lord,
Are found in all thy wayes,
By ev'ry one who keeps thy word,
And thy Commands obayes.
Remit (though great they are)
My ſinns, for thy Name ſake,
And, ſuffer him who thee doth fear,
His choſen-path to take.
5 Then, eaſ'd his hart ſhal growe,
His ſeed the Land ſhal fill,
And, he that feares the Lord, ſhall know
His Counſells, & his will.
Myne eyes attend on thee,
That thou maiſt me releaſe :
In mercie, Lord, returne to mee
Forlorne & in deſtreſſe.
6 My greefs enlarged are ;
Oh come, & me releeve,
My ſorrowes heed, regard my care,
And all my ſinns forgive.
Obſerve, oh Lord, my foes ;
Marke how abuſ'd I am ;
And (ſince I truſt in thee repoſe)
Defend my ſoul from ſhame.
7 Yea, keep thou me vpright ;

Be-

Becauſe, I hope in thee :
And, from all wrongs, & all deſpight,
Let Iſr'el ſaved be.

Remember not, oh Lord, *our offences* ; *but of thy meer Mercie blot out all our tranſgreſsions. Let neither the follies of our* youth, *nor the greatnes of any other ſinns, deprive vs of thy wonted* compaſſion. *Conſider our weaknes, our ſuf-frings, & the condition of our* adverſaries, *as motives of thy pittie* ; *That our ſinns beinge remitted, our fetters vnloſed, and thy ſecrets (even the miſteries of* Saving-grace*) revealed* ; *wee may in true meeknes, follow him, who is the* way, *the* Truth, *and the* Life ; *& be kept by thy ſpeciall* Grace *from all future ſinns & dangers, vnto our lives end.* Amen.

Another of the ſame.

ALoft, I raiſe my ſoul, oh Lord, to thee ;
And I in thee alone, my truſt have placed.
By thoſe therfore, that ſeek to miſcheeve me,
Oh, let me not be ſhamed, nor diſgraced.
Confound not thoſe who ſeek to do thy will ;
But, ſhame thoſe mē that Cauſeles have offended,
Direct thou me in thy Truths pathway, ſtill ;
For (Lord my health) on thee I have attended.
Eternall God, in mercie, thinck on me,
As it hath bene of old, thy gratious faſhion :
Forgot, let all my youthfull errors be ;
For thy love ſake, Remember thy compaſſion.
Great is thy grace, & great thy Iuſtice, Lord :
Therfor, thy waies to finful men thou ſhoweſt
Healp to thee meek, thou doſt, likewiſe, afford
Whē he is iudgd ; & guid'ſt him where thō goeſt.
In all thy waies, both Truth & Mercie be,

For

For ſuch, as have thy league, & word obſerved :
Keep therfor, Lord, thy grace in ſtore for me ;
(For thy nameſake) though I have ill deſerved,
Let thoſe, in whome thy ſacred feare is found,
In their deſired pathway, Lord, perſever.
Make true content, in all their ſoules abound ;
And, let their ſeed, poſſeſſe the land, for ever.
No man oh Lord, who ſtands in fear of thee,
Shall from thy league or Counſels, be debarred.
On thee, therfore, mine eyes attending be,
That from the net, my feet may be vnſnared ;
Pleaſd be, in love, to viſit me againe ;
For, lo, deſpis'd I am, & ſore deſtreſſed.
Quit me, from all my ſorrowes & my paine ;
For, my hart-greeſs (oh Lord) are much encræſed.
Regard my wants : Behold, & mark my woes ;
Remitting all wherin I have offended.
See, See, oh Lord, what numbers are my foes ;
And, what deſpights to me they have intended.
To help & ſave my ſoul, entreated be :
Thou art my Garde, oh ! keep me vndiſgraced,
Vpright, & pure ; becauſe, I truſt in thee :
And, from all Cares, let Iſr'el be releaſed.

Pſal. 26.

A Pſalm of David. *It ſetts downe ſome marks of the true* church *& of her members ; & perſonates her, iuſtifieing her ſelf againſt the ſecret imputations of her foes (from whome she deſires to be diſtingnisht) &c.* It is vſefull for thoſe members of Chriſt, who are falſly accuſed. *&c.*

GIve ſentence, now, oh Lord, with me ;
For, I have walk'd aright ;

And,

And, ſince I have relide on thee,
  Preſerve me ſtill vpright.
Proue thou my hart & Raines, oh God ;
  Search there, what thou canſt finde :
For, I the Paths of Truth have trodd ;
  And, bear thy love in minde.
2 With wicked men I have not ſate,
  Nor with diſſemblers gone :
Prophane Aſſemblies I do hate,
  And ſhunn the ſinners throne.
With hands waſh'd clean in ſimplenes,
  I'le round thine Altars goe ;
And there ; in ſongs of thanckſulnes,
  Thy wondrous works I'le ſhowe.
3 For, I that place affect, oh God,
  Where thou ſo much art fam'de :
Therfor, with ſinners, thirſting blood,
  Oh ! let me not be nam'd.
Their hands (their verie righthands) be
  with bribes, & miſcheefs fraught :
But, Lord, redeeme & pitty me ;
  For, I truths Paths have ſought.
4 In ſtedfaſt waies, with fixed feet,
  Firme ſtanding, I poſſeſſe :
For which, where great Aſſemblies meet,
  I, will the Lord confeſſe.

Give vs grace, oh Lord, *ſo to avoide the* ſocietie, *&* *practiſes of wicked men* ; *that neither our* conſciences *may accuſe vs, to be willfully guiltie of their crimes, nor thou condemn vs for* hypocrites, *when thou ſercheſt & iudgeſt the ſecrets of our harts. Ioine to the puritie of* manners, *a ſincere* devotion ; *that* honeſty *&* Religeon (*being knit & married together in our ſoules by thee) may never be divorced. Let our* zeal *alſo to thy* houſe

houſe, & our Love to thy Service, be ſuch as may diſtinguish vs from prophane worldlings ; *& ſo linck vs by* charity *to thy faithfull* members, *that we may continue thine to our lives end.* Amen.

Pſa. 27.

A Pſalme of David. *It expreſſeth confidence in God, & a longing to enioye the priveledges of his ſanctuarie. It vowes alſo to ſeek & ſerve him ; deſires Gods aſsiſtance, & exhorts to faith & perſeverance &c.* It is vſefull, for all Chriſtians, to theſe purpoſes.

GOd is my light, my health mine Ayde ;
My lifes defence : whome ſhould I fear ?
When wicked foes my death aſſayd,
They tript, & fell, & ruinde were.
I, therfor, will not faint, nor fly,
Although an hoaſt beſeigeth me ;
If God, will not this boone deny,
For which, I'le now a ſuiter be.
2 Ev'n that he grace to me afford,
My life-time in his houſe to ſpend ;
To vewe the beautie of the Lord,
And in his Temple to attend.
For, in his Tent, when dangers threat,
In ſecret, he ſhould me encloſe ;
Vpon a Rock, my footing ſet,
And, raiſe my head above my foes.
3 Then, in God's houſe, a Sacrifiſe
Of praiſes, I would alſo give :
Hear therfor, Lord ; & let my cries
A gratious Anſwere, now receive.
When thou doſt bid me ſeek thy face ;
Thy face I'le ſeek, my hart replies :
Reiect not therfor, nor diſgrace,

E Thy

Thy Servant who on thee relies.
4 Oh Lord, who didſt my ſoul preſerve
When, me my parents did forſake;
(Becauſe of them who me obſerve)
Now, plaine to me, thy path-waies make.
Yea, from the pleaſure of my foes,
Protect me Lord: for, lo; with lies,
Falſe witneſſes do me oppoſe;
And, cruel words they do deviſe.
5 That, had I not beleef to ſee
Gods grace (within that land of bliſſe
Where endles life ſhal granted be)
My ſoul had fainted, long e're this.
Attend thou ſtill vpon the Lord,
And faint thou not (*who e're thou art*)
Attend I ſay, vpon the Lord;
And, he ſhall fortifý thy hart.

It is an vnſpeakable favour oh Lord, to live where wee may peaceably aſſemble in thy houſe, *& obtaine thy comfortable preſence in thy bleſſed* word & Sacraments. *How many, oh* God! *how many? are deprived of this conſolation? And, oh how long? & with how little ſenſe of our* happines, *have wee enioyed this great* bleſſing? *Grant vnto vs, we beſeech thee, more thanckfulnes, leſt thou iuſtlie withdrawe thy abuſed* grace; *Give in due time, this great* Beniſit, *to all who vnfainedlie deſire it for thy glorie: In the mean while, vouchſafe them patience, to ſuſtaine their* burthen *without fainting; & let the hope of that, which is prepared for thie* ſaints, *in the* Land of the living, *ſtir vp them & vs, to a faithfull performance of our whole dutie towards thee, through the aſſiſtance of thy* holy-ſpirit, Amen.

Pſa. 28.

A Pſalme of David. *It craves Gods aſsiſtance, imprecate*

cates his Iudgments againſt the wicked, profeſſeth aſſurance in the divine protection, & aſcribes glorie, & powre, & thancks, to the Almighty, &c. It may be vſed as a prayer, and proteſtation of our faith in perſecution.

OH Lord My ſtrength, I crie to thee,
Give eare, & Silence do not keep:
Leſt, not vnlike to thoſe I be,
Which downe deſcend, into the deep.
Obſerve my Cries, & what I pray,
When to thine Arke, my hands I rear:
With ſinners, pluck me not, away,
Who ſpeake of peace, yet purpoſe warr.
2 Give them what their ill deeds require;
As they deſerve, ſo them reward.
For their lew'd works, pay them their hire,
Becauſe, thy works they nought regard.
Yea, ſeeing they thy works deſpize,
Deſtroy them, never to be raiſd:
But, hear my ſuite, & heed my cries,
And be thou, Lord, for ever praiſd.
3 For, thou art, Lord, my ſheild, mine ayde;
My ſtrength, of whome I hopeful am:
Therof, my hart is well apaid,
And, of thy praiſe, my Songs I frame.
Thy Chriſt, thou alway ſhalt protect:
Thou art his rock; &, ſav'd by thee,
Thine heritage & thine Elect,
(Bleſt, fedd, & magnifide) ſhall be.

Immortal God, *ſo manie & ſo great perills do alway threaten vs, that we are ſtill at the brinck of deſtruction; & vnles thou be gratious, we ſhall ſoone be ſwallowed vp. Hear vs therfor, when we cal on thee, in the Mediation of* Ieſus Chriſt; *& gather vs not among* Hypocrites, *or*

E 2 *notorious*

notorious Maleſactors; *But, when they shal receive their due reward, who by a diſſembled* Vnitie, *trouble the peace of thy* Church, *or dishonor thy* Name, *by* Atheiſme *or prophanes; let vs reap the frucſe of our* hopes, *to our ioyfull exaltation among thine* elect, *& to the glorifieng of thy* Mercie, *through* Ieſus Chriſt *our Lord.* Amen.

Pſa. 29.

A Pſalme of David. *It miſtically expreſſeth the powre of Gods voice (or evangelical word) over all ſorts of people, in all places.* It may be vſed to praiſe God, for having thereby *(according to this prophecie)* converted thoſe, who were naturally as obdurate as trees, mountaines, ſeilds, & brute-creatures.

AScribe, yee Mightie, to the Lord,
  Aſcribe al powre & fame:
Let him be in his houſe ador'd,
  And, honor yee his Name.
The Lord, commandeth, with his voice,
  The ſeas, & greateſt Floud;
And, when the thunder makes a noiſe,
  It is the voice of God.
2 With powre, the God of glorie, ſpeaks,
  And, awſull are his words.
His voice, the ſtrongeſt cedars breaks,
  That *Libanon* affords.
Eu'n *Libanon* & *Shirion* to,
  He makes to ſtart (through feare)
As Vnicornes & Bullocks do,
  That yonge & frightful are.
3 God's voice, between the flames doth flie,
  God's voice, the Deſert ſhakes:
God's Voice, doth *Cadeſh* terrifie,
  The Hinde, it Calfeles makes.

Yea,

Yea, with his Voice, the thickest grove,
To plainest veiwe he laies;
And, in his Temple, those things move
All tongues, to sing his praise.
4 The Lord, likewise, doth in the Floud
An endles rule possesse;
And, blesseth al the Folke of God,
With fortitude, and peace.

Honor & praise, be given to thee, oh Lord God, *for the powerful preaching of thy* word, *let the sound of thie voice be still in our eares. When we* rage *like a troubled* sea, *let it* calme *vs; When we are like over-loftie* Cedars, *let it* humble *vs; when we are as vnmoveable as* mountaines *(in our owne* opinions*) let it* shake *vs; when we are wanton like young* Bullocks, *let it tame vs; when we are as* rude, *or* barren *as a* wildernes, *let it* civilize *& make vs fructful; when we are* pregnant *with anie, mischeef, let it make our conceptions* abortive; *when we are ensnared among, the thick* bushes *of* ignorance, *or worldlie* Cares, *let it discover a passage out of* error, *& disentangle our harts from carnall* affections: *that, the whole world may be subiected vnto thee; & that we & al tongues may praise & magnifie thy* Name, *for ever & ever* Amen.

Psa. 30.

A Psalm or song of the dedication of the house of David. *It seems a thancksgivinge for the resurrection of Christ, whose true house or Temple, was his* Body. *It confesseth Gods gratiousnes, & mans weaknes, &c.* We may vse it, when, arising from our sinns, we resolve to dedicate our selves as tēples to the holy-ghost.

LOrd God, thy praise I will declare;
For why, thou me hast magnifide?
My foes insultings thou did'st bar,

E 3 And,

And, ſav'dſt me, when for help I cride.
Yea, from the dungeon & the pit,
Thou keptſt my ſoul & liſe, oh Lord;
Let all thy ſaints (remembring it)
With praiſe, thy holines recorde.
2 Thy wrath, abides not long in thee,
But, in thy ſavour, liſe appears;
And, joy ſhall in the morning be,
Though, over-night, there may be teares.
In my advancement, once I ſayd,
That nothing ſhould my foot remove;
Becauſe, my mountaine thou hadſt laid
So firmelie, Lord, by thy meer love.
3 Yet, when thy face thou didſt but hide,
I quickly was oppreſt, againe;
And, then, to thee againe I cride;
And in my crie, did thus complaine.
What profit will my bloud afford,
When, I, ſhal to the grave deſcend?
Oh! cann it ſing thy praiſes, Lord?
Or cann the duſt thy truth comend?
4 Lord, hear, & pittie take on me;
To ſuccour me, thy help employ:
That, chang'd to ſongs, my ſighes, may be;
My mourning-weeds to robes of ioy.
So, I, for ever, with my tongue
Will praiſe the, (oh my God my Lord)
And, in a never-ending ſong,
Thy mercies, thanckfully record.

Sweet Ieſu, *ſo great are thy* Mercies, *that in a night thou converteſt into* trivmphs, *the moſt deſperate* Afflictions; *yea, in the very moment of greateſt horrors, thou ſtrangly infuſeſt vnexpreſſible ioyes: yet, ſuch is our corruption, that vpon thy* ſavours, *we often build thoſe falſe* aſſuranſurances *which beget more* pride *then* thanckfulnes; *& ſo, we are iuſtly shakē againe frō our confidence; that (makinge the foundation thereof more firme (by true* humiliation *grounded meerly on thy* mercies) *we may ſtand immoveable for ever. Oh! grant, that by meditating thy* voluntarie-humiliation *we may deſcend to the true* Annihilation *& renouncing of our ſelves, & that by virtue of thy* Burial & Reſurrection *we may eſcape the Dungeons of the* Grave & Hell; *Change the* mourning-garmēt *of our fleſh, into the* robes *of immortalitie, & praiſe thee for thy mercies, world without end,* Amen.

Pſa. 31.

To the cheef Muſitian a Pſalm of David. *It perſonates Chriſt & his Church in perſecution; containes a large intermixture of many petitions, complaints &c, & admirably ſets forth the varietie of affections, incident to a ſoul, working out ſalvation with fear & trembling.* It is vſefull in great agonies & afflictions of minde, *&c.*

BEcauſe, I do on thee depend,
  (That ſham'd I may not be)
Lord, in thy Iuſtice me defend,
  And, quickly hear thou me.
Be ſtill my rock, my walled-bowre;
  And, me vouchſafe to ſave:
For, thou art my defenſive towre,
  And, all the ſtrength I have.
2 Be pleaſ'd (for my nameſake) to come
  And be my hopeful ſtay;
Direct thou me, & pluck me from
  Thoſe netts my foes do lay.
Thou art my ſtrength, & vnto thee
  My ſpirit I commit:
For, thou Lord God of Truth, art he
  Who haſt redeemed it.

3 I, them abhorr who lies approve ;
But, Lord, I truſt in thee :
And of thy grace, & in thy love,
My whole reioicings be.
For, me thou didſt from cares diſcharge ;
Thou knew'ſt my ſoul in woe :
My fettred feet thou didſt enlarge,
And keptſt me from my foe.
4 Have mercie, Lord, for I am vext ;
Mine eies with greef decay :
In ſoul & fleſh, I am perplext ;
Greef, waſts my life away.
My yeares, with ſigheng, ſhortned are ;
My ſight, to faile beginns :
My bones conſume, my ſtrength doth wear ;
And, al is for my ſinns.
5 My ſcornefull foes do me vpraid ;
My neighbours, more then they :
My freinds, to ſee me are afrayd,
And, far they fly away.
As one long dead, (vnthought vpon)
Ev'n pot-ſherd like, I fare.
I ſlander'd am of many a one,
And, round me, terrors are.
6 Yet (when to take my life fro me
They plotts againſt me layd)
Relieng ſtill, oh Lord, on thee,
Thou art my God, I ſayd,
Thou know'ſt the times, when me to take
From my perſueng foes :
Therfor, to me (for mercie ſake)
Thy cheerfull face diſcloſe.
7 Lord, let me not be made aſham'd,
Becauſe, thy help I crave :

But

But, let the wicked be defam'd,
  And, ſilenc'd in the grave.
Their lieng lips, for ever cloſe,
  Who murmur in deſpight,
Diſdainfull words, in ſcorne of thoſe,
  Whoſe courſes are vpright.
8 Oh! what great favours wilt thou ſhew,
  To ſuch as honor thee.
And bring to paſſe, in publike vewe,
  For them that faithfull be?
Thy ſecret preſence ſhal prevent
  The Tyrants hautie wrongs;
And, they ſhall in thy privie-tent
  Avoyd the ſtriſe of tongues.
9 Praiſe God; for, when I raſh-lie thought,
  That I quite loſt had binn;
Me, to a warlike Towne he brought,
  And, honord me therein.
My ſuites, & cries, he likewiſe heard:
  Yee ſaints of his, therfore,
The Lord your God, with good regard,
  Love, honor, & adore.
10 The faithfull, he doth keep from harme,
  And their proud foes contemn.
Be bolde: & he your harts will arme
  Who put your truſt in him.

Our ſinns (oh Lord) *bring on vs many great afflictions: They conſume our* fleſh, *blinde our* eyes, *rott our* bones, *fright our* harts, *& afflict our* conſciences: *They cauſe vs to bevprayded, ſcorned, betrayed, & perſecuted, by our* foes; *They make vs to be envyed, contemned, reproched, & abuſed among our* neighbours; *They occaſion, that we are miſcenſured, forſakē, yea & forgotten of our beſt affected* freinds; *and (which is worſt of all) they bring on vs thy* displea-

displeasure, *&* *make vs almost desperatly to forsake thee. Deliver vs (oh deliver vs) from these* evills: *but especially from the* sinns *which occasion them. Thou art our sole refuge, & the God into whose hands we have committed our* spirits: *So embolden vs therfor, in thy* grace, *that we, & the rest of thy* Saints *(seeing how great favours thou bestowest on all them that fear thee) may praise thy* Name, *for ever & ever,* Amen.

Psa. 32.

A Psalm of David Maschil. *It shewes the free forgivenes of sinn by grace,* Rom, 4. 6. *The danger of hidinge, the benifit of confessing our sinns, and the powre of timely prayer; It exhorts also, that we do not brutishly abuse the grace of God &c,* It should be sung, to remember vs of Gods mercies, & of these duties, &c.

A Blest estate, that man is in
Whose crimes the Lord forgives, & hides:
Ev'n he, to whome God laies no sinn,
And in whose hart no fraud abides.
Till I, my faults, did open lay,
My bones with paine were tired out:
Thy hand opprest me night and day,
And, I became like Summers drought.
2 My Trespas, I reveald therfore:
I shewd my secret faults to thee;
And vowd to hide my sinns no more:
So, thou, their guilt forgavest me.
For this: the Iust, on thee shall call,
At seasons when thou maist be found:
And he shall have no harme at all,
Though mighty Flouds enclose him round.
3 Thou art, oh Lord, my hiding-place,
Wherein, (when peril greatest growes)

From

From dangers, thou ſhalt me releaſe,
And, me with ſongs of health encloſe. *(Selah.)*
Thus, thou doſt alſo ſeem to ſay:
I will inſtruct thee with mine eye,
And, ſo inform thee in the way;
That thou ſhalt never walk awrie.
4 Then, be not like the Horſe or Mule,
That void of vnderſtanding be;
Which thou with Bitt, & Raines, muſt rule,
Leſt, els, they fling, or fall on thee.
The Sinners plagues grow more & more;
But, they finde grace, who truſt in God.
Let juſt, & righteous men therfore,
With Shouts, proclaime theyr joye, abrode.

It is not, oh gratious Redeemer, *our* Innocencie, *or any good which of our ſelves we can performe, that iuſtifies vs in thy ſight; but thy* free grace, *thy* hiding, *& thy* not-imputing *our ſinns. That, which thou expecteſt & accepteſt from vs, toward the procuring of this favour, is nothing els but humble* ſoules, *contrite* ſpirits, *vnfaigned* harts, *& ſincere* confeſſions; *which, thou thy ſelf alſo, muſt prepare & help perfect in vs, or we shall never perform them: no, though al the dangers & torments of the world were before our eies. Take therfor, from vs, our brutish ignorance; curb our head-ſtrong* wilfulnes; *Rain our vnbridled* appetites; *inſtruct vs, by thy favorable aſpect; &, ſo guide vs by the bridle of* reaſon, *& religeous awe; that (we being governed according to thy* will*) thou mayſt be found of vs in all troubles, at all ſeaſons; &, we reioice in thy mercy, for ever & ever,* Amen.

Pſa. 33.

It exhorts to praiſe God; *declares who are moſt obliged therevnto; In what manner we should performe this dutie, & for*

& for what principall cauſes &c. We ſhould often uſe it to put vs in minde how much we are obliged to praiſe God, &c.

YE Righteous, in the Lord reioice:
For, praiſe with Godly men doth ſute:
Praiſe God with Pſaltry, Harpe, & Voice,
And on the twice-five-ſtringed Lute,
To him, new ditties, ſing & play;
And tune them to the loudeſt kay.
2 For, God is righteous in his word,
His Actions, ful of truth appear:
His Bounty, all the world hath ſtorde:
His Darlings, Truth, & Iuſtice are.
The Heav'ns were form'd when he but ſpake;
His breath, did all their Armies make.
3 The ſeas huge waves, aloſt he rear'd,
The Deeps, as vp in ſtore, he layd:
Oh! let him through the world be ſear'd,
And make Earths-dwellers all afraide.
For, his Commandings are fulfill'd;
And all is done as he hath will'd.
4 God, makes the Gen*t*iles proiects vaine,
And, brings the Peoples plotts to nought:
But, his decrees, for aye remaine,
And, everlaſting is his thought.
Moſt ſurely bleſt therefore are thoſe,
Whome for his owne, the Lord hath choſe.
5 For, God from heav'n doth caſt his eye,
The Sonn's of meu to veiwe & knowe:
Yea, from his dwelling-place on high,
He marketh all on earth belowe:
Their hearts, alike, he ſhapeth to,
And heeds, ev'n ev'ry work they do.
6 Great Armies cannot ſave a kinge,

No

No ſtrong-mans powre his life preſerves,
The ſtrength of horſe, vaine ſuccours bringe ;
But, thoſe who fear him, God obſerves :
And, whoſoe're on him depends,
From dearth, & death, he them defends.
7 Our ſoul vpon the Lord ſhall waite,
Who hath our ſheild & ſhelter binn ;
And, he ſhall be our harts delight ;
Becauſe, his Name, we truſted in.
Oh ! let vs Lord, ſtill ſuccour'd be,
As we repoſe our truſt in thee.

Bleſſed God ! *at thy* word *al things were created, & by thy* providence *they are ſtil governed. Thou haſt faſhioned the harts of all men, to be in ſome meaſure capable of thy* grace ; *& obſerveſt how they emploie that* Talent. *Thy eternal* decree *remaines firme ; & therfor, theie whome thou* chuſeſt *shall be bleſſed for ever. Neither their owne ſtrength, nor any powre (but thine) is able to keep them ſafe : Thou therfor, on whome their ſoul waiteth, shalt prevent the* famine *of that which is the meanes of their* preſervation ; *& therby, keep them from* totall *or* final-falling. *Lord, make vs, to reioice in this vnſpeakable* mercie. *Encreaſe our* faith, *& continue vs in the meanes whereby we are to make our* Election *ſure. VVe beleeve it is alreadie granted ; & yet we praie for it, becauſe it is our dutie ; & becauſe we cannot chuſe but praie for that, which we beleeve, & hope, to obtaine, through* Ieſus Chriſt *our Lord,* Amen.

Pſa. 34.

A Pſalme of David when he changed his behaviour before Abimeleck, who drove him away & he departed. *It ſeems to typefy Chriſt, who being (as it were) diſguiſed by taking our nature, & infirmities, became therby contemptible to the great-ones of the world.* We ſhould ſing it to it to praiſe God, for diſcovering to vs, what is hid from the worldly wiſe, &c.

NOw ſhall the Lords, eternal praiſe,
The ſubiect of my ſong be made:
My Soul ſhall ſing it, all her daies;
The meek ſhall hear it, & be glad.
Let others come, & ready be,
To ioine in praiſing of his Name:
For, when I cri'de, he helped me;
And kept away my feared blame.
2 He lightneth ſuch as him obſerve,
And, no diſgrace vpon them falls:
He heares the pore, and will preſerve
From all his troubles, when he calls.
His Angell-gards, will them encloſe,
Who, of his God head, awfull be:
Therfor, his goodnes, vnto thoſe
Who truſt in him, come Taſt, & See.
3 Yea, fear the Lord, yee Saints of his:
For, he to ſuch will al things grant.
The Lions whelps their food may miſſe,
But, they that ſerve him, nothing want.
Yee Children come, attention give;
And I will teach th'Almighties feare,
How, yee long time on earth may live,
And, gaine a bleſſed-being, here.
4 Your tongues from ſlandrous words preſerve,
Diſſembling, let your lipps eſchewe;
Ill deeds avoid, good works obſerve,
Seek peace, & after it perſue.
For, God beholdeth ſuch as thoſe,
And heares the Righteous when they pray:
But, wicked men he doth oppoſe,
And, roots their Name & Fame away.

5 The

5 The Lord, will hear the Righteous crie;
From dangers he will them assure;
He, to the broken hart is nigh,
And, wounded Spirits, he will cure.
Although the Iust hath many greeves,
The Lord so helps, that they are gone;
In all his troubles, him releeves,
And keeps him sound, in ev'rie bone.
6 By sinn, the sinners death is wrought:
He shall not thrive, that hates the Iust.
But, God his servants lives hath bought;
And, faileth none that in him trust.

Hear vs oh merciful God, *in our present necessities, and preserve vs from those future evills which we may iustlie fear. Enlighten our* vnderstandings, *rectifie our* affections, *guide our* tongues, *sanctifie our* actions, *cure our diseased* bodies, & *heal our wounded* soules. *Let thine* Angells, *gard vs; let thine owne* eyes, *watch over vs; and let vs be so instructed in thy* fear; *that when our lion-like* adversaries *are emptie, we maie be filled with thy* goodnes, & *delighted in thy* sweetnes: *Grant, also, that when their memorial perisheth, we (being preserved sound both in* soul & body) *may enioie the promised blessing of* long-life, *even of* life-eternall *in thy heavenlie* kingdom, *for ever & ever,* Amen.

Another of the same.

AT al tymes with my tongue I'le blesse the Lord;
To sing of him I never will forbear,
But, in my Soul, his praise with mirth record;
And publish what the meek shall ioy to hear.
Come, therfor, helpe his praises to declare;
To magnify his Name, let vs agree.
Discharg'd I was, by him, of all my fear;

And

And, when his ayde I fought, he ayded me.
Enlightned are their eyes that look on him ;
And, no difgrace or fhame, or thofe cann fall :
For, he in all their troubles helpeth them ;
And hears the pore, when he on him doth call.
God's Angell-gards, round thofe that fear him, be
Encamped ftill to keep them from their Foes.
His greatnes, and his goodnes, taft, & fee ;
For, all are bleft, who truft in him repofe.
In him, let all his Saints, confine their fear ;
For, povertie from fuch reftrained is.
Kept hungry, oft, the whelps of Lions are,
But, they who fear the Lord, no goodnes miffe.
Let me from you (yee babes) attention gaine ;
That, I the fear of God to you may fhowe.
Mark alfo this (all yee that would attaine
Long life on earth, & happie daies, to knowe)
No fland'rous tales envre your tongues to tell ;
And, let your lipps diffembling fpeach efchewe :
Of wicked words beware ; Vprightly deal ;
Enquire our Peace, & after it perfue.
Plac'd are Gods eyes, vpon the Righteous race ;
He to their cries, an open ear doth lay :
Quite oppofite to finners, is his face ;
And from the land, he rootes their name away.
Right willingly, the Lord inclines his ear,
To hear, & fave the righteous, when they cry.
Sinn-wounded foules, & harts that broken are,
He never fhunns ; but, vnto fuch is nigh.
Though many greefs, vpon the Godly fall,
The Lord, will ev'ry one of them remove.
Vnbroke, ev'n all his bones, preferve he fhall ;
But, finn, the death of finful men fhal prove.
Whoe fo doth hate the Iuft, fhall hated be,

For

For, God his faithful ſervants wil redeem,
Yea, all their ſoules from thral he ſetteth free,
And leaveth none, that put their truſt in him.

Pſa. 35.

A Pſalm of David. *It containes divers petitions, & prophetical Imprecations, concerning the Adverſaries of* Chriſt, *& of his members; & perticulerly mentioneth ſome of thoſe miſuſages which he ſuffred by the Iewes &c.* We may properly ſing it, when we commemorate the Paſſion *&c.*

WIth ſuch oh Lord, as me oppoſe,
Vouchſafe to plead my right;
And, pleaſed be to warr on thoſe,
Who now againſt me fight.
Both ſheild & Buckler, take in hand;
Riſe, for my help, I pray:
Bring out the ſpear, & for me ſtand,
In my Perſuers way.
2 Say to my ſoul; Thy health, I am;
And, bring to ſhameful wrack,
All thoſe who ſeek my death or ſhame;
Yea, ſham'd repell them back.
Let them before God's Angell fly,
As chaff, before the winde;
Let them before God's Angel fly.
Through paths, vnſafe & blinde.
3 Since pitts they digg'd; &, therein ſnares
For me, vniuſtly, laid;
Let them be ſlaine at vn-awares,
In their owne trapps, betraide.
Then, Lord, in thee, my ſoul ſhal ioy;
Thy help, my mirth ſhall be:
And, all my bones, oh Lord, ſhal ſay,

F That

That none cann equall thee.
4 Thou fav'ft thee pore, & men oppreft,
From thofe that are too ftrong:
Thou free'ft the pore, who are deftreft,
From fuch as do them wrong.
Falfe witneffe rofe, & charged me
With words I never fayd;
And, that my foul might fpoiled be,
They, Good with Ill, repaide.
5 Yet, when great ficknes them oppreft,
In fack-cloth cladd, I mourn'd:
I fafted; &, into my breft,
My prayers back return'd.
I greev'd for them, as men bemone
A Brother or a Freind;
And fadly walk'd, as when that one
Bewailes his Mothers end.
6 But, when my greefs did me befett,
Their Merry-meetings were:
The bafer fort, in private mett,
And, none did fcofs forbear.
Yea, at their Feafts, in mock of me,
The Scorners gnafh'd their teeth.
No longer, Lord, fpectator be,
But, fave my foul from death.
7 My Darling, from the Lion fave:
So, thy great love, oh Lord,
Where many folk their meetings have,
I'le to thy praife record.
Oh! let not thofe who me defpize,
Deride my pore eftate;
Or, lear on me with fcornful eyes,
Whome they vniuftly hate.
8 They feek not Peace, but Projects lay

For

For them that peacefull be :
With gaping mouthes, A H ! H A, ſay they,
Our wiſh, we now do ſee.
Thou ſaw'ſt it ; Therfor, make no pawſe,
Nor abſent, long, abide :
But, wake, ariſe, & let my cauſe
By thee, Lord God, be tri'de.
9 Lord, judge me in thy righteouſnes,
That they deride not me ;
And ſay in hart, this Fall of his
Is that, which wee would ſee.
Oh ! never give them cauſe to ſay,
We have devour'd him quite ;
But, ſhame, & root them out, for aye,
That in my harme delight.
10 Let them, with ſhame, & ſcorne, be cladd ;
That have my ſoul defeas'd :
And, let them trivmph & be gladd,
Who in my cauſe are pleaſd.
The Lord be prais'd, let all men ſay,
That wiſh thy Servants Peace :
And, with my tougue, I'le all the day,
Extol thy Righteouſnes.

Oh bleſſed Redeemer ! *let thy grations aſsiſtance be alwaies readie to garde vs from the furious malice of our Foes : And, ſeeing their condition is not hidd from thee, let thy iudgments be executed vpon all thoſe who ſhall continue vnrepentant in their wickednes ; that thy* Juſtice *may be glorified, as wel as thy* Mercie. *Make vs, alſo, mindful (oh Chriſt) from what height of glorie, thou didſt voluntarilie humble thy ſelfe ; to what extream contempt thou wert abaſed ; how vnkindlie, yea, how deſpightfully handled (even by thoſe for whoſe Redemption thou wert pleaſed to deſcend) And, by thy example teach vs to be humble,*

F 2 *patient,*

patient, & charitable in our suffrings; that bearing thy crosse, *& imitating thy* virtues; *we may be pertakers of thy* exaltation, *who livest & raignest, world without end.* Amen.

Psa. 36.

To the cheef Musitian, a Psalm of David the servant of the Lord. *It mentions the impiety & corruptions of the wicked. It declareth also, the infinite Love, mercie, sweetnes, & Iustice of God &c.* It may be sung to bring to consideration, God's goodnes, whẽ the over-flowings of vngodlines circumvent vs?

MY hart, within me, sayes;
That, Sinners fear not God:
And, their self-pleasing course, displaies
Their hatefull guilt abrode.
Their words, are wicked wiles;
Nor wise, nor just are they:
Vpon their bedds they study Guiles,
And, cursed is their way.
2 The heav'ns, thy Mercy fills;
Thy Truth doth reach the skye:
Thy justice, Lord, or'e-topps the hills,
And, deep thy judgments lie.
Thou sav'st both man & beast;
For, Lord, thy grace excells;
And, vnderneath thy wings, in rest,
Man-kinde securely dwells.
3 With dainties of thy house,
They shall replenish'd be;
And, streames of blisse, they shall carowse:
For, Life doth flowe from thee.
Thy light is, Lord, our light:
Therfore (where thou art knowne)

Prolong

Prolong thy grace, that men vpright,
May make thy works, their owne.
4 Let not the foot of pride,
Oppoſe, or hinder me;
Nor let me be remoov'd aſide,
By hands that wicked be.
For, thence the overthrowe,
Of Sinners, firſt begann;
And, when they fell, they fell ſo lowe,
That, riſe they never cann.

VVee confeſſe (oh Lord) that by the corruption ſtill remaining in our owne harts, we are plainlie informed, how Sinn, *being firſt conceived in* thought, *will at laſt break forth into publike* Act, *if thy great Mercie prevent not. Vouchſafe vs, therfor, not onlie thy common* grace, *which thou ſpreadeſt over all; but be pleaſed alſo, to diſplaie over vs, the wings of thy ſpecial* Mercies, *that being nouriſhed in thy houſe with ſpiritual* Banquet *(ſuch as thy* word, *thy* Sacraments, *& the* Illuminations *of thy* Spirit) *we may eſcape the falling into thoſe offeces from which there is no riſing againe; Let thy Saving-grace, be extended alſo to thoſe who yet know thee not, to the multiplieng of thy* Elect, *through* Ieſus Chriſt *our Lord.* Amen.

Pſa. 37.

A Pſalm of David. *It propoſeth many counſells, & experimental Argnments, to move vs, not to be offended at the Proſperitie of world-lings, & to perſuade a patient perſeverance in well-doeng &c.* It is vſefull, to keep vs contented with our eſtates, & hopefull in all temptations, & afflictions &c.

AT Sinners, take thou no offence,
Nor vex thy ſelf, at ſuch as they:
For, they ſhall ſoone be ſwept from hence,

And, like the graffe confume a way.
Beleeve in God, & live vpright ;
So, where thou dwell'ft, thou fhalt be fedd :
And, if in him, thou take delight,
Of all thy hopes, thou fhalt be fpedd.
Commit thou, to the Lord, thy way ;
Truft him, & all fhall well be done :
Thy Iuftice fhall out-fhine the day,
Thy judgment, paffe the funn at noone.
Delight in God ; his leafure bide ;
And, fret thou not that others thrive ;
But, thy difpleafure lay afide ;
Left, thou offence, by vexing give.
Expect awhile, & thou fhalt fee
The wicked fall ; & men vpright
Poffeffors of the land to be,
When Sinners dwellings vanifh quite.
For, meek-men fhall poffeffe the land,
And, peace enioy (at full) therein ;
Though wicked men, do them withftand,
Confpire, & gnafh their teeth, & grinn,
God, fees & mocks the Sinners end.
His Blade, in vaine he drawes to fmite,
He fhall his Bowe as vainely bend,
To flay the pore, & men vpright.
His Blade, ev'n his owne hart fhall gore ;
His bowe fhall breake ; and, that fmall fhare
The Right'ous hath, fhall profit more
Then all their heaps, that wicked are.
It fhall be foe ; becaufe, the Lord
(Who breaks their arme, that are vniuft)
To Godlie-men, will healps afford,
Which never fhall deceive their truft.
Knowne to the Lord, are all their waies ;

Their

Their heritage will alwaies laft.
They fhall not feare in ev'll-daies:
Nor emptie be, when others Faft.
Lewd men (& they who parte have tooke
Againft the Lord) fhall, then, become
Like fatt of Lambes, or like the fmoke,
Which melts, or quite away doth fume.
Much, borrowe thofe; but, never pay.
The Righteous lends, & mercie fhewes.
Where he doth bleffe, right bleft are they;
Where he doth curfe, a curfe enfues.
No courfe he takes, but God will guide
His feet; & in his waye delight:
He falls not quite, although he flide;
Becaufe, God holds him, ftill, vpright.
Olde-age & youth, I now have feene,
Yet, faw no Iuft-man, or his feed,
Forlorne or begg; For, they have beene
So kinde; that they finde healp, at need.
Proceed thou in this way, therfore,
Depart from Sinn, tread virtues path;
That thou maift live for ever more:
For, God, in Iudgment, pleafure hath.
Quite, roots he out the Sinners race;
But, ftill, his faints preferved are.
The Land, they fully fhall poffeffe;
And, fafelie dwell, for ever, there.
Right fitt; for, they difcreetly talke,
The Lawe of God, they ponder, ftill,
And in their waies, directly walke;
Though Sinners wait, their life to fpill.
Still, therfor, God will them defend,
And, clear them, when arraign'd they be.
If thou, likewife, on him attend,

God, in the Land, will prosper thee.
The Sinners fall, thine eye shall veiwe:
For, I have seene them, like the Bay,
Spread wide, and make a goodlie shewe
Then, suddenly consume away.
Veiwe thou the Iust; Observe them all;
For, peace their later daies attends:
But, wicked men togither fall;
And, mischeef brings them to their ends.
Which comes to passe, because the Iust,
The Lord (at need) their helper have:
For they in him do put their trust,
And, them from Sinners, he doth & save.

Almightie God! *make vs contented with our* portion, *without medling in what appertaines to others. Let not the prosperitie of the wicked, cause vs to be envious, fretfull, or discouraged; considering the ficklenes, & peril of their estate: But, give vs grace to be rather carefull, that we discharge our owne duties. Make vs* faithfull, chearfull, patient, meek, charitable, prudent, diligent & constant *in the wayes of well-doeng; that so we may be delivered from* despaires, scornes, slanders, conspiracies, persecutions, wants, & *all other temporal disadvantages of this life; & be iustified in sight of the whole world at the* Resurrection: *where, it will be evident, that the florishings of the* wicked *were never worth our envie; & that (according to thy word) the later end of the* Righteous, *is the beginning of* Blessednes, *for ever more.* Amē.

Psa. 38.

A Psalme of David to bring to Remembrance. *It is a penitentiall Psalme, emploring the pacification of God's wrath, & expressing our natural miseries, & corruptions &c.* It is vsefull when we feel the guilt & punishment of Sinn, with a true repentauce, & harty

harty defire of pardon &c.

LOrd, chide not when thou wroth fhalt be,
Nor in thy rage, my finn chaftife;
For, deep thy fhafts do ftick in me,
And, ftrict, thy hand vpon me lies.
Paines in my flefh, thy frownes have bredd;
My faults have rob'd my bones of reft;
My flouds of Sinn, have drown'd my head,
And by their waight I am oppreft.
2 My wounds corrupt, & foule they growe;
My Crimes have caufd that thus I fare:
With forrowes, I am preffed lowe;
And, all day long, my mournings are.
My Raines are grip'd, & fore defeas'd;
Throughout my body I am fore:
A waftinge-greef on me hath ceaf'd;
And paind at hart, aloud I roare.
3 Oh Lord! thou know'ft what things I want;
My mournings are not hidd from thee:
My ftrength decayes, my hart doth pant,
Mine eye-fight alfo faileth me.
My freinds & kindred, fhunn my greef;
My lovers, hide themfelves away:
And, they who feek to take my life,
Clofe-engines, to enfnare me, lay.
4 Yea, they who for my harme awaite,
Speake words, that full of mifcheef are:
Yet, how al day they muze deceit,
I (hearing) will not feeme to hear.
Nay, I have ftood, as mute, as he
Whofe tongue is partcht, whofe throte is dry,
Whofe eares depriv'd of hearing be;
And, in whofe mouth is no replie.
5 For, I oh Lord, on thee relie,

And, anſwere I expect from thee :
Oh ! therſor, now attend my crie,
Leſt els my foes inſult on me.
For, if my foote but ſlip aſide,
They, in my fall, them ſelves delight ;
My feet (alas) are prone to ſlide,
And, ſtill, my greefs are in my ſight.
6 Beholde, for my offence I greeve ;
And, my tranſgreſſions I bewaile :
Yet, ſtill, my foes encreaſe & live ;
Yea, ſtill, my cauſles-foes, prevaile.
Moreover, they, who render ill
For doeng well ; have mee with ſtood,
And, borne me hate for my good-will,
Becauſe, I love the thing that's good.
7 Lord, go not far, therſore, from hence ;
From me, my God ! depart not farr :
But, make thou ſpeed in my defence ;
Becauſe, from thee, my ſuccours are.

Moſt awfull God ! *dreadfull is thy frown when we beholde thee angrie for Sinn : lothſome are our ſinns, when they appeare to a wounded conſcience: & vnſufferable our afflictions when our conſciences accuſe vs: VVe have ſinned, oh Lord, (we have ſinned) and are therfor tormented both in ſoul & bodie: yet, we beſeech thee deal not with vs according to our ſinns; but, for thy mercie-ſake vouchſafe vs a favorable correction, & thoſe remedies & conſolations which thou knoweſt beſt for our infirmities: VVhē thou art offended, our foes are not only miſcheevous vexations, but our kindred alſo forſake vs; our beſt beloved freinds afflict vs; & (which is yet more) we our ſelves are our owne tormentors. VVhatſoever therfor, betides vs (or whoſoever is iniurious) wee have nothing to replie, nor any to accuſe, but our ſelves. Oh ! pittie our diſtempers, hear vs, help vs, & deliver vs, for the*

bitter

bitter paſſion ſake of Ieſus Chriſt *our Lord.* Amen.

Pſa. 39.

To the cheef Muſitian to Iduthun a pſalme of David. *The Prophet reſolves a patient watchfulnes over the tongue; Bemoanes the vanitie, & miſerie of mankinde & petitions for God's mercie, &c.* It may ſerve to inſtruct & comfort vs, during the provocations of the wicked, & in other afflictions.

I Vow'd to keep my waies vpright,
And, that in words, I none would wrong.
While ſinners were, therfore, in ſight,
I ſhut my lipps, & ſtayd my tongue:
What er'e they ſayd, I ſilent ſtood;
Refraining words, though they were good.

2 But, greefs did then to ſtirr beginn,
Which, hot in me, my hart did make;
My thoughts inflam'd a fire within,
Which loos'd my tongue, & then I ſpake.
Lord, of my end, informe thou me;
And, what my dayes, & frailties, be.

3 For, loe, my life is but a ſpann;
It ſeems as nothing, in thine eyes:
Ev'n at his beſt, moſt vaine is man,
And, like the ſhade away he flies.
He tires himſelf, with needles paines,
And knowes not who ſhall reap his gaines.

4 On thee, therefore, I do attend;
My truſt, oh Lord, I place on thee.
From all my ſinns, my ſoul defend;
From flouting-fooles, preſerve thou mee:
For, I forbare to ſpeak a word,
Becauſe, it was thy doeng, Lord.

5 Thy hand, with blowes, doth me afflict;
Oh! take thy heavie ſtrokes away.

When

When thou for ſinn doſt man correct,
Thou, Moth-like fretſt their Forme awaie.
  Therfore, no cauſe of doubts remaine,
  That ev'ry man is wholie vaine.
6 Lord, hear my ſuite; my criengs hear;
Let not my teares vnmention'd goe:
For, as thy Gueſts, my Fathers were,
(And ſtrangers here) ev'n I am ſoe.
  Oh! ſpare, & grant me ſtrength, I pray,
  Before I paſſe from hence, for aye.

Give vs Grace, oh Lord, *that our tongues neither offend, by vndiſcreet or evill ſpeakings, nor by continueng ſilent whē we ought to ſpeake. Remember vs how short and vaine our lives are, & how foolish it is to wearie our ſelves, & conſume our time, for that which we may never enioy; looſing, in the meane while, aſſured bleſſings. Enable vs to ſuſtaine the* croſſe *(which thou shalt lay vpon us) without repininge, & lay no more on vs then thou shalt make vs able to beare. Deliver vs from the ſcorne of* fooles; *but eſpeciallie, from thoſe tranſgreſſions, by which our* beauty *is conſumed. Mark our* teares, *hear our* cries, *and ſpare vs in this our* pilgrimage, *vntill we have atained the ſtrength by which we may ſtand firm in thy favour, through* Ieſus Chriſt *our Lord.* Amen.

Pſa. 40,

To the cheef Muſitian a Pſalme of David. *It is applied vnto Chriſt,* Hebr. 10. *It praiſeth God for our Redemption, declares the aboliſhing of the* Ceremonial Law, *the obedience of Chriſt, & the preaching of the Goſpell, &c.* It is vſefull to commemorate Chriſts obedience; to give praiſe for former deliverances, & to pray for future preſervation.

MY conſtant hopes on God are ſett,
Who, when I cride, gave eare to me:

He

He brought me from the myrie-pitt:
Ev'n from the denn, where horrors be.
  Vpon a Rock, my feet he plac't;
  He fetled there, my ftanding faft.
2 And, that his praife I might declare,
A new-made fong, to me he taught;
Which many men fhall hear, with fear,
And, to depend on God, be brought.
  For, they, who truft in him, are bleft:
  And, they who pride & lies, deteft.
3 Thofe wonders, Lord, which thou haft wrought;
Thofe things (my God) fo many are
Which thou concerning vs haft thought;
That none cann them to thee declare:
  O Lord! to order them to thee,
  Is far too great a task for me.
4 No offrings thou doft now require,
But, only, that thy words I hear:
No Sacrifize confum'd in fire,
By thee, for finns, defired are.
  Then, Loe, *(I fayd)* I come, to be
  That, which thy *Book* foretold of me.
5 I ioy to do thy will, oh God!
Thy Law, is in my hart enrowld;
And, Lord, thy Iuftice, all abrode,
In great Affemblies, I have tolde.
  Thou know'ft my lipps thy Truth reveald;
  And, that my hart hath nought conceald.
6 I, made thy faithful-dealing knowne;
I, did thy faving-health declare:
I have not kept thy Love vnfhowne,
Nor hidd thy Truth, where hearers were.
  Therfor, to me thy mercy fhowe;
  Thy Truth, & Love, Lord, make me know.

7 For,

7 For, mifcheeves more then cann be tolde,
Have now enclos'd me round about ;
My finns, on me have layd fuch holde,
There is no place of looking out :
Their number doth my haires out goe,
And, therfor, faint my hart doth growe.
8 Oh Lord ! vouchfafe my life to fave,
With fpeed oh God ! affift I pray ;
That they with fhame. a fall may have,
Who feek to take my Soul away :
Let thofe that wifh amiffe to me,
With fhame & fcorne, repelled be.
9 With rooting-out, thofe men requite,
(And paie them with deferved fhame)
Whoe in thofe words of fcorne delight,
Which bring on me, difgrace, or blame.
But, give him ioy in his defires,
Who after thee, oh Lord, enquires.
10 Let them who love thy faving-health,
Confeffe thee Lord, for evermore :
For, thou art mindfull of my wealth,
And, heedeft me, though I am pore.
Lord God my helper, make thou fpeed,
To help me, ftill, at ev'rie need.

Allmightie God, *by whofe divine powre,* Iefus Chrift *was raifed out of the myrie* pitt *of the* Grave, *& with trymph afcended from the* Dungeons *of* Hell, *into the higheft heavens : Grant, that by his example we may continually offer vp the fweet, & ever acceptable* Sacrifize, *of* Obedience *to thy* Will. *Write thy* Lawe *in our* Harts ; *Let our* Tongues *publish thy* Righteoufnes, *& thy* Truth, *to all the world. And, though our manyfold Sinns make vs vnworthy of thy grace, yet deliver vs from that shame & punishmēt which they deferve, that our* Foes *may be difappointed*

pointed of their hope ; & that, we, (together with all thy Saints) *may ioyfully confeſſe thy great Mercie, through* Iefus Chrift *our Lord.* Amen.

Pfal. 41.

To the cheef Mufitian, a Pfalm of David. *It declares the reward of Charitie towards, the pore members of Chriſt ; expreſſeth the Hypocriſy of his foes ; Beſeecheth God's aſſiſtance, & praiſeth him for our exaltation by Chriſt.* It is vfefull, for thefe purpofes aforementioned. *&c.*

THe man is bleft that heeds the pore,
From dangers, God will him repreeve ;
He will preferve his life, therefore,
And, vnto him preferment give.
The Lord, will gard him from his foes,
When him they labour to furprife ;
Refrefh him, when that weak he growes,
And, make his bedd, when fick he lies.
2 In mercie, cure my foul I pray ;
For, Lord, ev'n thee, I did offend.
Vile words, of me, my foes do fay ;
And, wifh my fame & Life, had end.
When me they fpie, fair fhowes they make :
But, in their harts my harm defire ;
Which when they come abrode, they fpeake,
Where all my foes, my wrong confpire.
5 Some ill defeafe hath he (they fedd)
Hee's downe, & fhall no more arife :
Nay, he whome I have lov'd & fedd,
(My trufted-freind) did me defpife.
But, help me Lord, & raife, me now,
That, I their dealings may requite.
I fhall thereby, thy favour knowe,

If

If thou prevent my Foes deſpight.
6 Thou doſt maintaine my Righteouſnes,
And, in thy ſight ſtill placeſt me :
The Lord, the God of Iſr'el bleſſe ;
Oh ! let him bleſt for ever be. *Amen. Amen.*

Infuſe into vs, oh Chriſt, *ſuch brotherly compaſſion, & ſuch true Charitie toward thy pore members, that we may obtaine all timely conſolations in this life, & be well-comed with* Come yee bleſſed, *at the laſt-day. WVe confeſſe, there is a diſeaſe in our ſoules, diſenabling vs to performe this dutie ; and, as wee are neither truly compaſſionate to others, nor faithfull acknowledgers of thy love to vs ; So, we finde others iuſtly vnmerciful, in our Afflictions, & encreaſing our vexations, by neglect, conſpiracies, or bitter Cenſures: Yea, they whome wee have cherished & releeved, in their wants & ſorrowes, dovnthanckfully take part with our Oppreſſors. Oh ! deliver vs therefor, from our owne vnthanckfullnes, & want of charity, that we may be comforted by others, in our need ; & become more perfect and conſtant, in all good works, to the praiſe & glory of thy* Name. Amen.

Pſal. 42.

To the cheef Muſitian Maſchill for the Sonns of Chorah. *It miſtically expreſſeth a Chriſtian mans eſtate wandring through the Hopes, Doubts, & Feares, of this life &c.* It is vſefull, when inward or out ward afflictions tempt to deſpaire of God's love ; or, when we are hindred from frequenting *his aſſemblies, &c.*

LOrd, as that Hart which water wants,
So, longs, my ſoul for thee :
Eternal God ! ſo thirſts & pants
My ſoul, thy face to ſee.
My teares, are day & night my meat :

And,

And, when I hear them faie,
VVhere is thy God? the greef of it
Confumes my hart awaie.
2 For, heretofore I went among
Thy folke on holy-dayes;
Them, to thy houfe, I ledd along,
And, there wee fung thy praife.
My Soul, why art thou fo oppreft?
In mee, why art thou fad?
Still, praife thou God, & on him reft;
For, he will make thee glad.
3 My Soul, oh God! is faint in mee,
Yet, thinck on thee I will,
Though *Iordans* land I cannot fee,
Nor *Hermons* little Hill.
The, deepes vpon each other call,
When thy loud ftormes defcend;
And, over me, thy Billowes fall.
But, Lord, thou help wilt fend.
4 For day & night, I'le fing & pray
Oh God (my life) to thee:
My God my Rock; to thee, I'le fay,
Why thus forfak'ft thou mee?
Why am I fuffred ftill to mourne,
Afflicted by my foes?
VVhere is thy God? they fay in fcorne;
And, through my bones it goes.
5 My foul, why art thou fo oppreft?
Why art thou fad in mee?
Stil praife thou God; & on him reft
For; he my God will be.

How defirable (oh Holy-ghoft the Comforter) *are thy confolations to afflicted fouls! & how thirftely fwallowed, being mingled with our teares! Our finns oft greeve thee; therfor, thou iustly greevest vs to make vs sensible of our vnkindnesses: Therfore, wee are somtime censured as Hypocrites; & have all our piety & devotion mentioned with scorne, to our vexatiō: Therfor, mischeeves like waves, follow vs, one after another; yea, & therfor also, our owne consciences so accuse vs, that wee are somtime sorrowfull to the death, & almost desperate of thy favour. But, blessed* Spirit, *speake thou (oh speake thou) comfortably to our soules; & to whatsoever outward miserie thou expose vs, (yea though we appear miserable to our selves) be thou still our* God, *& our* Comforter, *that our sorrowes may at the last be turned into ioy, to thy glorie & our everlasting consolation.* Amen.

Psa. 43.

The Prophet *prayeth for assistance, promiseth to be thanckefull, & concludes, with rowzing vp his deiected Soul to persevere in praising, & relieng on God. It may be sung, to keep vs vndiscouraged in our spiritual greevances.*

LOrd, judg thou me & plead my right
  With such as cruel be;
From wicked men, that vse deceit
  Oh God! deliver met.
For, since thou Lord, my fortresse art
  Why shouldst thou fro me goe?
Why should I walke so sad in hart
  Oppressed by my foe?
2 Mee, let thy light & Truths bright raies,
  Vnto thy dwelling bring:
And, at thine Altars; to thy praise
  Oh! God my Ioye, I'le sing.
My Soul, why art thou so opprest?
  Why art thou sadd in mee?
Still praise thou God, & on him rest:
  For he my God will be.

VVhen

VVhen our foules are afflicted, expofe vs not (oh God*) to fuffer longe, the fcornes of our Adverfaries; nor leave vs to the terror of thofe cruel iudgements which our owne confciences do often pronounce againft vs: But, when wee are moft feverely iudged by the world, & by our owne felves, doe thou abfolve vs. Depart not from vs, when wee are compaffed about with iniuries, neither give vs over to thofe melancholy cogitations which will oppreffe our harts when forrowe hath entred into our foules. But, let the truth of thy* promifes, *& the light of thy* countenance, *fo appeare to vs, that we may be revived thereby; to the encreafe & continuance of our confolation; and, that (depending alwaies on thee as our fole comforter) we may magnifie thy Name for ever & ever.* Amen.

Pfa. 44.

To the Cheef Mufitian, for the Sonns of Chorah *The Church pleads for God's mercie, becaufe hee is her auncient deliverer; & becaufe he is yet, her only Truft, though shee hath long fuftained the fcornes & oppreffions of Tyrants, &c.* It may be vfed, when the Church or commonwealth is afflicted, *&c.*

Oh God! thy work's in Ages paft
  Wee heard our fathers tell:
How, thou the Gentiles forth didft caft,
  And, broughtft them there to dwell.
For, nor their fword nor Arme it was
  By which that land they gaind
But, Lord, thy hand, thyne arme, thy grace,
  And favour, them fuftain'd.
2 Oh Lord my God, my king thou art,
  Thy *Iacob*, ftill, defend,
And, we fhall thofe through thee fubvart
  That harme to vs intend.

G 2 Wee

Wee through thy Name ſhall tread them lowe,
That vs reſiſt, oh Lord ;
For, I depend not on my bowe,
Nor truſt I to my ſword.
2 Wee from our foes were kept by thee,
And thou didſt work them ſhame :
In thee therſore, much joy'd were wee
And, wee did praiſe thy Name.
Yet, now diſgrac'd, thou throw'ſt vs by ;
Our Hoaſt thou doſt forſake :
Before our foes, thou mak'ſt vs fly
And, ſpoiles from vs they take.
4 Thou makeſt vs the Gentiles meat,
And, vs like ſheep they ſlaie ;
We, ſcattred, & for ſale, are ſett
To thoſe, who nothing paie.
At vs our neighbours laugh & ieer,
Of vs, they proverbs make :
The people round vs, mock & flear ;
At vs, their heads they ſhake.
5 Diſgrace is alwaies in my ſight ;
And, redd with ſhame, I grow,
To hear the ſcornfull words of ſpight,
And, railings of my foe :
Yet, wee, oh Lord, forget not thee,
Nor from thy cov'nant ſtray ;
Nor changed in our harts are we,
Nor gone out of thy way.
6 Nay, though (oppreſt, in death's black ſhade)
Wee lodg'd with Dragons, lie :
Thy Name, wee not forgotten had,
Nor to ſtrang Gods did crie.
Yea Lord, thou know'ſt (who know'ſt each thought)
That, daylie, for thy ſake,

We

We fare like sheep, to slaughter brought
And, so our deaths wee take.
7 Lord, wake, & rise; why sleepst thou so!
Reiect vs no for aye.
Why shouldst thou disrespect our woe,
And hide thy face away?
Behold, ev'n to the dust wee make
Our soules & bodies bend:
Redeem vs for thy mercie sake;
Arise, & vs defend.

Deliver vs, oh Lord, *from all our adversaries: & make vs to be still mindfull what wee have aunciently heard concerning thee, from others; & what experience we our selves have had of thy iudgments and Mercies, from time to time: that, neither our prosperities make vs arrogate any thing to our selves, nor our Afflictions or persecutions cause vs to blaspheame, or forget thee. Yea, though we should become the scorne & laughing-stock of our Neighbours, a prey to our foes, & be alwaies as the sheep appointed for slaugher; yet, keep vs vnchanged in the true* Religeon, *& in our* love *to thee: That, thou (to whome both our outward* Trialls, *& our inward* sinceritie, *is ever knowne) mayst in due time, help & save vs whome thou hast redeemed, through* Iesus Christ *our Lord,* Amen.

Psa. 45.

To the Cheef Musitian vpon Shosannim for the Sonns of Chorah Maschil. *It is, as it were, Christ's marriage-song, and setts forth the glorie of that bridegroome & of his Spouze.* It is vsefull to stir vp our spirituall affection to Christs, &c.

MY tongue shall prompt the writers penn,
My thoughts of thee, oh King! to tell:
For, thou excellst the Sonns of men;

And, on thy lipps, all graces dwell.
God, wil thee bleſſe, for evermore.
Great Conquerour, vnto thy ſide,
With honor, gird thy ſword, therefore,
  And, forward in thy Triumphs ride.
2 Thy Righthand ſhall, by deeds vpright,
(By Truth, & Meeknes) wonders doe:
Thy ſhafts, thy foes, to death ſhall ſmite,
And make the people ſerve thee to.
Eternal is thy Throne of ſtate;
Thy Scepter, from all wrong is free;
Thou Iuſtice lov'ſt, thou Sinn doſt hate;
  And therfor, God anointed thee.
3 Yea, thine owne God, thy head anoints,
Ev'n with his oyle of Ioyfulnes;
And, thee (above thy Mates) appoints,
The place of Sov'raigne to poſſeſſe.
The pretious Robes, which thou put'ſt on
Of *Aloes*, *Caſſia*, & of *Mirrh*,
Smell round about thine yv'rie throne,
  When, they thy hart have cheared, there.
4 Kings daughters, have at all times bene
Among thy Maides of honour, found:
And, at thy righthand, ſtands the Queene,
In *Ophir* gold, arayd, & crown'd.
Hear, daughter, & my words reſpect;
Forget thy fathers kindred, now:
And, that the king may thee affect,
  Him, for thy Lord, acknowledg thou.
5 Then, ſhall the Daughters come from *Tyre*,
And, bring rich preſents vnto thee;
The wealthy, ſhall thy grace deſire,
And, Suitors, for thy favours be.
The Daughter of the King, doth wear

An

An vpper garment wrought with gold :
But, if her in-ſide ſhould appear,
You, all perfections would behold.
6 Her, to the kinge, preſent they ſhall,
In Robes which are by needels wrought ;
Ev'n with her fellowe Virgines all,
(Attending her) ſhee ſhall be brought.
They ſhall into his pallace come,
With ioyfull hart, & merry chear :
And, ſhee, ſhall in her fathers Roome,
To be her comforts, Children bear.
7 Great Kings, (on earth) ſhee, them ſhall make ;
And, cauſe, that men in future daies,
Such notice of her Name ſhall take,
That nations all, ſhall ſing her praiſe.

Moſt amiable Bridegroome *of our ſoules, (whoſe excellencies ravish, with ſpirituall affections, all thoſe who cann apprehend the beamings of thy maieſty, with true faith.) Proceed on, in the manifeſtation of thy powre; Enflame our harts by the viſion of thy* perfections ; *make our perſons acceptable by the reflection of thy* beauties ; *enrich vs outwardly with the goldē embroideries of* goodworks ; *adorne vs inwardly with the Iewells of* Divine graces ; *and let thy* holie-Spirit *bring vs vnto thee, acompanied with ſo many vnpoluted Affections ; that, thou maieſt take pleaſure in our comelines ; and, that we, forgetting our carnall deſires, (and wholie renouncing our ſelves) may have our full contentation in thy dear embraces ; and enioy all the priveledges belonging to thy* Spouze, *for ever and ever.* Amen.

Pſa. 46.

To the cheef Muſitian for the ſonns of Chorah, a ſong vpon Alamoth. *It expreſſeth on Aſſurance of*
G 4 *Gods*

God's protection, & the reasons thereof, with an exhortation also, to give notise of God's powre. It is vsefull to vs, for those purposes, &c.

GOd, is my strength, when dangers are ;
 A ready healp approved :
Therfore, wee would not stand in feare,
 Though all the world were mooved.
No, though the Flouds had flowed-o're
 The highest earthlie dwellings ;
And Seas did make the hillie shore,
 To tremble at their swellings. (*Selah.*)
2 There is a River, which doth glad
 The place where God resideth ;
And, happie is that Cittie made,
 Because, he there abideth.
Her, vn-remoov'd, & firme to sett,
 He, timelie vndertaketh ;
And, though Realmes rave, & heathens frett,
 Earth melts, when he but speaketh.
3 The Lord of hoasts, our part will take ;
 Vs, *Iacobs* God, protecteth. (*Selah.*
Oh come therefore, & notise take
 What wonders God effecteth :
What wast, & spoiles, when he shall please,
 Among mankinde he sendeth ;
And, how he makes, both warr & peace,
 As far as land extendeth.
4 He cuts the spear, he breakes the bowe,
 And, he the Charret fireth :
Be still, saith hee, & also, know
 Your God the same requireth.
I will divulge my fame abrode
 To ev'ry ethnick Nation.
The Lord of Hoasts, ev'n *Iacobs* God,

(With

(With vs) is our Salvation. (*Selah*)

No distrust have our soules, oh Lord, *of thy loving protection; yet when the contract betwixt thee & vs was first published, the whole world of our enimies raged at our preferment; & all the Corruptions of our Nature did furiously oppose our vnion: And, but that wee were strengthned by thy continuall presence (& refreshed by the ever-flowing River of thy grace) they had shaken (& perhaps overthrown) our Constancie. Oh! continue thy assistance to our comfort, & their further vexation. Protect vs from every evill; confirm vs in all goodnes; and so break the weapons & engines of vngodlines; that, all the world may extoll thy works, &, wee continue, for ever, in thy Salvation, through* Iesus Christ *our Lord* Amen.

Psa. 47.

To the cheef Musitian, a Psalme for the Sonns of Chorah. *It provoketh to reioicinge, for the Ascention of Christ; praiseth him, for subiecting the world to his spiritual dominion; & for vniting Iewes & Gentiles &c.* VVee should vse it to those purposes.

TO God, all people, ioyfullie
Clapp hands, with exultation;
For, dreadfull is the Lord, most high,
Great king of ev'ry Nation.
He, vnto vs, by his great powre,
Much people hath subjected;
And, made our heritage, the flowre
Of *Iacob*, his elected. (*Selah*)
2 With trumpets, & with merry noise,
Is God the Lord ascended:
Oh! let him be (with joyfull voice)
In songs of praise, commended.
Of God our kinge, the praise now sing;

Sing praiſe, & honour do him.
The Lord, of all the world is king;
Sing praiſe, with knowledge, to him.
3 God ſitts vpon his holy throne
Or'e all the Gentiles raigninge;
And, calleth ev'ry willing-one,
To *Iacobs* God pertaininge.
For, vnto God (whome ev'rie tongue
With high applauſe commendeth)
The worlds protection doth belonge;
And, he the ſame defendeth,

Eternal Sonn God, *great in powre, terrible in Iudgment, King of Kings & Lord of Lords; who ſitting on the right-hand of thy Father, haſt ſubiected the world to thy* Dominion, *& elected vnto thy ſelfe out of all Nations thoſe* willing-ones *who are obedient to thy* Call. *Oh grant, that wee may not hide thy* Talent, *or belie thy bountie, (by their perſwaſions, who tell vs that,* thou expecteſt to reap where thou ſowedſt not) *but, let vs thanckfully, acknowledge thy* Common grace: *When we are particulerly called, let vs runn vnto thee by thy aſsiſting Spirit; & obtain that ſpeciall Favour, which makes a ſure* Election, *and from which there is no* falling. *So, we ſhall ſee that* Truth, *at which ſo many ſtumble; & with cheerfull harts & triumphant voices, aſcribe our Salvation, wholy, to thee; & all honor, & powre, & glory, to thy Maieſty, now & for ever more.* Amen.

Pſa. 48.

A Pſalm & ſonge for the Sonns of Chorah. *It extolls the Lord, & the place of his dwelling; confeſſeth his mercy, his Bounty, & exhorts others to conſider & publish he ſame.* Wee, above many other Nations, ſhould vſe this, to praiſe God for our Syon, *&c.*

The

THe Lord is great, & great his Fame
Should in his holy mountaine be:
For, *Syon* is a goodly Frame;
The praise of all the world, is shee.
Shee north-ward stands, & shee doth hight
The Cittie of the King of might.
2 The Lord, is knowne to be her garde;
For, when great kings against her came,
They much admir'd; admiring, feard;
And, fearing, fledd away with shame:
Ev'n with such pangs, & suchlike feare,
As women that in travaile are.
3 For, thou, didst raise an Easterne winde,
Which all the shipps of *Tarsus* brake:
And, Lord of Hoasts, now true we finde,
What others of thy Cittie spake:
Yea, wee have heard, & now wee see,
That, God will still her keeper be. *(Selah)*
3 Within thy Temple, wee oh God,
Vpon thy loving-kindnes thought;
Thy Name is published abrode;
With Justice, thy Right-hand is fraught:
And, in thy Iudgments, *Syon* shall
Reioice, with *Iudah's* daughters all.
Through *Syon* goe; about her walke,
Her Bullworks marke, her Turrets heed;
That, of her beauties you may talke
And, tell her glories to your seed:
For, God in life will be our guide;
And, in our death, our God abide.

Thou art worthy oh Lord God, *to receive honor, & praise & powre; for, thou hast beautified, & soe fortified thy* Cittie *the* Catholick Church; & thy *auncient promises concerning her, are so gratiouslie fulfilled, that many*

*ny famous Nations, Kingdomes & potentates, (who despi-
sed & opposed her small beginning) having, since, vewed
her (with reverence terror & admiration) are driven back
from their Idolatries & ashamed of their malitious Inten-
tions. Make vs oh God! faithfull Citizens of this thy* Citty,
*& delighted, so to observe & publish the beauties & prive-
ledges thereof, that the number of her inhabitants may be in-
creased, & that wee & they, may there live, vnder they
protection, for ever & ever.* Amen.

Psa. 49.

To the Cheef Musitian a Psalm for the Sonns of Chorah. *It declares the common vanity, & the folly of men in honor &c.* It is vsefull, to comfort the weak Christian against the scandalls of the crosse; & strengthens him that is offendeth at the prosperities of the wicked *&c.*

YEe dwellers all on earth, give eare,
Both rich & pore, & high, & lowe;
For, musings deep, I will declare,
And, wisdom from my tongue shall flowe.
Dark Problems I will harken out,
A Ridle to my harpe, I'le sing;
For, of that day, what should I doubt,
Which, all my faults, will round me bring?
2 They, who their trust in Riches have,
And, glorie in their wealths encrease,
Their brothers life, shall neither save,
Nor with his God, procure him peace.
For, soules redemptions are so deare,
That, no man cann sufficient have
To purchase life, for ever, here;
Or, scape the Dungeon of the grave.
3 Men see, both fooles & wisemen die,

And,

And, that their gettings others waſt:
Yet, to their Names, their lands they tie,
And, thinck their houſe will ever laſt.
But, man's vaine honor ſoone decaies,
Ev'n as the brutiſh creature dies:
And, (though their ſeed, their courſe do praiſe)
Their waies are neither ſafe, nor wiſe. *Selah*
4 Like ſheep, they food for death are made,
Who ſhall a cov'ring on them laie:
Their glories in the grave ſhall fade,
And, Iuſt-men riſe more bleſt, then they. *Selah*
Deſpaire not then, though ſome thou ſee,
Surpaſſing thee in place, or pelſe:
Since, God, thy ſoul from hell will free,
And, home receive thee to him ſelf.
5 For, though their life more bleſt they thought,
(And, others did their path commend)
They to their grave ſhall carry nought,
Nor ſhall their pompe to them deſcend.
No; to their Fathers, they muſt paſſe,
And lie in darknes quite forgott;
For, fooliſh men in honor'd place,
Are like the beaſt, which dies, to rott.

*It is a Riddle (*oh Father of Wiſdome*) that happines, should be attained without* wealth honours *and ſuch tranſitorie things; Therfor, worldlings magniſy them ſelves, & applaud others, according to their temporal acheivments; but when Sinn followes at the heels to Iudgment; when the grave shall devour our beauties; & when the price of Soules is required; then, their vainty will be apparent. Grant therfor, oh* Lord, *that neither the worlds eſteem of ſuch things, make vs to overvalue them; nor our want of them, to be diſcouraged; but, let vs be fully contented in our ſalvation by thee: So, when they perish like beaſts, (& are con-*

consumed & forgotten in the grave) who were honorable & rich, without vnderstanding; wee, whome they iudged vnhappie, shal at the Resurrection arise blessed and glorified, through Iesus Christ, *our Lord,* Amen.

Psa. 50.

A Psalm for Asaph. *It propheceis of the last Iudgement, & summons Iewes & Gentiles there vnto; it declares by what lawe they shall be iudged; Reprehends Hypocrites; & exhorts to Repentance, &c.* It is vseful, to warne that wee be not hypocriticall; in regard, all shall one be disclosed, &c.

THe Lord our God, th'Almightie-one
  Hath spoke, & summon'd all,
That are betwixt the rising Sunn,
  And places of his fall.
God's glorie, *Syon,* first will showe.
  With noise, approch will hee;
Before him, burning fire shall goe,
  A storme, shall round him be.
2 Through heav'n & earth, he shall, aloud,
  His folke to iudgment call;
His Saints, that Sacrifizes vow'd,
  Appear before him shall.
His Iustice, heav'n shall shewe abrode;
  For, God the Iudge will be.
Hark *Isr'el* ; for, ev'n I, thy God,
  Will thee accuse, saith hee.
3 I, for thine Offrings blame thee not,
  Which were my due of olde;
Nor Bullock ask I, neither Goate,
  Out of thy Stall or Folde.
For, I, more heards of Cattell owne,
  Then all the Mountaines yeald;

To

To mee all Beaſts, & Birds are known,
  That live in wood or feild.
4 If I were hungrie, doſt thou thinck,
  (Since all the world is mine)
Thy Goates bloud, I would ask to drinck?
  Or, feed on Bulls of thine?
No; rather pay, in thanckfulnes,
  Thy Vowes; and call on me:
So, I ſhall pittie thy deſtreſſe
  And, have due praiſe from thee.
5 But, to the wicked, ſaies the Lord,
  How dareſt thou to prate
Of my commands, & of my word,
  Whilſt thou doſt Counſell hate?
For, when thou doſt a Theef perceive,
  A ſhare with him thou tak'ſt;
Thou, in Adulterie doſt live,
  And, wicked words thou ſpeak'ſt.
6 Thy Brother, (thine owne Mothers ſonn)
  Thou cauſles, doſt revile.
I, ſilent was, & thou haſt done
  Theſe wicked things, the while.
Yea, thou haſt therevpon ſuppos'd,
  That, I, was like to thee;
But, all thy folly ſhall diſclos'd,
  And, now apparent be.
7 Yee, that of God forgetfull are,
  Of this, Remembrance have,
Els, I ſhall you in peeces tear,
  When there is none to ſave.
For, I am glorifide of thoſe,
  That give due praiſe to mee,
And, ſuch as well their lives diſpoſe,
  By ſaving health ſhall ſee.

Al-

Almighty God, *who with maiestie & terror, shall come to iudge the world & require an Account of everie one according to the Talent receaved (especially of us, who are* Saints, *by an ordinarie & visible* Callinge*) give vs grace to offer the acceptable Sacrifize of Righteousnes & true obedience. Let not our Religeon be meerly formall, without the fruites of good life. Let vs not be of those hypocriticall talkers & professors of thy word, whoe hate reformation, & vncharitably censure their owne Brethren; neither let thy long forbearance of our Sinns cause vs any way to abuse thy mercies: but, grant rather, that we may so vnfainedly embrace thee in our harts, & so truly serve thee in our lives, that thou maist be glorified by vs, & wee saved by thee in the last Iudgment,* Amen.

Psa. 51.

To the cheef Musitian a Psalme of David when Nathan the prophet came vnto him, after he had gone into Bethsheba. *It personates a man trulie penitent; and, a true confession, contrition, & purpose of amendment, is the subiect of this Psalme,* Everie true penitentiarie may sing it in his humiliation, &c.

OH Lord, of thy abounding Love
To my offence, remissive be:
My Follies Purge, my Sinn remove,
And, of thy grace, daigne grace to me.
For, still, my fault before me lies;
Yea, by my selfe, I am accus'd:
Thee, thee alone, my conscience cries,
Ev'n to thy face, I have abus'd.
2 Which, here I do confesse, oh Lord,
That, when to censure thou art brought,
Men, true my finde thy Truthfull word,
And, judge thy Iudgments as they ought,

For,

For, (sinfull though my parents made,
My Beeing, & my Birth to bee)
From thee, a secret grace I had,
  To forme the Truth thou seek'st in mee.
3 And, if I purg'd with hysope were,
Mee, thou shouldst make more white than snowe
Yea, thy *Glad-message* when I heare,
The bones thou brak'st, will heathfull growe,
Then, from my faults, thy face divart;
Blot all my follies out of sight;
Creat in me a spotles hart,
  And, make my Spirit, Lord, vpright.
4 Oh! let me not rejected be;
Take not thy Holie-ghost away;
To joiefull health, restore thou mee;
Let thy free Spirit be my stay.
So, I will other Sinners guide,
To seek thy grace, & walk thy waies;
And, (if my bloudie sinn thou hide)
  Thy Iustice, oh my God, I'le praise.
5 Which praises, that my tongue may sing,
My lipps, oh Lord my God, vnclose:
For Burnt-oblations I would bring;
But, thou hast quite reiected those.
A greeved Soul, a contrite hart,
Is God's best-liked Sacrifize:
With such, oh God! thou pleased art;
  And, such thou never shalt despise.
6 As thou art pleas'd, Mount-*Syon* blesse,
And wall about *Ierusalem*.
The Sacrifize of Righteousnes,
Shall then obtaine thy good esteem.
Yea, thou shalt then their Guifts receive,
And, they shall all their Offrings pay;

H Ev'n

Ev'n whole Burnt-offrings they ſhall give,
  And, Oxen on thy Altar ſlay.

Oh Lord! our owne Conſciences accuſe vs, & will pronounce thee iuſt if thou condemn vs: for though it might ſomewhat moove thy compaſſion, to conſider our diſabilities, by Original Polution; yet, knowing what grace thou haſt ſecretly infuſed, both, to reſiſt that naturall corruption, and to forme alſo within vs that Righteouſnes which thou requireſt; wee have no excuſe (no hope) but to appeal to thy mercie. To thy Mercie therfor, wee appeal, beleeving to be perfectly purified by the ſprinckling of thy dear Sonns bloud. Oh! forgive vs for his ſake; Reſtore vs to thy favour; repaire what is decaied in ſoul or bodie; & ſo comfort, renue, guide, & ſtrengthen us, by the continuall preſence of the Holy-ghoſt; that our converſation may be more vpright; & all our future endeavours become acceptable; to thy glorie, to the Saving of our Soules, & to the conſolation of other penitent Sinners, through Ieſus Chriſt *our Lord:* Amen.

Pſal. 52.

To the cheef Muſitian Maſquil a Pſalm of David when Doeg the Edomite came & told Saul, & ſaid vnto him, David is come vnto the houſe of Abhimelech. *It miſtically, perſonates the Elect, vpbraiding their perſecutors, foretelling their ſhamfull ruine, & reioicing in their owne deliverances, &c.* It is vſefull in perſecutions.

WHy vaunt'ſt thou Tiraunt of thy wrong?
  God's love will ſtill the ſame appear,
Although thy miſcheef-working tongue,
Faines lies, as keen as Razors are.
Thou, evill more then Good reſpect'ſt;
Thou loveſt falſhood more then right: *(Selah.)*
All

All harmefull ſpeaches thou affect'ſt,
And, tongues which publiſh forth deceit.
2 But, thee from hence, the Lord ſhall tear,
And, from the Land thy dwelling take. *(Selah.)*
The Iuſt ſhall ſee the ſame with feare,
And, ſport at thy deſtruction make.
Yea, they ſhall ſay ; Loe, this was hee
Who ſought not God to make him ſtronge ;
But, labour'd how he great might be,
By getting wealth, & doeng wrong.
3 Then, as for mee, I proſper ſhall
As Olive trees that have their place
Within Gods holie temple wall,
And, ſtill depend vpon his grace.
There, Lord, I'le ſpread abrode thy fame ;
Yea, then, I'le praiſe thee for thy love,
And, truſt for ever in thy Name ;
Which, all thy Saints will well approve.

Deliver vs oh gratious Lord, *from the cruell inſolencies & falshood of thoſe, who ſeek their* Advancement *by iniurious & wicked meanes. Preſerve vs alſo from the guilt of their abhominations ; but eſpecially from being ſo shameles, as to make vaunts of oppreſsion, or of any other ſinn. Diſenable, & root out of the land, all ſuch inſolent Offenders ; that the Righteous floriſhing as green Olive trees, & beholding thy Iudgments, may with reverent awe, reioice in their ſubverſion who are freinds to* Vnrighteouſnes ; *& (with a fearles confidence in thy love) magnify thy Holy* Name, *for ever & ever.* Amen.

Pſa. 53.

To the cheef Muſitian Maſchil, A Pſalm of David. *It is almoſt the ſame with the* 14. *Pſalm. And may be vſed* to minde vs that our Nature was wholie depraved, and that wee should desire the comming of Christ, by whome wee are to be renewed, &c.

THe foole, doth God in hart denay,
 And, all corrupt are growne;
Perverse & wicked is their way,
 There is no Righeous-one.
For, God from heav'n his eye declin'de,
 Man's of-spring to behold;
And, searched who did seek to finde,
 Or, know him as they should.
2 But, all their waies prepostrous were;
 All, fillthie & vnsound:
None sawe he live vprightlie, there;
 Not one good man, he found.
Ev'n brutishlie, fond Sinners eat
 God's people, as their bread.
They, seek not God; and horrors great
 They feel, where is no dread.
3 The Lord will breake the bones of them
 That have beseiged thee;
And, thou shalt shame them, since, of him
 They disrespected be.
Would wee God's healp from *Syon* had!
 For, *Iacob*, triumph shall,
And, Isr'el, will thereof be glad,
 When them he brings from thrall.

Free vs, oh Lord, *from that vniversall corruption which overspreadeth our* Nature; *that wee neither become so foolish to deny thee in our harts, nor so perverse as to dishonour thee in our waies. Soe behold our* polutions, *that thou maist cleanse vs from them; Soe consider our* weaknes *that thou maist breake the bands of all our foes; So make vs to* fear *thee, that all our other feares may be turned into ioye;*

ioye; And cause vs to be so desirous of that salvation, *which was promised out of* Syon, *that (being delivered from the thraldome of sinn and death) wee & every true* Israelite, *may triumph in our Salvation & Redemption through* Iesus Christ *our Lord.* Amen,

Psa. 54.

To the cheef Musitian on Neginoth Maschil. A Psalm of David when the Ziphims came & said to Saul, doth not David hide himself with us? *It mystically prophecied the Iewes trecheries & tirannies against Christ &c.* It is vsefull, when wee are (or have beene) betraied or persecuted by false brethren, *&c.*

DEfend mee Lord, for thy Name sake,
In thy great powre, adjudg thou mee,
Of all thy suites quick notise take;
And, let my words well heeded be.
For, Strangers do against me rise,
And, Tirants for my life have sought,
(Not setting thee before their eyes)
Although my healp, thou still hast wrought,
2 The Lord, my Soules vpholders, gards;
His Truth hath chas'd my foes away;
And, them with Vengance he rewards:
For which, my Vowes I'le freely pay.
To laud thy Name is wel approv'd
And, I oh Lord, thy praise will sing;
Because, my greefs thou hast remoov'd
And, on my foes, my wish dost bring.

Encline thine eare (oh mercifull father) vnto all our iust petitions, & suffer vs not to be oppressed by our professed foes, nor to be betraied into their hands, by those Aliens vnto thy Truth & Goodnes, from whome wee have better deser-
H 3 *ved:*

ved; But, as thou haft bene alwaies heretofore our Healper (and the vpholder of them who have befriended vs.) So, continue, we pray thee, to reward our freinds, according to their kindnes; to requite our foes according to their defervings; & to deliver vs from all our forrowes, through Iefus Christ; To whome with thy bleffed Spirit, wee will offer vp the free Sacrifize of praife and thancksgivinge, now & for ever. Amen.

Pfa. 55.

To the cheef Mufitian Neginoth Mafchil, a Pfalm of David. *It perfonates the faithfull, complaining & petitioning againft the inhumanitie of their foes. It deciphers, alfo, falfe brethren; declares their deftruction, & the fecuritie of the* Elect. It may be vfed as the former.

OH God! my praiers hear;
Hide not away thine eare;
But, hear, & caft on mee thine eye.
For, loud my foes doe roare;
The wicked greeve me fore;
And, therfore Lord, thus loud I crie.
2 With wrongs, they mee perfue,
A wrathfull fpight they fhewe,
And, I, at hart am greatlie vext:
Deaths torments mee oppreffe,
I fhake through fearfullnes,
With horrors great, I am perplext.
3 I fayd; Doves wings, had I,
To reft, I then would flie.
Lo, then farr hence I would abide.
I, then would hafte away,
And, in fome Defert ftay
Which frõ the Tempeft mee fhould hide. *(Selah.)*
4 Deftroy & flitt their tongues;
For, ftrife, oh Lord, & wrongs,

Pof-

Poſſeſſe their Cittie night & day;
  In midſt thereof I ſpi'de
  Sinn, fraud, & guile abide;
  Theſe, in her ſtreats, ſtill made their ſtay.
  5 A foes contempt, or ſcorne,
  I could have ſhund or borne;
But, mee no publike foe abus'de:
  It was my truſted Peer;
  As freinds, wee freindlie were,
And, wee God's houſe togither vs'd.
  6 Arreſt them, Death & Hell,
  With whome ſuch Miſcheevs dwell:
For, I, vpon the Lord will call.
  To God, at night I'le pray,
  At morninge, at nooneday;
And, mee both hear, & ſave, he ſhall.
  7 In warr, he gave mee peace,
  And, mee will ſtill releaſe:
Ev'n me, the Lord will hear, and ſave.
  But, God will puniſh them: *(Selah.)*
  For, they his feare contemn;
Becauſe, that they no Changes have.
  8 Their hands, the Peace did breake,
  (Where they a league did make)
And, though their ſpeach moſt freindlie were,
  Yet are, ſometime, their words,
  Like darts or naked ſwords.
Let God, therefore, thy Burthen bear.
  8 For, God is thy defence,
  He gardeth innocence;
And, Sinners downe to Hell will thruſt.
  Not half their daies they live,
  Who murther or deceive:
But, in the Lord I put my truſt.

H 4 *Many*

Many & grevous (oh Lord) *are those troubles which exercise thy Children; especially in those places, where* prophanes, *or* false worship *is openly approoved: but, the greatest afflictions are occasioned by* Hypocrites, False breathren, *& those who abuse vs vnder cullour of Religeon, or by pretences of dearest Amitie. Defend vs therfor, oh* God, *from those harmfull Serpents; Give vs the wings of Dovelike innocence, to carry vs above their snares: Grant us those enterchanges of Prosperitie & Adversity, which may keep us both in thy Feare, & Love: Suffer not the tribulations of the world, nor the temptations of the Devill, nor the miseries of the Flesh, to oppresse us: But, let us lay all our burthens vpon thee, confidently; Trust in thee firmly; Seek thee duly; love thee sincerely; & enioy thy gratious protection for ever more* Amen.

Psa. 56.

To the cheef Musitian vpon the mute Dove in the Desert, a golden Psalm of David, when the Philistims took him in Gath. *It typically personates the* Church *in persecution, & is a prayer, & a complaint against her Foes, acknowledging Gods regard of her suffrings, professing assurance in him, & promising to be thanckfull &c.* It is vsefull to those ends. *&c.*

HAve Mercie Lord, for, man hath sought
To swallowe vp, & mischeeve mee.
My Foes with mee have daylie fought;
And (Lord most high) they many bee.
Thou art my hope, when doubts arise,
Thy word hath brought me comforts, to,
On thee alone, my hart relies,
And, fearles is, what Flesh cann do.
2 They wrest my words, Lord, ev'rie day;
To worke me harme, they still devise:

They

They meet vnseene, they mark my way,
And, how they might my Soul surprise.
Therfore, in thy just wrath, oh God!
Correct them for this Crime of theirs:
And, as thou dost my Faults record,
  Recorde, & botle vp my teares.
3 For, thou wilt save me, Lord, I knowe;
When thee I seek, my Foes flie back:
Thy promise makes mee joyfull growe,
And, of thy word, my songs I make.
My, trust, oh God! is all in thee,
And, of man's powre, I fearles am.
Thy vowes are all perform'd on mee
  And, I will praise thee for the same.
4 For thou hast freed my Soul from death;
From falls, thou dost my footing stay,
To walke, by thee, within that Path,
  Which leads to Life, a lightsome way.

Oh thou faithfull preserver of all who put their trust in thee! Our visible & invisible Adversaries do continually seek the destruction of our soules & bodies, by many secret & mischeevous devises: But, our trust being placed vpon thee, wee need not fear the malice of any Adversarie. Grant vs grace therfore, so to depend on thy promises, & so to lament our errors (with tears of true Repentance) that as our enimies mark our wayes to entrap vs, wee our selves may mark them to prevent ensnarings; & that thou observing their hatred, & our penitence, mayst cause vs to walke ioyfully, in the way of eternal life, through Iesus Christ. Amen.

Psal. 57.

To the cheef Musitian Altaschith, A Psalm of David, when he fledd from Saul in the Cave. *It myſtically expreſſed the* Iewes *perſecutinge Chriſt, even vnto the Grave, wee that are his members, & partake in his ſuffrings, may ſing it, to declare our iniuries, & to pray, & praiſe God, for deliverances. &c.*

LOrd, grant (oh grant) me thy compaſſion;
For, I, in thee my truſt have placed.
Diſplay thy wings for my Salvation,
Vntill my greefs are over-paſſed.
To thee I ſue (oh God moſt high)
To thee, that canſt all want ſupplie.
2 From their deſpights who ſeek to rend mee,
Let help, oh Lord, from heav'n be daigned,
And let thy Truth & Love defend me;
For, I with Lions am detained:
With men inflam'd, whoſe biting words,
Are ſhafts, & ſpears, & naked ſwords.
3 Let over heav'n Gods praiſe be reared,
And through the world, his glorie ſhowed.
For, they who netts for mee prepared,
(They who my ſoul to ground had bowed)
Ev'n they, who in thoſe trapps are caught,
Which for my fall, their hãds had wrought. *Selah*
4 Oh God! my hart now ready maketh,
My hart is for thy praiſe preparing;
My Tongue, my Harpe, my Lute awaketh
And, I my ſelfe, betimes vprearing,
Will ſpeake & ſing, in praiſe of thee,
Where greateſt throngs of people be.
5 For, Lord, thy Mercies forth are ſtretched,
As farr as are the Sphears extended;
Thy Truth vnto the Clouds hath reached
And, thou thy ſelf art high aſcended
Let, ſtill, thy, Fame & praiſe, oh God!
Through heav'n & earth be ſpread abrode.

Oh

Oh Lord to whome Mercy belongeth, *have mercy vpon vs; & let the* Wings *of thy* protection *be gratiously spread over vs, vntill the* Stormes *of this life be overpast: For, so great & so manyfold are those dangers, & those Miseries wherewith wee are alwaies enclosed, by spirituall & temporal foes; that they have brought our bodies to the* Grave, *& our soules near vnto* Hell. *Oh! let thy* Truth *&* Love *defend vs from our Lion-like persecuters; that our* Harts *(being timely cheared) our* Thoughts, Words & Actions, *may harmoniously agree in manifesting thy praises. And, seing thy holy Spirit hath plainely declared the* Vniversality *of thy proffered* Grace; *let not vs presume to sett Limmits there vnto; but publish thy glorieas vniversaly as thou hast extended thy Mercies, through* Iesus Christ *our Lord. Amen.*

Psa. 58.

To the cheef Musitian Altaschith Michtam of David. *It reprehends & characters, that Serpentine generation, whoe are obstinate enimies to the Gospel of Christ, & prophecies & illustrates their destruction, &c.* It is vsefull to encourage vs against their malice, &c.

YEe congregation, said yee right?
Yee Mortalls, are your Doomes vpright?
No; for you muse on works of Sinn:
Your hands with mischeevs filled are,
You from your Births vntoward were;
And, from the wombe have liers binn.
2 Your poyson, like the serpents, flowes;
Deaf-Adder-like, your eares you close,
Though powrfull Charmes are wisely sung
Oh God! their mouthes of teeth disarme;
And, that their Fangs may do no harme,
Make tootheles (Lord) the Lion's young.

3 Like

3 Like ſudden Flouds, their ſurie ſlale;
When they would ſhoot; their arrowes, breake:
  Yea make them quite conſume away.
Like ſnailes, conſume them from the earth;
Or els, like ſome vntimely birth,
  Deſtroy, them, er'e they ſee the day.
4 Before wee feel them, prick or burne,
Them, whirle-winde-like, Lord, overturne;
  And ſweep them hence, in wrath alive.
Which Vengance, when the Righteous vewe,
(And vewing Sinn receive her due)
  They, joyſull thancks, to thee ſhall give.
5 Yea, they ſhall trample on their bloud,
Who have bene Foes to doeng good;
  And ev'rie man ſhall ſay, & ſee,
That Righteous men ſhall have their meed;
And, that there is a God, indeed,
  By whome the world ſhall judged be.

Keep vs, oh LORD, *from having fellowship in the* Congregations *of thoſe, who are perverted in their* Iudgment, *miſcheevous in their* Converſation; *Draf to good* Inſtructions, *Obſtinate in their* hereſies; *& willfull continuers in all their natural* Corruptions. *Deliver vs from their malice; Breake their Inſtruments of miſcheef; and let their deſerved confuſion fall ſuddenly vpon them: That, the Faithfull Congregation, may vewe it; & that all men may ſee & confeſſe thee, to be the Righteous* Iudge *of the world, & the rewarder of all thoſe who put their truſt in thee.* Amen.

Pſa. 59.

To the cheef Muſitian Altaſchith Micham a Pſalm of David, when Saul ſent & they watched the houſe to kill him. *It cheefly prophecied the Iewes dogged*

dogged crueltie to Christ, & that they should be preserved to wander in a vagabond Condition (as wee see at this day) for an example to others &c. It serves to warne vs, that wee resist not God's grace once offred. &c.

MY God, protect mee from my Foes;
  From them, who strive with mee:
From Sinners gard mee, & from those,
  That bloodie-minded be.
For, loe, the mightie do combine;
  They waite my soul to teare:
And, without cause or fault of mine,
  With speed there to prepare.
2 Lord God of Hoasts, & Isr'el, wake,
  To heed & succour mee:
The Gentiles Curbe, & vengance take,
  Where sinns malitious be. *(Selah)*
At night, like Doggs, they Bawling come,
  They round the Cittie goe
And slanders ranck, & threatnings, from
  Their Mouths, & lipps, do flowe.
3 For why, say they, none hears the same;
  But, God shall them detect:
The Gentiles also to defame,
  His ayde I will expect.
For, God's my strength, God healpeth mee,
  Preventing grace bestowes;
And, what my hart requires to see,
  Inflicts vpon my Foes.
4 Oh Lord our help, disperse with shame,
  Disperse them by thy powre;
But, lest my Folke forget the same,
  Them, doe not quite devoure.
Vntill their tongue, all words of spight
  And falshood, vttred hath;

And,

And, when their pride is at the height,
Conſume them in thy wrath.
5 Yea, Lord, conſume them vtterlie,
Till, notiſe they obtaine,
That, God, throughout eternitie;
Doth over *Iacob* raigne. *Selah*
At night, vnto the Cittie wall
Like doggs they ſhall retreat;
Without it, they ſhal barke & bawle,
And whine, for want of meat.
6 But, in the Morne, aloud I'le ſing,
Both of thy powre & grace;
And ſpeake what ſuccours thou didſt bring
When ſore deſtreſt I was.
Ev'n vnto thee, oh God my powre,
My praiſe-full ſong ſhall be:
For, thou art my deſenſive Towre,
And, gratious vnto mee.

Iuſt Avenger of all malitious iniuries; According to thy promiſes thou haſt ſubiected the Gentiles *to thy* Sonns *Dominion, & ſcattred the* Iewes *(with a* Cain-*like marke preventing their vtter extirpation) that ſo, their vagabond life may be a perpetuall memoriall, both of their crueltie, & of our* Savious *Paſſion. Let all thoſe who ſhall make themſelves partakers of their malitious hereſie (without repentance) be partners in their puniſhment; and let them hunt through the earth in error, bawling like doggs without the walls of thy new* Ieruſalē *(for an example to all Ages): But, let ſo many of them as have bene miſſeled, by ignorance only (without willfull malice) oh let them, returne from their obſtinacie, in the Evening of their life (or of this world) & let them hunger & thirſt after the true* Meſſiah; *that in the* Morning *of their & our* Reſurrection, *we may, altogether, praiſe & glorifie thy holy Name.* Amen.

Pſa. 60.

To the cheef Muſitian vpon Shuſhan Eduth Michtam *of David*, to teach when he ſtrove with Aram Naharaym & with Aram Zobath, when Ioab returned & ſlew of Edom in the ſalt vallie 12000. *It bemones the preſent calamitie; mitigates it by remembring God's promiſes; Deſires his conduct; & profeſſeth Aſſurance in him.* It is vſefull to encourage thoſe who fight vnder God's banner. &c.

OH God! wee are deſpis'd of thee,
  And, in thy wrath diſperſed be:
  But, now returne to vs againe.
Thou ſmot'ſt our land, & Loe it quakes,
Oh! ſtopp the breach, for, ſtill it ſhakes;
  And, many cares thy folk ſuſtaine.
2 A giddie wine thou mad'ſt vs drink;
Yet, they that feare thee, do not ſhrinck
  They Truths diſplaied Flagg to beare. *Selah*
Oh! that thy Darling, ſafe may be,
Let thy Right-hand or'eſhaddow mee;
  And, bowe thou downe to me thine ear.
3 Then (as God's holy voice declar'd)
All *Shechem*, ſhall by mee be ſhar'd;
  I'le *Succhoth* Dale by Line receive:
I'le *Gilead* & *Manaſſeth* take;
Mount *Eph'rim*, I my gard will make;
  In *Iudah*, I, my law will give.
4 My ſervile worke ſhall *Moab* doe;
O're *Edom* I will fling my ſhoe;
  And *Paleſtine*, of mee ſhall boaſt
For, who to *Edom* is my Guide?
Or to the Cittie fortifide,
  But, God, that had forſook our Hoaſt?

5 That

5 That Lord, who did our Hoaſt forſake,
Shall of our greeſs an ending make:
For, man's vaine help wee do contemn.
Through God, we valiant Acts have done,
Our Foes, by him, ſhall downe be throwne
And, Hee ſhall ſet his feet on them.

Notwithſtanding our many outward Afflictions make vs appeare as reprobates in the worlds opinion; & though (by reaſon of our ſinns) wee our ſelves are ſometime half afraids, that thou, oh God, *haſt forſaken & deſpized vs: yet, havinge among vs the* Enſigne *of* Truth *as a teſtimonie of thy favour; wee beleeve that thy ſpirituall kingdome ſhall be continued with vs, & be eſtablished in thoſe places alſo, which are not yet of thy viſible* Church. *Fulfill oh Lord, our hopes herein; that wee may breake through the fortifications of the miſtical* Babilon, *& that thy Spirituall Armies may be victorious, through the conduct of our Lord & Captaine* Ieſus Chriſt. *Amen.*

Pſa. 61.

To the cheef Muſitian a pſalme of David. *It deſireth God's aſſiſtance; confeſſeth former protections, & promiſeth future truſt in him. It containes alſo, a prediction of Chriſts kingdome, a petition for Grace, and a vowe of thanckefulnes.* To theſe ends it may be vſed.

LOrd, let my plaint attention move,
When greev'd at hart I lie;
And, lead mee to the Rock above,
When from Earth's ends I crie.
For, as a Cittie fortifide,
From foes thou gardeſt mee,
Within thy Tent, ſtill, ſafe I bide;
Thy Wings my Cov'ring bee. *Selah.*
2 Thou hear'dſt my vowes, & gav'ſt mee ſhares,
With

With ſuch as fear thy Name ;
And, ſpar'dſt the king, till hee in yeares
An aged man became.
Oh ! let thy Truth & Mercie, Lord,
Preſerve him ſtill by thee ;
That, ſtill thy praiſe I may record,
And pay my vowes to thee.

Hear our Prayers, oh Lord, *& let our cries come vnto thee. So firmlie eſtablish vs on that* Rock *whereon thy* Church *is founded, that it may be our* Bullwork *of defenſe in all dangers. Cover vs with the wings of thy Mercie; Succour vs in thy* Tent ; *& be gratious vnto vs, from what place, or in whatſoever affliction, wee call vpon thee: That ſo (having an outward portion among thoſe who profeſſe thee, & performing thoſe vowes, which wee made vnto thee in our Baptiſme) wee may be continued in thy favour, vntil we shal be admitted into thy triumphant* Church, *& enioy life eternall with* Chriſt Ieſus. *Amen.*

Pſa. 62.

To the Cheef Muſitian to Iduthan a Pſalm of David. *It profeſſeth truſt in God* ; *threatens & Characters out, Antichriſt & his Members*; *Exhorts to faith in Chriſt*; *& declares the vanitie of man & of all tēporall aſſiſtances &c.* It may be ſung to encreaſe Piety, Faith, Hope, & the contempt of temporall Vanities, *&c.*

STill wait thou, oh my Soul, on God ;
For, he my helpe doth prove,
My Rock, my Garde, my Safe-abode ;
Whence, none cann mee remove.
Thoſe, therfor, who conſpire my fall,
His Blade ſhall root from hence,
And, ſhake them like a rotten wall,
Or, like a broken ſence.

2 They feek my fhame; They lies commend;
And hate when faire they fpeake. *Selah.*
My Soul, therfore, on God attend;
Thy hope, him only make.
For, God (my ftrength, my healp, my fort)
From harme will fuccour mee:
My praife, my garde, my firme fupport,
And my fole truft, is hee.
3 In God, yee people, alwaies hope;
To him, your harts declare:
For, he will prove a certaine propp,
When men deceitfull are. *Selah.*
Men high & lowe, are leffe in weight,
Then things that are moft vile:
Truft not therfore nor take delight,
In wealth, in wrongs, or guile.
4 For, once God faid, & oft I heard,
That, God (both ftrong & kinde)
On all men, will beftowe reward,
As he, defert fhall finde.

Grant oh Lord, that wee may alway, fo patiently attend on thee, that perfecutors, falfeteachers, *and all they who feek our fall or dishonour, may be quite fubverted or converted. Make vs ever mindfull how ftrong a fupporter thou art vnto all thofe who put their truft in thee; & how iuft a rewarder of every one according to his deferving. Seeing alfo, wee cann have no fafe affurance in the beft men, nor in the beft outward meanes (without thy fpeciall Affiftance), let vs never depend vpon them; much leffe, feek to be fecured, or to profit our felves, by fraudulent or wicked practifes: But endeavoring rather, to fulfill all righteoufnes for thy fake; and making our petitions to thee only; let vs depend wholie on thy protection, for ever and ever,* Amen.

Pfa.

Publications of the Spenser Society.
Issue No. 32.

THE

PSALMS OF DAVID

TRANSLATED INTO LYRICK-VERSE.

BY

GEORGE WITHER.

PART II.

PRINTED FOR THE SPENSER SOCIETY.

1881.

The Spenser Society.

COUNCIL.

LIST OF PUBLICATIONS.

For the First Year 1867-8.

Issue

1. The Proverbs and Epigrams of John Heywood. Reprinted from the Original Edition of 1562.
2. The Works of John Taylor the Water Poet. Reprinted from the Folio Edition of 1630. *Part I.*

For the Second Year 1868-9.

3. The Works of John Taylor the Water Poet. Reprinted from the Folio of 1630. *Part II.*
4. The Works of John Taylor the Water Poet. Reprinted from the Folio of 1630. *Part III.* (*Completing the volume.*)
5. Zepheria. Reprinted from the Original Edition of 1594.

For the Third Year 1869-70.

6. The ʽΕΚΑΤΟΜΠΑΘΙΑ or Passionate Centurie of Love, by Thomas Watson. Reprinted from the Original Edition of (*circa*) 1581.
7. Works of John Taylor the Water Poet, not included in the Folio Volume of 1630. Reprinted from the Original Editions. *First Collection.*

THE

PSALMS OF DAVID

TRANSLATED INTO LYRICK-VERSE.

BY

GEORGE WITHER.

PART II.

PRINTED FOR THE SPENSER SOCIETY.

1881.

Printed by Charles E. Simms,
Manchester.

CONTENTS.

THE PSALMS of DAVID *Tranſlated* Into LYRICK-VERSE, according to the ſcope, of the ORIGINAL. And *Illuſtrated, with a Short* Argument, *and a breiſe* Prayer, *or* Meditation; *before, & after, every* Pſalme.

By GEORGE WITHER.

Imprinted *In the Neatherlands* By Cornelius Gerrits van Breughel. M. DC. XXXII.

(*Lowndes*, p. 3966; *Hazlitt*, No. 17.)

Pſa. 63.

A Pſalm of David when he was in the wildernes of Iudah. *It may be ſung by thoſe who are afflicted in the wildernes of this life, hungring & thirſting after righteouſnes. It expreſſeth their longing to be partakers of the publike worſhip, who are debarred from the ſame; & may be vſed alſo by them, &c.*

OH God! my God thou allwaies art;
For thee, betimes, I ſeeking pant,
With longing ſoul, & thirſting hart,
Ev'n as the land, which raine doth want.
Yea, Lord, my ſoul doth long, full ſore,
Thy powre & glorie to behold,
As I have ſeene them heretofore,
Ev'n in thy holie-place of olde.
2 For why! thy love doth life ſurpaſſe;
And, I therfore will ſing thy praiſe:
Thy Name, I'le all my lifetime bleſſe,
And, vnto thee my hands I'le raiſe.
For, when I minde thee on my bed,
And muze vpon thee in the Night;
It fills me, as with marrowe fedd;
And I with ioye thy praiſe recite.
3 Since, me thou healp'ſt in my deſtreſſe;
Beneath thy wings I gladd remaine,
My Soul, to thee doth cloſelie preſſe;
And, thy Righthand ſhall mee ſuſtaine.
But, they ſhal to their grave deſcend,
Whoſe purpoſe is my ſoul to ſlay:
Thy Sword ſhall bring them to their end,
And, they ſhall be the foxes prey.
4 The king, & they who ſwear, in truth,
By God's great Name; in God ſhall ioy:
But, he ſhall ſtop the liers mouth,

I 2 And

And, ev'rie perjur'd soul destroy.

Cause vs to seeke thee timely (oh Lord *our* God) *and when wee are wandring in the deserts of this life, let vs hunger and thyrst after thee and thy righteousnes; that wee may be satisfied according, to thy promise. Let our muzings be vpon thee, both in the* night *of our* Afflictions, *and vpon the* bedd *of our* prosperities. *Let the contemplation of thy powre and glorie fill vs, as with marrowe and fatnes: Let thy Love be pretious vnto vs; yea, more pretious vnto vs then our lives: Let the wings of thy Mercy, and the powre of thine Arme, so shaddowe and protect vs, that (both our Lionlike & foxlike Adversaries being destroied, and the mouth of all vnrighteousnes being stopped.) VVee and thy whole* Church *may reioice in thy Salvatoon, for ever and ever.* Amen.

Psa. 64.

To the Cheef Musitian a Psalme of David. *It prophecies the Iewish malice against the Messiah at his passion; and that accordinge to their owne imprecation, the avengment of his bloud should be vpon them and their children, &c.* It serves to minde vs, what manner of foes wee have, and for what assistance wee may hope, *&c.*

LOrd, hear my voice, & me acquite
From terrors of the foe;
And from their plotts, & feirce despight
That mischeefe seek to doe.
For, they like swords, their tongues prepare;
With words, like arrowes keen,
They shoote the righteous without fear,
With quicknes, & vnseene.
2 Themselves in Mischeefe, strong they make,
Their plotts they thinck vnspide;

And,

And, ſearch how that effect may take,
  Which in their harts they hide.
But, God ſhall wound them with a ſhaft,
  Before they be aware ;
So, they ſhall fall by their owne craft,
  And their owne ſentence beare.
3 Thereat, beholders all, ſhall flie,
  And, ev'rie man, with feare,
The works of God ſhall magnifie,
  And, ponder what they are.
The righteous alſo, with delight,
  On God, their hope ſhall build :
And, they that are in hart vpright,
  Shall with true joie be filld.

Oh Lord, *wee have ſo manie viſible, and inviſible Adverſaries, ſecretly and continually plotting our deſtruction; that our Soules are afflicted with great terror. Some, by whiſpering of ſlanders, or by privie conſpiracies, ſeek to endanger our bodies; Others, by hidinge falſe Doctrines vnder appearances of Truth, or masks of pietie; or els, by inſinuating carnall or ſpirituall wickedneſſes (before wee be aware) deeplie wound our Conſciences; and very dangerouſly peirce our Soules with venemous arrowes. Oh* God ! *break, and quench theſe fierie darts of* Sathan ; *Deliver vs from their cunning Proiects; ſhoot back their arrowes into their owne boſomes; and let their predictions be fulfilled on themſelves: But, grant that wee may ſtill depend on thee; & that being delivered from all our terrors, wee may ſerve thee in* holines & righteouſnes, *all the daies of our life* Amen.

Pſa. 65.

To the Cheef Muſitian a Pſalme & ſong of David. *It acknowledgeth God's manifold benifits ; Firſt, those which are peculier to the Elect; & then, his Vniversall providence over all his Creatures &c.* Wee should sing it to those ends. &c.

IN *Syon*, Lord, thine honor lies;
 There, vowes to thee are brought:
Ev'n there, thou answer'st all mens cries,
 And, of all Flesh art sought.
Though many sinns do me oppresse,
 From them thou purgest mee;
For, thou thy Chosen-one dost blesse,
 And bringst him near to thee.
2 Within thy courts & holie-place,
 His dwelling he doth gaine;
Ev'n there, where wee shall (of thy grace)
 Our wished fill obtaine.
Thou in thy Iustice dreadfull art,
 Yet, in thy grace wee stand;
And thou the hope of all men art,
 That live on sea, or Land.
3 Girt round with powre, thy Vigor laies,
 A ground-work for the hills:
The noise of seas & Flouds it staies,
 The peoples rage it stills.
Thy signes, remotest Clymates feare;
 Thee, daye & night they praise;
Their Lands to visite, thou hast care;
 And, rich encrease it paies.
4 To water all their furrowes there,
 Thy River overflowes:
To feed them, corne thou dost prepare;
 And, blessest that which growes.
Thou Crown'st the year with plentiousnes,
 And, fat thy paths are made:
It dropps vpon the wildernes

And

And makes the mountaines glad.
5 Faire flocks, their fruitfull meadis adorne;
Their vallies freſhlie ſpringe,
And, are ſo filld with cropps of Corne;
That they do laugh & ſing.

In thy viſible Church, *oh* Father of Mercie, *thine honour & thy Grace are moſt evident: Nevertheles, thy Mercie is not ſo confined, but that thy Church inviſibly extends it ſelf into everie corner of the earth; yea, thy overflowing River makes vp thy harveſt even in thoſe deſerts where wee behold no fertilitie; & there (thou having regard as well to the ſoule as the bodie) viſiteſt them, not only with temporal, but with ſpiritual Bleſſings. For which thy great providence & mercie, wee bleſſe thy holy name; beſeeching thee, ſo to moiſten the clodds of our harts with dewes from above, that wee whome thou haſt planted in thy viſible Garden, may not, be leſſe fruitfull then thoſe, to whome thou haſt not yet vouckſafed the ſame priveledges; But grant that both wee & they (according to what we have received) may bring forth fruites acceptable vnto thee, through* Ieſus Chriſt *our Lord.* Amen.

Pſa. 66.

A ſong a Pſalme. *It praiſeth God both for temporall & ſpirituall bleſſings, eſpecially for the great benifit of our univerſall Redēption, which is typically expreſſed, by allusion to the Iewes deliverance from the Egiptian bondage &c.* It may be ſung to praiſe God for our deliverances from ſinn & the Devil. &c.

YEe kingdomes all, God's praiſe expreſſe;
In ſongs, exalt & laud his Name:
To him, his dreadfull Acts confeſſe;
And, how his Arme his foes doth tame.
Let all the world before him bowe,
With ſinging to his Name & him; *Selah.*

I 4 And,

And, let all men more heedful growe,
  What dreadfull things he did for them.
2 The ſea he dri'de, & through the Maine
Wee walk'd on foote, him praiſing there.
He hath obtain'd a boundles raigne,
And, of all Nations, he hath care.
He will not let the Rebells thrive. *Selah.*
Oh ! bleſſe our God, & ſing his praiſe ;
For, he preſerves our ſoul alive,
  And, he from ſlipps our footing ſtaies.
3 By thee, oh God ! wee prooved were,
Like ſilver tried & refin'de :
Thou didſt entrap vs in a ſnare,
And round our loines afflictions binde.
Above our heads, thou mad'ſt men ride ;
And, through both Flouds & fires, we came :
But, thou didſt reſt, at laſt, provide ;
  And, I will praiſe thee for the ſame.
4 Ev'n in thy houſe thoſe vowes I'le pay,
Which in deſtreſſe were ſworne by mee ;
Fatt Rams & Bullocks I will ſlay,
And burne ſweet incenſe vnto thee. *Selah.*
Come hither, yee that feare the Lord,
And, hear what for my ſoule he wrought,
When his aſſiſtance I emplor'd,
  And, him with praiſe-full voice beſought.
5 If any ſinn, my hart affects,
The Lord, will then withdraw his eare ;
But, ſurelie, God my ſuite affects ;
For, he my vocall moane did hear.
Oh ! let him ever praiſed be,
For not reiecting my requeſt :
And, for his Mercie ſhew'd to me,
  Oh ! let him be for ever bleſt.

Bleſſed

Bleſſed be thy Name (oh gratious God) for all thy benifits; eſpecially for our many ſpiritual deliverances, which are, everie day as wonderfull now, as when the Redd-ſea *was dried vp. For, through* Seas *of terrors, &* Deſerts *of tribulations, wee paſſe many Dangers, many trialls, & many enterchanges of Adverſitie & proſperitie in this life, to refine & prepare us for a bleſſed habitation; &, that without impeachment to thy Iuſtice, wee may be made capable of thy free-Mercie. Oh! root out of our harts that affection to ſinn which interrupts thy hearing of our prayers; and grant that (by ſacrifizinge our brutish affections, & offring vp the ſweet Incenſe of a Faith fruitfull in Good works) wee may declare our ſelves thanckfull vnto thee; and that wee & our Oblation may be made acceptable through the Merrits of* Ieſus Chriſt. Amen.

Pſa. 67.

To the cheef Muſitian vpon Neginoth, a Pſalme a ſong. *It expreſſeth a longing for the vniverſall ſpreading of that ſaving grace which is offred to* Iewes, & Gentiles; *& shewes the bleſſednes which will ſucceed the ſame. It is daylie ſung in our Liturgie for the enlargment of the Catholick Faith.*

THy bleſſing, Lord, beſtowe;
Shewe vs thy glorious Face *Selah.*
That, all the world, thy waies may knowe,
And, ſee thy ſaving-grace.
2 Let all men give thee praiſe;
Let all ſing praiſe to thee:
Let nations all ſing out thy praiſe,
For, thou their Iudge muſt be.
3 God, is the Nations kinge, *Selah.*
Let Nations all therefore,
Let Nations all, vnto him ſing,

And praiſe him ever more.
4 Then earth ſhall give encreaſe ;
And, God, whoſe Folke wee are,
That God, ſhall vs vouchſafe to bleſſe,
And, him, the world ſhall fear.

Allmighty God, *vouchſafe, that wee whome thou haſt alreadie enlightned with a gratious meaſure of thy* Saving-knowledge, *may ſo evidently enioy alſo, thy protection, & the continuall brightnes of thy Favour; that all the Nations of the world, beholding the benifit of thy Service may be allured to ioyne with us in magnificenge of thee. Let alſo, a due conſideration, that thou art* Vniverſall king, *makes vs beleeve that thou haſt provided means of ſalvation for all thy Subiects: and let the remembrance that thou art vniverſall* Iudge, *make vs all, ſo fruitfull; that thou maiſt be vniverſally feared, & glorified; & wee bleſſed world without end.* Amen.

Pſa. 68.

To the cheef Muſitian a Pſalme or ſong of David. *It is a prophecie of Chriſt Heb.* 4. 8. *Herein, by alluſion to ſome paſſages in the* olde Teſtament, *many* Evangelical *myſteries are shaddowed out (to witt) the* Reſurrection, Aſcention, ſending of the holy-ghoſt, Callinge of the Gentiles, *&c. It is vſefull to commemorate thoſe myſteries, &c.*

LEt God ariſe, & all his Foes affright,
Let thoſe that hate him, be deſpers'd & flie;
Let Sinners, paſſe like ſmoke out of his ſight,
And melt like wax which in the fire doth lie.
But, from the Iuſt, let him expel their ſadnes,
And make them glad in him, with perfect gladnes.
2 Oh! prais *Gods name,* who rides above the *ſphears*
His *Name Eternal* in your Songs commend;

For,

For, in his holy-place, he ſtill appeares
The *Orphanes* Father, & the *widdowes* freind.
He captives frees, he ſtrangers entertaineth,
And for the proud, a fruitles land ordaineth.
3 Whē thou didſt, *Lord*, thy peoples paſſage make
(And, waies, for thē through *deſerts* vaſt prepare)
At ſight of thee, both heav'n & earth did ſhake;
Yea, *Sinai* ſhook, when *Iſr'els* God was there.
Thou gav'ſt thy *flock*, ſweet raines as need required
And, mad'ſt thē ſtrōg, whē they were weak & tired.
4 There dwelleth now, thy *Congregation*, Lord,
Where, for the pore thy goodnes roō had made:
Whē thou thy ſelf hadſt firſt proclaim'd the word
Great Armies, thē, of *Preachers*, there they had.
Kings troupes did flie, & *shee* the ſpoile divided,
Who came not forth, but, in her tent reſided.
5 Ye ſhal be made (tho lodg'd with pots ye were)
As fair as doves, with gold & ſilver wings,
As white, as ſnowe in *Salmon* did appeare,
When there, the Lord diſperſed mighty *Kings*.
Like *Bashan* hill, God's holy mountaine ſheweth,
And, *Bashan*-like, all other hills or'e veweth.
6 This hill is God's, & hee inhabits here;
Then why inſult yee foe, yee meaner hills?
God's charrets, twice ten thouſand Angells are,
And, he, by them, in holy *Sinai* dwells.
Aſcending high, ev'n thraldome, he enthralled,
And bought vs guiſts, whē we his foes were called.
7 Thus *God* hath done, that he might dwel in vs,
Oh! let this God, our ſaviour, bleſſed be; *Selah.*
For, with good things, he dailie lodeth vs,
And, God of Life, & Lord of death is hee.
He breaks the heads of thoſe, that him receive not
And wounds the crown of him, that ſinning leavs not.

8 From

8 From *Bashan*, & the deeps I wil (saith God)
Bring back my Folk as once frō thēce they came
That thou maist wash thy feet, in thy foes bloud,
And, that thy dogs, may come & lick the same:
For, they, oh God my king! thy goengs heeded;
They saw, how in thy house, thou hast proceeded.
9 The singers first, the minstrells next had place,
With whom, the maids, on timbrels plaieng wēt:
And then, the Choire of Isr'els blessed race,
Did all in one, to praise the Lord, concent.
There went young *Beniamin's* & *Iudah's* Guiders,
And *Zabulon's*, & *Nepthalies* Providers.
Oh Lord! whoe bid'st that we should courage take
Cōfirm thi work which thou for vs hast wrought;
At *Salem* then, (and, for thy Temple sake)
To thee by kings, shal guifts of price be brought.
Their brutish troupes, that armes do love to carrie
Rebuke, disperse, & make them tributarie,
11 Then *Egipts* kings will seek vnto the Lord,
And *Chush* will then, to God advance her hands.
His praise therfore, yee kingdomes all record,
And, sing aloud his praises, all yee Lands.
For, whē he rides, the sphears his horse he maketh
And lo, his voice is thunder when he speaketh.
12 All powre & praise, ascribe to God alone,
For, his renowne is through all Isr'ell spread;
God is in heav'n, the great Almighty-one,
And, in his holy-place, is full of dread.
His peoples powre, by God is much encreased
(By Isr'els God) let him therefore be blessed,

Eternal Sonn of God, *who art ascended vnto the right-hand of thy* Father, *& shalt come againe with maiestie to be our Vniversall* Iudge; *Deliver vs from the thraldome of* Sinn, *by the powre of thy Righteousnes: And (though wee have*

have yet our converſations among Dragons, *& in defiled habitions) make us innocent as* Doves, *& as vnpoluted as the mountaine ſnowe. Encreaſe the meanes of publishing thy* Goſpel ; *and preſerve Vnitie, order, & good diſcipline, in thy* Church : *that the comelines thereof may allure all beholders, to deſire fellowſhip in thy Congregation ; that, hereticks, hirelings & contentious perſons, may be reprooved & reformed, or cutt of ; that, they who are, yet, without, may be received into the Covenant ; that wee who are admitted, may be confirmed, without waveringe ; & that the* God head *may be feared, & praiſed, & bleſſed, now & for ever more* Amen.

Pſa. 69.

To the cheef Muſitian Shoſannim a Pſalme of David. *It perſonates Chriſt taking vpon him our ſinns & infirmities ; humbling him ſelf before his Father ; declaring the Condition of his Adverſaries ; shewing the bitternes of his paſsion ; ſignifieng the iudgments prepared for Sinners ; & prayeng for his Elect &c.* Chriſts members may vſe it to thoſe purpoſes.

HEalp Lord, for, Flouds encloſe my Soul,
In groundles depths I am bemir'd,
Above my head, great waters rowle,
My parched throate, with cries is tir'de.
Mine eyes are dim'd in ſeeking thee,
Moe then my haires, my Foes are growne,
My ſpoilers are too ſtrong for me ;
And, take as theirs, what is mine owne.
2 Thou knoweſt how I am too blame ;
But, for my ſake, let none of thoſe
(Lord God of Iſr'el) ſuffer blame,
Who do in thee their truſt repoſe.
For, I ſuſtaine reprochfull ſcorne,

And,

And, am disgraced for thy sake.
My brethren, of my mother borne,
 Of mee, likewise, a stranger make.
3 Zeal to thy house, hath worne mee out,
Thy scorners, my reprochers be;
My Fastings, & my teares they flout,
And, when I mourne, they laugh at mee.
Of mee, the Rulers, evill, spake;
The Drunckerds, made of mee their songs:
But, Lord, my moane, I timelie make,
 In Mercie, mark therefore my wrongs.
4 Mee, by thy Truth's protection keep,
That miry-depths, nor spightfull-foes,
Devouring-Flouds, nor whirl-pooles deep,
Nor Dungeons Mouth my soul enclose.
But, Lord, of thy abounding grace,
(For thy Love-sake) returne, & hear;
To mee, thy servant show thy face,
 And, in my need, incline thine ear.
5 Drawe nigh, & save, & sett thou free
My soul, from those who bear me spight;
For, all my wrongs, are knowne to thee,
And, all my Foes, are in thy sight.
Rebukes & scornes, my hart nigh broke,
With greefs opprest, I made my mone;
But, where I did for pittie looke
 They would (alas) afford me none.
6 They, for my meat, did gall prepare,
Sharp Vineger to quench my thirst;
Their Bourd, therfore, shall them ensnare,
And, Blessings, be to them accurst.
Their eye shall be depriv'd of sight;
A cure-les greef, their back shall shake;
God's heavie wrath, shall on them light,

His

His Vengance, them ſhall overtake.
7 None ſhall in their abiding-place,
Or in their Tent, be dwelling found;
For, whome thou ſmot'ſt, thoſe they did chaſe,
And, greeved him, whome thou didſt wound.
More ſinfull ſtill, they ſhall become,
And, in God's Iuſtice have no ſhare,
Nor in that book of life have roome,
Wherein, the Iuſt enrowled are.
8 But, I, that pore & ſcorned am
Shall by thyne ayde, oh Lord, be raisd;
For which, I'le magnify thy Name,
And, in my ſongs, thou ſhalt be praisd.
And, that, oh Lord, more pleaſes thee,
Then, horn'd & hooſed Oxe to give;
Which, when the Meek (thee ſeeking) ſee,
It ſhall with ioye, their hart revive.
9 God's praiſe, yee heav'ns & earth declare,
Him praiſe thou ſea, & all in thee:
For, to the pore, he lends his ear,
And, he doth ſett the pris'ner free.
He, *Syon* ſaves in time of need,
And, Iudah's Townes he will erect,
To be for thoſe, & for their ſeed,
Who ſerving him, his Name affect.

Oh Lambe of God! *which taketh away the ſinns of the world*, have mercie vpon vs. *Thou, that haſt taken on thee our ſinns, felt our infirmities, & ſuffred all which wee deſerved*, have mercie vpon vs. *Thou, who for our ſalvation, dideſt bear the vnkindneſſes of kindred & familiers, the reproches of Neighbours, the ſcornes, & oppreſsions of ſtrangers, the reproofs of Magiſtrates, & the contempt of the baſeſt people*, have mercy vpon vs. *Thou, who for our ſakes, haſt endured, inſufferable torments of the bodie, the*

the vnſpeakable agonies of the ſoul, & taſted the gall & vinegar of everie bitter paſsion, have mercie vpon vs. *Deliver us from them who ſeek to crucifie thee againe, in thy members. Raiſe us by thy* Reſurrection, *whome thou haſt redeemed by thy* paſſiō; *Glorifie us by thy* Aſcentiō, *in life eternall, whome thou haſt ſecured frō* Damnation, *by thy* Death & Buriall; *And, for that which thou haſt done, & prepared, for thine* Elect; *let heaven & earth praiſe thee world without end* Amen.

Pſa, 70.

To the cheef Muſitian a Pſalme of David to bring to Remembrance. *The Church praies for deliverance from her perſecutors; prophetically imprecates their confuſion; & deſires the proſperitie of the Godlie, &c.* It may be ſung when oppreſſors inſult over vs. &c.

DEferr not Lord, thy ſuccours longe
  But, bring my Foes to ſhame;
Ev'n thoſe, who plott my ſoul to wronge,
  Bring back, with loſſe & blame.
On them who skoffe, & flout at mee,
  Beſtowe the Scorners hire:
But, make them glad, & ioye in thee,
  Who after thee enquire.
2 Still, *God be prais'd*, let all men ſay,
  Who, on his ayde relie;
And, make, oh Lord, no more delay,
  For, in great want, am I.
I will no other aide emplore,
  Then, what thou ſhalt afford;
To bring me ſuccours, now therfore,
  Thy healp, defer not, Lord.

Healp vs, oh Lord; *for thou only art our* healper, & *wee have no other hopes but in thee. Make us, not the ſpoile or or scorne of those, who desire, & practise the destruction of our soules: But, grant rather, oh God! that all they who fear thee, may be comforted in our speedy deliverances; Reioice in thy Mercies; relie on thee in their necessities; & ascribe all thancks, honour, & glorie to thy blessed* Name, *for ever more.* Amen.

Psa. 71.

The Church *acknowledgeth God's preservation of her in her severall* Ages, *& from her manyfold Oppressors, desiring to be preserved also, in her last & worst age. &c.* wee, on whome the worst Age is come, should vse it as a prayer, to be delivered from the same.

KEep me from shame; for, Lord in thee I trust;
 Incline thine ear, to healp & set mee free:
Yea, save thou mee, oh Lord, as thou art iust,
My Rock, my Fort, my Refuge daigne to be;
 For, *Lord* my strēgth, thou help dost promise me.
2 Mee from the powre of sinnful men defend,
And from their hands, oh Lord, that cruel are.
My soul, on thee did in the wombe depend,
And, since my birth, thou hast of mee had care:
 For which my tongue shal stil thy praise declare.
3 Thou art my hope, though wondred at I be,
And, I will sing thy praises all the day.
When I am weake & old, Lord, leave not mee:
For, with despight, my haters mee gainsay,
 And, for my soul, they plotts & engines lay.
4 God, leaves him quite (say these) persue & take;
He, now, hath none to rescue him from thral.
But, come, oh God! & speed to healp me make;
Oh come! & smite my soules Oppressors, all,
 Bring scorn & shame, on those who seek my fal.
5 Thē, still, I'le hope; thy love I'le still commend;

K Yea,

Yea, ftill, relate what favours thou haft done :
And, of thy grace, fince I perceave no end,
Thy ftrength, Lord God, I will depend vpon,
  And, magnifie thy Righteoufnes alone,
6 Till now, oh God ! thy Marvailes I have told,
As from my youth I have bin taught by thee :
Oh leave me not, when I am gray & olde,
Till Ages all, thy powre have learn'd of mee ;
  And, then extold, thy Iuftice, Lord, fhall be.
7 None ever did fuch works as thou haft wrought ;
And, though my foul thou keptft awhile in paine,
At laft, as one who from the grave was brought,
Me, to my ioyes, thou didft reftore againe ;
  For which, my harpe, to praife thy Name, I ftrain,
8 My tongue, likewife ; in fetting out thy prais,
Oh thou cheef faint of *Ifr'el* ! part fhal bear ;
So fhal my foul, whofe price thy bountie paies,
And, ev'rie day, thy Iuftice I'le declare,
  Becaufe, my foes defam'd, & ruin'de are.

Oh Lord, in the wombe wee had extraordinarie nourish-mēt & breathing for our bodies, & (no doubt) our foules had there, a due nourishment by thy Spirit. Being borne, wee are brought into thy vifible Church by Baptifme, *& long time after fuftained by thee, both in foul & body, without having any outward work required at our hands ; & when we are capable of the outward Covenant, al thou requireft is but to give thee that hart which thou haft prepared fo to doe. Yet helps vs, oh God, in this dutie ; & never leave us in our own hands. And as thou haft in all her former ages, preferved thy* Church, *both from the rage of* Iewes, Gentiles, *& Heriticks ; fo, in this her old & worft age, preferve her from thofe* Hypocrites *& lukewarm* profeffors, *who have added feacret mifcheeves, to publike oppreſsions. Yea preferve her, & us, oh* God, *from thofe, & all other Adverfaries, that*

that thy Truth *may be continued to all ages; the ioye of her* Children *reſtored; & thy bleſſed* Name *glorified, for ever and ever.* Amen.

Pſa. 72.

A Pſalm for Solomon. *It ſetts forth the maieſtie of Chriſt & his kingdome* (for, only, of that *Salomon* are many paſſages of this Pſalme verified) *it declares his Univerſal iudicature; The Churches happines therein; His marvailous Incarnation; The extent, Riches, & peaceablenes of his Kingdome &c.* Wee ſhould ſing it to glorify God for thoſe things &c.

THe King oh God! with judgment bleſſe,
And, give thy Iuſtice to his Sonn;
That, to thy people, in deſtreſſe,
With judgment, Iuſtice may be done.
Then, Truth & Iuſtice floriſh will,
On ev'rie great & little hill.
2 Then, pooreſt men ſhall be ſecure,
For, he will all Oppreſſors tear;
And, whilſt the ſunn & moone endure
From age to age, they, him ſhall fear.
On Earth, like dropps deſcend he ſhall;
Like thoſe, which on the Fleece did fall.
3 The Iuſt, ſhall whilſt he rules have peace,
So long as doth the moone remaine:
He from the River to the ſeas,
(And quite throughout the world) ſhal raigne,
The ſalvages, adore him ſhall,
And all his foes, before him fall.
4 *Arabia's* prince, & *Saba's* Kinge,
The Lords of Seas, & Ilands to,
Shal guifts to him, with homage, bring;
So ſhall all Kings, & people doe.

For, when they crie, he setteth free,
The pore & meek, that helples be.
5 The pore & humble he respects,
He saves their soules that healples are:
From fraud & force, he them protects;
For, in his eye, their bloud is dear.
To him, they *Sheba's* gold shall give;
And, he shall prais'd, & prayd for, live.
6 His Corne, shall from a handfull, growe
To cover all the mountaines topps;
Like *Libanon*, his fruit shall showe,
And fill the Citties with his cropps.
His Fame through Ages, all shall runn,
As everlasting as thee sunn.
7 In him, the Nations all abrode,
Shall blessed be, & praise him to;
Oh praise the Lord! ev'n *Isr'els* God,
For, he alone cann wonders do.
Still, blessed be his glorious Name,
And, earth still filled, with his Flame. *Amē. Amē.*

Sweet Iesu *who being invisible in thy* Deitie, *didst become visible in thy* humanitie, *by descending miraculously into the* Virgines *wombe, like raine into* Gideons *fleece; Grant wee beseech thee, thy divine spirit may so infuse it selfe into our harts that* (Iustice, Peace *&* Charitie, *encreasing & continueng vpon the earth) all thy afflicted Children may be comforted & secured; the barbarous Nations converted; thy Kingdome enlarged; thyne enimies be brought into subiection; thy feilds become abundantly fruitfull; & heaven & earth be filled with thy glorie, world without end,* Amen.

Psa. 73.

A Psalm for Asaph. *It expresseth, how the faithfull are*

are sometime discouraged, by the prosperities of the wicked; & is an excellent description of such conflicts as are between the Flesh & the spirit in everie Christian. &c. We may vse it, to comfort vs in such tẽptations, & to remember vs whither to repaire in such conflicts.

NO doubt, God counts his Isr'el dear,
  And, loves the righteous man;
Yet was my foot quite gone, wel-near
  And, I to fall begann.
For, when I fooles did honor'd vewe,
  And Sinners lifted high,
And that nor sick, nor weak they grewe,
  Their weal I did envie.
2 From greefs like ours, they seemed free,
  Their pride & Cruelties.
To them as clothes or bracelets be;
  And, fatt stuffs out their eyes.
They have their wills, & are so base,
  To boast of Sinns & wrongs:
And neither earth nor heav'nly place,
  Escapes their evill tongues.
3 To such Ful-springs, as wel as they,
  God's Children seek to goe:
For, God (the God most high) they say,
  Regards not what wee do.
Lo, wicked men the world possesse,
  And, wealth & honors gaine;
But, wee have cleans'd in righteousnes,
  Our harts & hands in vaine.
4 Yea, wee still pininge goe (say they)
  Lamenting all day long:
Yet, thus I, speak not, lest I may,
  Thy weaker Children wrong.
I sought a reason for the same,

K 3 But,

But, I no cauſe deſcern'd
Till to the houſe of God I came,
And, there their end I learn'd.
5 On ſlipp'rie ſeats, them ſett thou haſt,
From whence with ſhame & feare,
Ev'n ſuddainly, they downe are caſt;
And never more appeare.
For, as a dream (when thou doſt wake)
Thou doſt their Forme deface:
At ſuch therefore, offence to take,
Thou ſeeſt, how fond I was.
6 But, ſtill, with mee thou doſt abide,
Thou hold'ſt my Right-hand faſt;
And, by thy Counſells, mee ſhalt guide
To Glory's throne, at laſt.
In heav'n or Earth, account I make
Of nothing but of thee:
And, though my ſoul & Fleſh be weake,
Thou alway ſtrengthneſt mee.
7 For, thou oh God! my portion art;
And, thou ſhalt them deſtroy,
Who runn a whooring in their hart,
Another, to enioy.
Becauſe, right good, the ſame doth ſeem,
To God, approching near,
(And, placing all my truſt in him)
His works I will declare.

Direct thou ſo (*oh* Lord) *all our* works, words, & thoughts, *that wee neither murmur at any afliction where with wee are exerciſed, nor be diſcouraged in thy ſervice, becauſe the wicked are more flourishing, for a time. VVee confeſſe it is oft our frailty to iudg of thy love by outward proſperities; & that great Adverſities have tempted ſome to call into queſtion thy providence, to the shaking & endange-ring*

ring of their Faith. But, grant (wee pray thee) that by frequenting thy houſe *& vſing the meanes of* Perſeverance, *wee may be ſo informed touching the fickle eſtate of wicked men, in proſperitie (& of that happines which thou prepareſt for conſtant profeſſors of thy Truth) that wee never commit ſpiritual fornication againſt thee: But, that chuſing thee for our portion, & ſupporting our weakenes by thy ſtrength, wee may continue in thy* Fear, Favour & protection, *to our lives end.* Amen.

Pſa. 74.

A Pſalm for Aſaph. *It myſticallie propheeied what havoke ſhould be made in the* Church, *by aluding to the deſtruction of the material Temple; & God is deſired to vouchſafe his wonted Mercie, in regard of the Foes outrage; but, eſpecially, for his owne honour ſake.* It is a prayer for the Church in perſecution.

OH God! for ever, why deſpis'd are wee?
Why is in rage, thy paſturage laid waſt?
Oh minde thy Flock, redeem'd of old by thee,
(That heritage, which dearly bought thou haſt)
Ev'n *Syon* mount, whereon thy Name is plac't.
2 Come Lord (oh come) deſtroy for evermore,
The Foe, that on thy holy-place hath preyd;
Thy foes, that in thy Congregation roare,
Who, there, for ſignes, their enſignes have diſplaid
And, on the carved works their axes laid.
3 For, as if they ſome grove were hewing downe
With Axe & Maul, the coſtly works they breake;
They flaming fires, into thy houſe have throwne;
Thy name's cheef ſeat, a place prophane they make
And, in their harts, of ſpoiling all, they ſpeake.
4 Throughout the Land, thy houſes burned be;
Yet, to declare the date of this our woe,

K 4 Nor

Nor viſions now, nor Prophets word have wee.
Lord, when ſhall end, theſe ragings of the Foe?
Shall he blaſpheam thy Name, for ever, ſo?
5 No more, thy hād (thy right-hād) Lord, withhold :
Within thy breſt, the ſame no longer hide :
For, thou oh God ! thou art our king of old,
And, here on earth, for vs thou didſt provide,
When, by thy powre, thou didſt the Sea divide.
6 The Dragons Heads thou woundedſt in the floud ;
Leviathan's vaſt heads, thou didſt prepare,
In places wilde, to be thy peoples food :
Yea, frō dry rocks, thou hewdſt our fountains there
And ma'dſt firm land, where mighty waters were.
7 Thine, is the day, the night is alſo thine ;
Thou ma'dſt the light, & thou did'ſt form the ſunn
The world, within her *Zones*, thou didſt confine ;
& ſhewdſt what cours, times hot & cold ſhould run
Lord, mind thoſe things, & what the foe hath don.
8 Obſerve, how fools blaſpheā thy name oh *Lord?*
Thy Turtles life, defend from Sinners wrongs :
Obſerve our greefs, & thinck vpon thy word ;
For, to the world, a darkſome denn belongs,
Which harbors fraud, inhumane deeds, & wrōgs.
9 That ſo the pore (vnſham'd) may praiſe thy name,
To plead thy cauſe (thine owne juſt cauſe) ariſe ;
Obſerve how fooles, thee daylie do defame ;
Yea, bear in minde, thy Foes malitious cries,
And to what height, their ſhouts againſt vs riſe.

Oh Lord God, *dreadful in iudgmēts & infinit in mercies! the devaſtation typified in thy Material* Temple, *is fulfilled vpon thy ſpirituall* Sanctuary. *Thy open Adverſaries batter the maine Fabrick without, whilſt* Schyſmaticks *&* Hypocrites *breake downe the Ornaments within: & betwixt both; terrors, confuſions, & diſſentions are ſo increaſed, that thy*

thy Church, *is indangered. Have mercie vpon the people whome thou haſt bought, & (as heretofore) shew thy ſelfe the* King & protector, *of thine* Inheritance, *to the confuſion of thy blaſpheamers. Though not for ours, yet, for thine honour ſake, let neither the temporall enimies of thy viſible* Church, *make ſpoile thereof; nor our ſpirituall* Deſtroier, *deface thoſe* Temples *of thy holy-ſpirit which are erected in our harts: But, keep them alwaies vndefaced, vnpoluted, & fitting receptacles, for thee & thy Graces, through* Ieſus Chriſt *our Lord.* Amen.

Pſa. 75.

To the cheef Muſitian Altaſchith, a Pſalme or ſong for Aſaph. *God is praiſed for his ready healp. Chriſt promiſeth to ſupport & iudge his* Church. *Oppreſſors are reprooved, & the different portion of them, & of the Godly, is declared.* It is vſefull, to comfort againſt the inſolencies of ſpiritual foes.

THee Lord, wee praiſe & magnifie ;
  To thee wee thanckfull are :
For, that thy Name approcheth nigh,
  Thy wondrous works declare.
When I the people have aſſum'd,
  I, Iuſtice will maintaine :
For, when Earth's dwellers are conſum'd
  Her pillers I ſuſtaine. (*Selah*)
2 To Fooles, I ſaid, more prudent growe ;
  To Sinners, thus I ſpake,
Your horne (your horne) advance not ſoe,
  Nor, ſuch proud boaſting make.
Nor Eaſt, nor weſt, advancements come,
  Nor from the Mountaines flowe ;
But, God him ſelf preferreth ſome,
  And, ſome doth overthrowe.

K 5 3 From

3 From his full Cupp, within his hand,
He mixt redd-wine doth poure;
Which ev'rie Sinner in the land,
Shall dreggs & all devoure.
But, I of *Iacob's* God will fpeak,
And alway fing his praife:
The hornes of Sinners I will break;
And, high, the Righteous raife.

Oh Chrift, *the Sonn of God! fo eftablish thy Kingdome in our harts, that Righteoufnes may be continued in the Land. Support thofe whome thou haft raifed to be as it were pillers in thy* Church *or* Commonwealth; *keep them from being fo impudent, or vaine glorious in their preferment, as if it came either caufuallie, or by their owne Induftrie, or defervings: But, fo caufe thē & us to perceive thy purpofe & thy providence, both in our feverall advancements, & humiliations, that we may the better difcharge our perticuler duties. And, when thou shalt fill out the* redwine of thy wrath *to all obftinate malefactors, let us be refreshed by taking the* Cupp of Salvation, *which thou haft prepared for all them, who shall be iuftified, through the merrits of* Iefus Chrift *our Lord* Amen.

Pfa. 76.

To the cheef Mufitian a Pfalme or fong for Afaph. *It is a Triumph-fong to praife God, for that knowledge of him, which he hath vouchfafed vnto his* Church *typified by Iudah, Ierufalem, & Syon. It glorifieth Chrift alfo, for his conquefts over finn, Death & the Devill.* The vfe is manyfeft.

IN *Iurie*, God is knowne full well;
His Name's in Ifr'el great:
He, in *Ierufalem* doth dwell,
And, *Syon* is his feat.

Shaft,

Shaſt, ſword, & ſheild, he battred there;
 Yea, there he wonn the Feild; *Selah*
And, more his powrs, and honors are,
 Then ſpoilers Burroughts, yeald.
2 The ſtrong are ſoilde; their dream is flowne
 Their ſtrength has not prevaild:
For, at the God of *Iacob's* frowne,
 Both horſe & Charret faild.
Thou dreadfull art, & none, oh Lord,
 Thine angry looks cann bear;
For, when thy voice from heav'n is heard,
 The Earth is dumbe with fear.
3 The meek on eatth, when thou to ſave,
 And judge them (Lord) ſhalt pleaſe, *Selah.*
Thou by man's wrath, ſhalt honour have,
 And, his hot rage appeaſe.
To God make vowes; & preſents give
 All yee that round him are.
For, he doth kings of breath deprive
 And makes great princes fear.

Glorify thy ſelf, oh Lord God! *in thy holy* Catholick Church, *by the final overthrowe of all her enimies: Let thy powre break all their Inſtruments of miſcheef: Let the preaching of thy* Goſpell, *& the thundring of thy Iudgments (which have already deſtroyed the powre, & made fruſtrate the Dreames, of the old heathnish Idolaters, & their falſe Philoſophie) vtterly overthrowe the ſtrength of that carnal wiſdome, which at this day ſtandeth in oppoſition to thy Truth. Let our furious diſſenſions be appeaſed, & let the frowardnes, rage, & blind zeal of all men, become a meanes of encreaſing thy glory; to the confuſion of thy ſtouteſt oppoſers, & to the Salvation of the meeke harted, through* Ieſus Chriſt *our Lord.* Amen.

Pſal. 77.

To the cheef Muſitian to Iduthun a Pſalm for Aſaph. *It expreſſeth thoſe interchanges of Doubts, Hopes, Feares, Comforts & Aſſurances, through which wee work our ſalvation with fear and trembling.* It ſerves to minde vs of our fraile condition ; & ſhewes how to order our throughts in ſpiritual combats.

TO God, ev'n to the Lord, I prayd,
And, hee did hear my moanes ;
Both day & night I ſought his aide,
With never-ceaſing groanes.
My hart no comforts entertain'd,
But fixt on him her thought ; *Selah.*
And ſo I greev'd, & ſo complain'd
That, lowe my ſoul was brought.
2 Mine eyes from ſleep hee did with holde,
With paine, I loſt my tongue :
I mus'd on daies, & yeares of olde, .
And what was once my ſong.
Yea, all alone, at night I lay,
Thus muſing in my minde ;
Lord, wilt thou caſt mee quite away,
And, never more bee kinde ?
3 Is thy compaſſion loſt out right ?
Shall thy firme promiſe faile ?
Haſt thou for got thy Mercie quite ?
O're Love, ſhall hate prevaile ?
No ; this my frailtie is, quoth I,
And, theſe, but changes are,
Wrought by the powre of God moſt high,
Which, I, in minde will bear.
4 Thy works, & wonders paſt, oh Lord,
I'le therfor muſe vpon ;

Thy

Thy former Acts, I will record,
And, shewe what thou hast done.
Thy walkings, in thy house, declare,
That, there's no God like thee :
And, what thy powre & marvailes are,
Thou mak'st all people see.
5 For *Iacob's*, & for *Ioseph's* race,
Thine arme did purchase aide ; *Selah*
And, seas, & Flouds, to vewe thy face,
Were troubled & afraide.
The Clouds did melt, the Vapours crasht,
Thine Arrowes, forth were shott,
Thy thunders roar'd, the lightnings flasht,
And, Earth a trembling got.
6 Thou wentst through seas with steps vn-eide,
Thy paths were in the Deep ;
And, *Moses* did with *Aron*, guide
Thy people, there, like sheep.

Father of mercy, *& God of all consolation (who hast often tymes, gloriously, & miraculously hertofore delivered thy Children, & made safe passage for them through horrible Feares troubles perills & temptations) be mercifull vnto us, wee beseech thee, in all our inward & outward afflictions ; especially, when our sinns cause thee to exercise us with such* chaunges, *as may make us fearfull we have lost thy favour. VVee deserve to be deprived of thy compassion, & of all those comforts & protections, which wee have long enioyed, by thy free grace: Nevertheles, grant that wee never fall quite away from thy regard, but may so returne alwaies vnto thee; that our frailties may be pitied, our penitence accepted, our petitions entertained, & wee continued in a full fruition of all thy mercies, & gratious promises, in* Christ Iesus. Amen.

Psa. 78.

Pſa. 78.

Maſchil, for Aſaph. *It commemorates the Iewes obſtinate incredulilitie, with God's plagues & Mercies interchangeably ſent among them vntill the tyme of* David. Wee ſhould vſe it, to warne vs of God's long-ſuffring toward the whole humane Nature, whoſe perverſenes, is here miſtically ſet forth, *as alſo, the ſen ding of the true David, Ieſus Chriſt.*

NOw to my Law (my people) give thine eare,
&, wel obſerv what weighty things are tolde:
For, lo, my lipps a problem ſhal declare
And, plainely ſing, grave ſayengs, dark, & old:
That, nether what our Fathers have revealed,
Nor what we know, be from our babes concealed.
2 God's powr & praisfull wonders I will blaze,
His Teſtaments, to *Iacob*, I will ſhowe;
How he, likwiſe, in Iſr'el ſetled lawes,
Which they were bound to let their childrē know
That ſo, they might to their next ages teach them,
And, Age to age, for ever after preach them.
3 That they, in God, a faithful hope might place,
And not forget his works, or his command,
As heretofore their Fathers head ſtrong race,
Whoſe hart, with God, vprightly did not ſtand;
Like Ephr'ims brood, who bows & weapōs bearing
Forſook the Feild, the day of battell fearing.
4 Gods law they brak, his cov'nant they did ſlite
And on his works or marvailes never thought:
Yet, many ſignes & wonders in their ſight,
In *Zoan* feildes, & *Egipt*-land he wrought.
To make their way, the ſea, in twaine he cleaved
And, high on heaps, the rowling waters heaved.
5 A pillerd-Cloud, by day he made their guide,
A Column-

A Column-fir'd, to clear the night he ſent.
More over, he the Rocks did then divide,
And ſtreams like ſeas, along the Deſert went.
From craggy flints, ſweet waters forth he bruſed,
And ſprings from thēce, like Rivers were diffuſed.
6 But they went on to move his anger, ſtill,
And much provokd the wrath of God, moſt high,
By tempting him their luſtings to fulfil,
And craving fleſh, their longings to ſupplie.
For, with diſtruſt, they ask'd if God were able,
In that wilde place, to furniſh out a table. (ſmot,
7 Springs flowd indeed (ſed they) when rocks he
But, can he bread & fleſh as wel provide?
Which when God heard, with *Iacob* he was hot,
And, in his wrath he did with *Iſr'el* chide;
Becauſe, no faith to his firm promiſe giving,
They ſtill remain'd in truſtles vnbeleeving.
8 He naitheles, the gates of heav'n vnclos'd,
And made the clouds, raine *Manna* for their meat
The bread of heav'n, among them he diſpos'd,
And Angells food, vnworthy men did eat.
A wind South-Eaſt-by Eaſt, he then ordained,
And fleſh as duſt, & foules as ſand, it rained.
9 Theſe fild ther camp, & fluttred round their tēts
Til they were cloid with what their luſt perſu'd:
Yet none of them his fleſhlie minde repents;
which God avengd, ev'n whē the meat thei chewd
For, his feirce wrath, on *Iſr'el* down he poured,
And, of their cheefs, the fatteſt he devoured.
10 Yet, ſin'd they ſtil, & ſet his works at naught;
For which, their time he waſted out in vaine,
(Afflicting them, til after him they ſought)
And, then in ſhew, they did repent againe.
Yea, then his powre to bear in mind they ſeemed,
And

And ſaid, he was the God that them redeemed.
11 In which altho he knew their flattring mouth
And lieng tõgues, did nought but falſhood ſpeak;
Tho, him, their hart affected not in truth,
And, tho, they ſtil his holy League did break,
Of his meer grace, he naitheles forgave them,
And, from his wrath, ev'n he himſelf, did ſave thẽ.
12 For, them to be but fleſh, in minde he bare,
And gone like windes, which never ſhal retire;
That they perverſe eu'n in the Deſerts were,
Yea, that ev'n there, they much incens'd his yre,
Provoking him, by falſe & fain'd repenting,
The holy-one of *Iſr'el* diſcontenting. (thought,
13 Nor on his powre, nor on thoſe daies they
Wherin he from their foes did ſet them free;
They minded not, the ſignes in *Egipt* wrought,
Nor thoſe which they in *Zoan* feilds did ſee:
How, he with bloud, the wholſom ſprings diſtaſted
How, them with flies of divers kinds he waſted.
14 How, he with frogs their ſtubborn foes anoyd
How, their encreaſe, the Caterpillers pild.
How, then, the Locuſt al their fruits enioy'd
Nor how the froſt, their vines deſtroid & kild;
Nor how, cold haile, & burning bolts of thunder,
Did flay their flocks, & break their trees aſunder.
15 For, he did hurl on them his furious wrath;
To them, both fears, & harmful-ſprites he ſent;
Vnto their deaths, his rage did make a path,
And then, to wrack, both men & cattel went;
He, of their lives, their eldeſt-born bereaved
Through *Egipt*-land, where *Cham* his lot receaved.
16 Then, like a flock, his people forth he led,
Through places wilde cõducting thẽ like ſheep.
He kept them ſafe, without all cauſe of dread,
Whil'ſt

Whil'ſt he, their foes o'rewhelmed in the deep;
And alſo gave, when al this grace was done them,
That holy hill, which his right-hand had won thē.
17 Before their face, the gentiles thēce he took,
And what was theirs, to Iſr'el gave by lot,
Yet ſtil, almighty God they did provoke,
And his commands, they ſtill regarded not;
But, being like their Fathers, double-harted,
Like broken bowes, from him, aſide they ſtarted.
18 The *Lord* was wroth & Iealous when he ſaw
Their Images, & their hill-alters rear'd,
And, ther-vpon, from Iſr'el did with drawe
His former love, & ſo incens'd appear'd
That, of his place among them, he repented
And left his Tent in *Siloh*, vnfrequented.
19 By thraldom then, he took way their powr,
He gave their ſtrength & glorie to their foe,
He cauſ'd the ſword his people to devour,
And with his Land, exceeding wroth did grow.
Conſuming heat, their yongmens vigor tired:
Their maides, by none, in wedlock were deſired.
20 Then by the ſword, his preiſts away he took,
Whome to bewaile, the widdows were not ſpar'd
But, lo, the Lord from ſleeping then awook,
As when with wine a mighty man is chear'd.
Their hinder parts, with ſecret-ſores he wounded;
And al his foes with laſting ſhame confounded.
21 Then he the Tent of *Ioſeph* did refuſe,
And Ephr'ims tent he did likewiſe reiect:
But, *Iudah's* tribe it pleaſed him to chuſe,
Ev'n *Syon* hill, which he did beſt affect;
And, there, aloft he rais'd his habitation,
To be as firm, as is the Earth's foundation.
22 He from the flocks, his ſervant *David* choſe,
L From

x 161

Frō bigwombd ewes, & from attending sheep:
His heritage, to him, he did dispose,
And *Iacob's* flock, & Isr'els heards to keep.
So, with pure thoughts, discreetly thē he guided,
And, food for them, sincerely he provided.

O Lord God! *we have often bitterly censured the* Iewes, *not considering that their* storie, *is a* Problem, *mistically decipheringe our condition: Or that wee, like* David *by* Nathan's *parable, are therby, made Iudges & condemners of our selves. If we overlooke the course of our lives, we shal finde verified in our owne persons, all those things which are mentioned of that* People. *VVe have the like Covenant of grace; wee have had miraculous deliverances both temporal & spiritual; some of us have tempted him as long (& longer) in this* wildernes *of our Pilgrimage; Our murmurings, desparings, longings, yea our frowardnes & infidelity hath bene as much as theirs; VVe have had as many several pardons to winn us; as many enterchanges of prosperity & Adversitie, to reform us; & have had them, also, for our examples; yet are as disobedient & as negligent as they. Oh Good God, lay not this to our Charge; but, grant we may so apply what thou hast left written of them for our warning; that the fear of thy* Iudgments, *& the love of thy* Mercies, *may reclaime us; and that our great Sheapherd (ev'n the true David Iesus Christ) may guide us out of our* wandrings, *& bring us out of this* wildernes, *into his eternal* Rest, Amen.

Psa. 79.

A Psalm for Asaph. *It is vsefull for any perticuler Church, when it is tirannised over, by* Turks, *hereticks, or such like members of* Antichrist: *For the* Church *of* Christ *(whose persecutions & martirdomes were prefigured by those which fell on* Ierusalem*) is here personated, pray-*

eng

ing, & expressing her suffrings, &c.

VPon thine heritage, oh God!
The Gentiles, Ryots de commit:
Within thy Temple, they have trod,
And, wasted & prophaned it.
The bodies of thy saints, bestrowe
The feilds about *Ierusalem*;
Their blood, ev'n in the streets doth flowe,
And, birds & beasts do feed onthem.
2 Their bones without a grave remaine,
And, all our neighbours vs defame:
Oh Lord, how long shal wee sustaine,
Thy burning rage, thy iealous flame!
Let thy incensed wrath be pour'd.
On heathen lands, that knowe not thee;
For, they thy *Iacob* have devour'd,
And, quite consum'd his dwellings be.
3 Remember not our follies past,
(Oh God! from whome our help doth flowe)
But thy sweet grace, Lord, let vs tast;
For, wee are brought exceeding lowe.
Healp (for thy Mercy's cause) wee pray,
For thy Name-sake, forgive our sinn;
Lest, els, of thee the heathen say,
Where is their God, they trusted in?
4 But, let it bee (before our eyes)
Of all the Gentiles vnderstood,
By hearing of the pris'ners cries,
And, by revenging of our bloud.
Them, save likewise (ev'n through thy might)
That vnto death appointed be;
And seaven fold, oh God! requite
Our neighbours scornful spights to thee.
5 So, wee thy pasture-sheep, oh Lord,

Will give thee praife, & thancks therfore,
Yea wee thy praifes will record,
From age to age, for ever more.

Looke downe, oh Chrift, *vpon the perfecutions of thy* Church ; *behold the bloud of thy* Martirs ; *the prophanation of thy holy* Ordinances ; *the fcornful vpraidings, & the great calamities, which are publikely inflicted on many true profeffors of thy* Gofpel (*even among thofe who are their* neighbours *in* Belief) & *in the very ftreets of thine owne* Cittie. *Though our finns have deferved more; yet, for thy merciefake, & for thineowne honor fake, compafsionate our humiliation, forgive our offences, & let thy difpleafure be rather manifefted againft thofe who are enimies to thy Truth. So, they, who have (in derifion) queftioned thy regard of us, shall be affured thereof, by thy avenging our caufe; & we being fecured from our Oppreffors, shal magnify thy holy Name for ever & ever. Amen.*

Pfa. 80.

To the cheef Mufitian vpon Shofannim Eduth a Pfalm for Afaph. *By the allegory of a Vine, is expreffed God's great care of the Iewish* Church, *typifieng alfo, the* Chriftian Church, *whofe complaints & defires in her fuffrings, are here expreft.* It may be vfed by any congregations of the faithful, when they are delivered vp to their foes &c.

HEar thou, that Flock-like, *Iofeph* guideft,
And twixt the Cherubims refideft ;
Now, *Ifr'els* Paftor fhine thou clear :
To *Beniamin's* & *Eph'rims* vewe,
Thy ftrength before *Manaffeth* fhewe ;
And, to defend vs, drawe thou near.
2 Returne, & of thy grace affure vs ;
For, that alone will fave & cure vs.

Oh

Oh Lord of hoafts; wee thee entreat:
For aye therfor, clofe not thime ears
Though, long, thou mak'ft vs drinck our teares,
And giv'ft vs weepings for our meat.
3 Our Neighbours are at ftrife about vs,
Thou mak'ft our foes to fcorne & flout vs,
Lord God of Hoafts! our forrow flake:
To fave vs, caufe thy face to fhine:
For, thou from *Egipt* broughtft this Vine,
And, threw'ft out Nations for her fake.
4 The place, thou hadft before fo tilled,
That, rooting well, the land fhee filled,
And cov'red mountaines with her fhade:
Her boughs did Cedar-like extend,
Shee, branches to the fea did fend,
And, to the River, fhee did fpread.
5 Why of her hedge haft thou bereft her?
Why to the fpoile of ftrangers left her?
And of the feirce vntamed fwine?
The Forreft herds, have her or'ethrowne;
Oh Lord of Hoafts! from heav'n look downe,
Behold, & vifite this thy Vine.
6 That Vine, which thy right-hand hath cherifht
That branch, which for thine owne was nourifht,
Is burn't, & fpoild, while thou doft frowne:
Oh! fend, for our defence to ftand,
That Sonn of Man, whome thy Right-hand,
Hath arm'd, & chofen for thine owne.
7 Then, we fhall never more denie thee;
But, being ftill revived by thee,
For ever, call vpon thy Name.
Oh Lord of Hoafts, convert vs nowe,
A gratious look, on vs beftowe,
And, thou fhalt fave vs, by the fame.

Notwithſtanding (oh gratious Father) *thou doſt often water us with our owne teares, & expoſe us iuſtly to the beaſts of the Forreſt (even to our owne brutish appetites) & though our vnthankfulnes hath worthilie deſerved that wee should be chaſtiſed with many ſtormes of Adverſitie : Yet, Remember, wee beſeech thee, that wee are plants of thine owne* Vineyeard, *& branches of that goodly* Vine, *which thou haſt elected for thy ſelf. Behold, & viſite us with a favourable aſpect; repaire thoſe decayed Fences, through which any* ſtrang luſt, *or* ſwiniſh Condition, *hath broken in vpon us. Let our Foes (by whome wee are perſecuted) our neighbours (by whome wee were mocked, or preyed vpon) & our brethren (who were cenſorious beholders of our afflictions) become witneſſes alſo, of thy renewing Favours: That we may be comforted in thee, & continue for ever hereafter, conſtant in thy fear & ſervice, through the aſsiſtance of that* man of thy Right-hand, Ieſus Chriſt *our Lord.* Amen.

Pſa. 81.

To the Cheef Muſitian on Gittith a Pſalm for Aſaph. *It is vſefull to commend vnto us the obſervation of our Chriſtian* Sabaths *& Solemnities, which are piouſly to be regarded in all Ages; becauſe we commemorate in them our* Deliverances, *from our ſpiritual* Bondage, *typified by the* Egiptian-thraldom. &c. It vpraideth man's in gratitude, & neglect of God &c.

IN God our ſtrength, let vs reioice;
To *Iacob's* God, let vs now ſing,
And in our Pſalmes, to help the voice,
The tym'brel, harpe, & Pſalt'rie bring.
The Moone renewing, trumpets blowe,
And, when the ſolemne feaſtings be :
For, *Iacobs* God, long time agoe,

In

In Ifr'el, did this lawe decree.
2 This Teftimonie he prepar'd,
When *Iofeph* came from *Egipt*-land
And liv'd where hee a language heard,
Whofe words he did not vnderftand.
From Burthens, & the potters task,
Thy hands & fhoulders I did free,
I help'd, when thou for help didft ask,
And, heard thee from the ftorme, faid he.
3 Ev'n at the waters of debate *Selah.*
I fayd (that I might prove thee there)
Oh *Ifr'el* mark, what I relate,
And, to my words incline thine ear.
Thou fhalt no other God's at all,
But me the Lord thy God, receive;
For, thee I brought from *Egipts* thrall,
And, will thy largeft askings give.
4 But *Ifr'el* did my words contemn;
Of me, my people would have none:
So, to their pleafures left I them,
Who, after their owne lufts are gone.
Oh! had my people mee obayd,
If Ifr'el had my waies perfu'de,
I on their foes my hand had laid:
Their haters, I had foone fubdew'd.
5 My Foes had then obayd my powre,
And, I had ftill my Folk vphild:
I, them had fedd with pureft flowre
And, with rock-hony, them had fild.

Make us ever mindfull, oh God, to magnify thy Name *for delivering us from our fpiritual Bondage; But, at thofe times which thy* Church *(according to the laudable cuftome of the* Patriarks) *hath fet apart to commemorate thy extraordinarie* Mercies, *let us, efpecially, performe this,*

 dutie;

dutie; neither falsly counting it superstitiō to meet in the publike solemnization of thy praise; nor vnthanckfully omit the continuation of so necessarie a service. Give us grace also, to consider that it is no constraining Decree of thine, which hath made any of us vncapable of thy free grace, *but that it is meerly our owne* wilfulnes, *which compels thy* Iustice *to leave us to our owne wills, if we be cast off: So, we shall be kept the more obedient to thy commands; & thou (who renewest the* will, *before thou exactest obedience from it) shall accept the willingnes for the* deed; *& in due time work in us the* Deed *also, to our eternall salvation through* Iesus Christ. Amen.

Psa. 82.

A Psalme for Asaph. *It may be sung at our publike Iudicatures, before them who administer in the great affaires of* Church *or* Commonwealth; *to minde them of their duties, &c. For, it instructs & reproves* Princes, Pastors *&* Magistrates, *abusing their Authority, declares the reward of their Iniustice, & invokes God to take the iudicature to himself.*

GOd stands, where he doth see
The *Lords* to Counsell goe;
And, when the *Gods* in Iudgment be,
He judgeth what they do.
22 Yee Nobles, wherfor, then,
Are yee vnjust so long?
Why favour yee, vngodlie men
To do the righteous wrong? *Selah.*
4 The pore, young Orphanes greev'd,
The needie & opprest,
Should by your Iustice be releev'd,
And from proud hands releast.
4 But, yee are men vnwise,

And

And walk without the light :
Ev'n you, on whome the land relies,
Are out of order, quite.
5 You, therefore, whome I call
The fonns of God moft high,
(And termed *Gods)* like men, fhall fall ;
And, like fuch Princes dye.
6 Thy felf, oh God ! advance
And, give the world her doome ;
For, thine by due Inheritance,
All nations are become.

Grant almighty God, *that they to whome thou committeft the government of thy* Churches *or* Commonweales, *may not (as it often happneth) Be their greateft oppreffors: But give thy grace (oh heavenly Father) to all whome thou fetteft in Authority, that they (confidering whofe powre they have, what they were and what they fhalbe hereafter, may become fo wife, in them felves, & fuch lights to others; that Righteoufnes may be advanced, Vngodlines fuppreffed, the pore & fatherles releeved, all abufes reformed; and that fuch* Dignities, *may be ftill conferred & continued, to the publike profit, & to thy eternal glorie,* Amen.

Pfa. 83.

A Pfalme or fong for Afaph. *It may be vfed as a prayer againft the* Leagues & Confederacies *of the* Churches *foes, fuch as* Pagans, Turks, Hereticks *and* Falfebrethren ; *for, the whole Lift of them, is here typically regiftred, vnder their Names who were enimies to the* Iewifh Church.

BEe filent Lord, no longer now,
To fpeak, oh God, no more forbear :
For lo, thy foes do furious grow,

And, proudly rais'd thy haters are.
They plot, thy people to betray,
And, thy intirest freinds to take ;
Come, & of Isr'el, now (say they)
  A nameles nation wee will make.
2 As in one League, all these combine,
And, are against thee Lord, agreed ;
Ev'n *Edom* land, & *Ism'els* line,
And *Moab's* race, & *Hagar's* breed.
Philistim's, *Gebal*, *Ammon*, *Tyre*,
Huge *Amaleck*, & *Ashur* to,
To help the Sonns of *Lot*, conspire,
  Assisting them in all they do. *Selah.*
3 But, Lord, like *Madian* make thou them,
Like *Sisera* and *Iabin's* traines,
Who slaughtered were by *Kishon* stream,
And, lay like dung on *Endor* plaines.
Their dukes, like *Zeb*, & *Oreb* make,
Like *Zeba* end *Zalmana's* Peers,
Who said, they would God's houses take,
  And his Possessions, to be theirs.
4 Lord, wheel them round, as turn'd wee see
The dust or chaf, when whirl-winds blowe.
And, let thy wrath, among them be
Like flames on hills, where woods do grow.
Yea, let a dreadful storm arise,
Persueng them with death & shame :
Let feares & troubles, them surprise,
  Vntill they seek, & praise thy Name.
5 So, when that men behold their fall,
They shall confesse, there none cann be,
Whome wee ETERNAL ought to call
Or sov'raigne of the world, but thee?
Permit not, oh Lord, *those enmies to praile who have made*

made Leagues *&* confederacies, *against thy* Church; *But, as heretofore thou hast overthrowne al those Nations who were great oppressors of thy ancient people the* Iewes (*& who were* types *of our confederated Adversaries) So, wee beseech thee, bring to suddaine destruction, all the plotts enterprises and combinations, of Turks, hereticks, vnbeleevers, & false brethren. Protect vs also, we pray thee, from the snares, powre & subtilties, of our spiritual foes; that thou being known our defender & our trust being alwaies in thy defence, wee may not fear the powre of any adversaries; But, for our manyfold protections, praise & magnify thy* Eternal *name, through* Iesus Christ *our Lord.* Amen.

Psa. 84.

To the cheef Musitian a Psalm for the sonns of Chorah. *It setts forth the soules longings, to be pertaker of the blessed* Communion of saints, *& the fruition of God; It shewes also, the happines of such, & their demeanour in this vale of their Miserie. &c.* It is vseful, to stir vp in our soules, on ardēt love to God & his house *&c.*

OH Lord of Hoasts! how pleasant are
Thy dwellings, & thy courts to me?
In soul & flesh, for entrance there,
Eternal God, my longings be.
The Sparrow findeth an abode
The Swallow builds, & breedeth, to,
(Oh Lord of Hoasts! my King, my God)
Ev'n at thine alters, thus they doe.
2 Right blessed, all thy houshold be,
For, they are singing, still, thy praise: *Selah.*
And, blessed are, the strong in thee,
Who in their harts affect thy waies.
As, through the vale of tears they goe,
They find sweet springs of comforts there,
And, they from strength to strength shall growe,

Till

Till they with God, in *Syon* are.
2 Lord God of Hoasts, give ear to me,
And, mark, oh *Iacob's* God, my moane. *Selah.*
Oh God our sheild ! behold & see,
The face of thy *Anointed-one.*
For, in thy house, one day is more,
Then thousands, any other where ;
And, I had rather keep thy dore,
Then live in pompe, where sinners are.
3 For, as the Sunn, thou shinest bright,
And, wee from thee our light receive :
Thou art the sheild of men vpright,
And, thou dost grace, & Glories give.
From such as walk the righteous way,
No needfull things withheld shall be ;
For ever blest, therefore, are they
Who trust (oh Lord of Hoasts) in thee.

Kindle in our harts oh Lord, *such an affection to thee, & such a longing after thy spiritual habitations, that wee may obtaine the measure of* grace *in this life, that will fit us for the portion of* glory, *in the life to come, which thou hast prepared for all those, who do hunger & thirst after thee. Number us among thy* houshold-servants ; *Make us to take pleasure in thy* will, *& in thy* presence, *above all earthly preferments* ; *So enable us to walk from strength to strength, that wee may become strong* Walkers *in thy waies* ; *and so instruct us to make a comfortable vse, of all those afflictions, which wee suffer in our* Pilgrimage ; *that wee may sincerely acknowledge, our safetie, our honor, our sustenance, & all our temporal & spiritual happines to be only, from thee, oh God, who livest & raignest, world without end* Amen.

Psa. 85.

To the cheef Musitian a Psalm for the sonns of Chorah.

Chorah. *The* Church *acknowledgeth God's benifits*; *deſires their continuance*, *& the forbearance of his wrath &c.* Wee may ſing it to praiſe God for his bounty to his Church & kingdome, & to deſire the continuatiō of our happines, by ſtil vouchſafing Mercy with his Iuſtice.

THou haſt, oh God, thy Kingdome grac'ſt
  And, *Iacob's* thrall repeald;
Thy peoples faults, thou pard'ned haſt,
  And all their ſinns conceald. *Selah.*
Thine anger, thou haſt quite appeas'd,
  And, thy juſt wrath for borne;
Oh Lord of Hoaſts, now thou art pleas'd
  Let vs to thee returne.
2 For, why ſhouldſt thou ſtill wroth remaine?
  And vexed rather be,
Then chear thy people's harts againe,
  That they may joy in thee?
To ſave vs, Lord, thy favour ſhowe,
  And, let vs hear (in peace)
Thy word among vs preached ſoe,
  That wee from ſinn may ceaſe.
3 Then, ſhall thy ſaving-health abide;
  Near thoſe who fear thy Name;
And, in our Land, ſhall ſtill reſide,
  Thy glories & thy fame.
Then Truth & Love ſhall meet & kiſſe,
  And, Iuſtice, Peace embrace;
Yea, Truth on earth, & Righteouſnes
  From heav'n ſhall ſhew her face.
4 The Lord, with ev'rie needfull ſtore
  Shall make our Kingdome flowe;
And, ſend his Righteouſnes before,
  That wee his way may know.

Oh

Oh Lord, *wee acknowledge that from tyme to tyme, thou haſt bene exceeding gratious to thy whole* Church, *& to this parte thereof in perticuler: For, when thy Bleſsings made us wanton, thou didſt alwaies humble us by thy fatherly corrections; & when thou hadſt worthilie afflicted us according as thy wiſdome ſawe cōvenient, thou didſt ever mercifully comfort, & reſtore us againe to thy favour. Continue, oh* God, *wee pray thee, this thy gratious reſpect vnto our infirmities; & grant, wee may ſo repent of our ſinns, ſo vnfainedly profeſſe thy Truth, & ſo diligently practiſe the works of righteouſnes: that,* Honeſtie *&* Religeon (Faith *&* Good-works *may inſeperably be vnited in every one of us; & that the abundance of thy temporall & ſpiritual bleſſings, may be powred forth on this* Kingdome, *& on thy whole* Church *for ever & ever.* Amen.

Pſa. 86.

A prayer of David. *It perſonates Chriſt in his humiliation, prayeng in the behalfe of his myſticall body, for ſeveral neceſsities thereof; intermixing ſome vowes of praiſe, & acknowledgments of Gods Attributes &c.* It is an vſefull, forme of prayer, in many temptations, & afflictions.

LOrd, hear me, for great wants I have;
 My ſoules defender be:
My God! thy Saint, & ſervant ſave,
 Who puts his truſt in thee.
That, thou thy grace to me afford,
 My daylie crie requires;
Thy ſervants hart, revive, oh Lord!
 Which vp to thee aſpires.
2 For, thou good Lord, ſoone pard'neſt all,
 Who ſeek thy grace to finde;

Oh!

Oh ! hear me (now to thee I call)
  And, bear my ſuite in minde.
My dangers, I, to thee will ſhow,
  That thou maiſt healp aſſigne ;
For, there is no ſuch God, as thou,
  Nor any works like thine.
3 All nations whome thou didſt creat,
  Shall praiſe & worſhip thee ;
For, thou alone (oh God) art great,
  And, great thy wonders be.
Teach me thy waies, & in thy fear,
  My ſoul to thee vnite :
So, never ſhall my hart forbear
  Thy praiſes to indight.
4 I ſcap'd the grave, by thy large grace,
  When proud & cruel foes,
(Who ſet not thee before their face)
  To take my ſoul aroſe.
Oh God ! thou art a gratious Lord,
  Long-ſuffring, kinde, & free ;
With Truth & Love, moſt largly ſtor'd :
  Now therefore, pitty mee.
5 Return, oh Lord, & mee revive ;
  Let mee thy favour have :
Thy ſtrength to mee thy ſervant give ;
  Thy Handmaids of-ſpring ſave.
Yea, for my good, vouchſafe ſome ſigne,
  That, all my foes may know,
I am a Favorite of thine ;
  And, bluſh, they wrong'd me ſoe.

Almighty & moſt mercifull Father, have pitty vpon vs according to thine infinite goodnes & compaſſion. Let vs not alwayes wander after our owne imaginations ; nor be continually exerciſed with ſuch Afflictions as may make vs the ſcorne

ſcorne of all that hate vs; but according to thy infinite mercy & vnparaleld goodnes, Have mercy vpon us: And not on vs only, but on all thoſe people whome thou haſt created; that, according to thy promiſe, they may all ſerve & praiſe thee. Setle them & vs, in thy Truth; guide vs in thy waies; & ſo reſtore & confirme vs in thy ſavour, by ſome apparant ſignes of thy love, & ſpeciall grace; that our adverſaries may be ashamed of their hatred, & we thanckfull for al thy Mercies, through Ieſus Chriſt *our Lord,* Amen.

Pſa. 87.

A Pſalm or ſong for the ſonns of Chorah. *It deſcribes the ſcituation & glorie of the* Church *typified by* Syon; *prophetically declareth, that all Kingdomes shall be incorporated into that* Citty of God; *& that all Nations shall there obtaine their* New-birth *&c.* It ſerves (*among other vſes*) to informe, that God's Church excludeth no Nation &c.

THe Lord, hath his Foundations plac'd
 Above the higheſt mountaines crownes;
Yea, *Syons* ports, he more have grac't
Then all the reſt of Iacob's Townes:
 And, glorious things, are ſam'd abrode
 Of thee (oh Cittie) lov'd of God. *Selah.*
2 For, Gods account, as borne in thee,
Egiptians, if they him deſire;
Nay; though from *Babell* ſprung they be
From *Chush*, *Philiſtia*, or from *Tyre*.
 For, he hath ſayd, that all on earth
 In *Syon*, may renew their Birth.
3 The God moſt high will ſtrengthen her,
And shall record each faithfull ſoul,
As having had firſt-beeing, there: *Selah.*
When hee his people doth enrowl.

For,

For, there are, all that play or ſing;
And, thence proceeds each bleſſed thing.

Thou, oh Lord, *art no acceptor of perſons, but every one that feares thee; & worketh righteouſnes (of what place ſoever he be, or from whom ſoever he were deſcended) hath promiſe, of admiſſion into thy* Church, *& to be regeſtred as a free-borne Citizen of thy ſpiritual* Syon. *Make vs thanckfull, Oh God, for this large priveledge; And, ſeeing none are exempted, but ſuch as wilfully exclude themſelves (ſeeing alſo it is manifeſt to thee only who they are) let vs hope charitably of all men, whilſt there is time of grace and repentance; endeavoureng, by our prayers, inſtructions, freindly reproofs & good examples, as much as wee are able, to bring them, to become the Members of this* Corporation; *& to enioy a Chriſtian fellowship with us, in* Chriſt Ieſu *our Lord.* Amen.

Pſal. 88.

A ſong or Pſalm for the Sonns of Chorah, to the cheef Muſitian vpon Mahalath Leanoth Maſchil of Heman, the Ezrahite. *It perſonates Chriſt & his members complaining of his & their ſorrowes, contempts & ſuffrings &c. And it is full of paſſionate petitions & expoſtulations.* We may vſe it in private or Publike afflictions.

LOrd, of whoſe aſſiſting might,
I was never yet denied;
All the day, & all the night,
I, to thee have call'd & cried:
Now, regard my wofull plight.

2 Let thine *Ear,* thy *Minde,* thine *Eyes,*
To the *dropping, pleading, cryeng;*
Of my *Teares,* my *Cauſe,* my *Cries,*
Grant me, *hearing, weighing, eyeng;*

For, my soul afflicted lies.
3 I, to Death, am drawing nigh,
And am priz'd as one interred;
Like a strengthles man I lye,
As algeady slaine, and buried:
Free among the dead, am I.
4 Yea, as one forgot of thee,
(Or, as from thy hand Abiected)
Darksome pitts, my lodging be,
And in Dungeons deep afflicted,
Thy strict hand oppresseth me.
5 All thy, waves I doe sustaine,
Thou dost make my Lovers flee mee; *Selah.*
And my freinds fro me restarine:
Shutt I am, where none cann free me,
Then, how cann I teares refraine?
6 Lord, my greefs to thee I showe,
With my hands to thee vp-raised.
Cann the dead thy wonders knowe?
Or thy Love or truth be praised,
By the Sonns of Death belowe? *Selah.*
7 Cann, thy Marvailes, thee vnfold,
Who in darknes, quite are blinded?
Or thy Iustice, there be tolde,
Where, is nothing said or minded,
Which was done in times of olde.
8 Vnto thee, oh Lord I crie,
And, my suites, prevent the Morninge;
Oh! why dost thou cast me by?
Still fro mee thy presence turninge,
Who am greev'd, & like to dy?
9 Fro my youth oh Lord, till now,
Mee, thy terror hath destressed,
Nigh distract, it makes me grow;

For,

For, thy wrath hath mee oppressed,
  And, thy feares have brought me lowe.
10 They, besett me ev'ry day,
Floud-like, flowing altogether ;
And no freinds, to help me, stay
(Lovers, nor Familiers neither)
  For, thou driv'st them all away.

Help vs, oh gratious Redeemer, *so to bear the manifold infirmities & afflictions of our* flesh ; *so to endure the contempts, neglects, & iniuries of the* world ; *& so constantly to sustaine all the Assaults of our spirituall Adversaries ; that (though we be deprived of all outward Freindships & consolations) wee may be inwardly satisfied, & comforted, against every terror, in every temptation. Let vs seek soe earnestly & soearly, for thy assistance, that (escaping the spiritual* blindnes, *which makes vncapable of thy* praise ; *that dungeon of vtter* Darknes, *in which thy* Righteousnes *is obscured ; & that everlasting* Death, *from which there is no* Resurrection *) we may enioy thy blessed presence, where we shall magnify thy* Mercies, *for ever & ever.* Amen.

Another of the same.

LOrd God, my healper ! day & night,
  To thee my moanings are :
Admit my suites vnto thy sight,
  And, my complainings hear.
For, in my soul, great sorrowes be,
  My life drawes nigh the grave,
As one inter'd, they count of mee,
  And, little strength I have.
2 As he, that's dead, & buried long,
  Death's free-man I became ;
As one, out of thy presence flung,

M 2 I quite

I quite forgotten am.
Thou laidst mee in the lowest ward,
Where darksome Dungeons are :
On mee thine Anger presseth hard ;
And, all thy stormes I bear. *Selah.*
3 Thou hast my freinds fro me restraind,
My Lovers, mee despize ;
I, fast in prison am detain'd
And, sorrow dims mine eyes.
Oh Lord ! all day to thee I sue,
My hands, I meekly raise :
Thy wonders, cann men buried shewe ?
Or, wake to sing thy praise ? *Selah.*
4 Lord, cann the grave thy Love expresse ?
Thy Faith, cann ruines teach ?
Thy wonders, or thy righteousnes,
Cann dumb Oblivion preach ?
Betimes, oh Lord, I will erect,
My suites & cries to thee ;
Why shouldst thou then, my soul reject,
And, hide thy face fro mee ?
5 My soul is pain'd ev'n to the death ;
And all my life I bear,
The heavy burthens of thy wrath,
Thy terrors, & thy fear.
They clos'd mee round, like waters deep,
Where, whilst begirt I lay
Fro me, my Lovers thou didst keep,
And hidst my freinds away.

Psa. 89.

Maschill of Ethan the Ezarite. *It celebrates the mercy, Goodnes, Iustice, & powre of God &c. Mentioneth his* League *with* David, *& mystically declares, that these covenants belong to his spiritual seed, in the cheef place, &c.*

It

It inſtructs vs, who are the right heyres of the promiſes. &c.

NOw, in a ſong of endles praiſe,
Thy Mercies, I will ſing, oh Lord;
And vnto all ſucceeding dayes,
Thy faithfulnes I will record:
For, I have ſayd, that thy great Love,
And Mercy, ſhalbe raiſed high;
And, that thou ſhalt in heav'n above,
Thy Faith, confirm & magnify.
2 Thou haſt both vowed & decreed,
To *David*, thine Elected-one,
To multiply his faithful ſeed,
And build him vp an endles throne. *Selah.*
Which heav'n ſhall to thy praiſe declare,
In works to be admired at.
And, where thy Saints aſſembled are,
Thy Faithfulnes they ſhall relate.
3 For, whome like thee, doth heav'n afford?
What earthly Kings thy equalls be?
Who, art among they Saints ador'd,
And, fear'd of all that wait on thee?
Oh Lord of Hoaſts, what Lord is found
So faithful or ſo ſtrong as thou?
Who ſetts the raging ſeas, their bound
And, calm'ſt them, when thy furious grow?
4 Thou didſt afflict all *Egipt*-land,
As one made weake, by wounds & blowes;
And, by the powre of thy ſtrong hand,
Thou haſt diſperſed all thy foes.
Thine, heav'n & earth & all things be,
For, thou alone didſt all things frame.
The North & South, were made by thee;
And Eaſt & Weſt, extoll thy Name.

5 Strong armes thou hast, with powrfull hands,
And, where thou dost thy Throne prepare,
With Iudgment, Iustice alwaies stands,
And, Truth & Love thy Vshers are.
Oh! blest are they who know thy voice:
Thy look shall chear them in their waies;
They, in thy Name shall still reioice:
And, them, thy Iustice high shal raise.
6 For, thou art, Lord, our strengths renowne,
Our horne shall by thy favour spring:
Thou art our strong defensive Towne,
The Saint of Isr'el, & our King.
By vision, thou didst once declare,
And, to thy Holy-one disclose,
That thou a healper wouldst prepare,
Among thy people to be chose.
7 I have, saidst thou, my David found;
My holy oyle on shall flowe:
By mine owne Arme, he shall be crown'd,
My hand, shal strength on him bestowe.
His Foe, shal do him no disgrace,
The Sonn of sinn, he shal not fear;
For, I will smite, before his face,
All them, that his Opposers are.
8 My faith & love, on him shal stay,
My Name, his honour shall maintaine;
His hand shall make the seas obay,
His right-hand shall the flouds restraine.
His Father, he shal knowledg me,
His God, his Rock, & his defence:
For, he my eldest borne shalbe,
And, King of ev'ry earthly Prince.
9 To him, I still, will mercy grant,
He shall enioy my promise given;

Succes-

Succeſſors, he ſhall never want;
His Throne ſhall ſtand as firme as heav'n?
And, if my Lawes his Children break,
If they ſhall fro my precepts flye,
My ſtatutes, if they ſhall forſake,
 Or, from my Iudgments walk awry;
10 Their ſinns with ſtripes I wil correct,
And, ſcourg them, when amiſſe they do;
But, thoſe whome I do well-affect,
My Love, will never quite forgoe.
For, once ev'n by my ſelf I ſwore,
I would no lye to *David* make;
My League I will not break therfore,
 Nor change a word, of that I ſpake.
11 Lord, thus thou ſaydſt, & that a Throne,
Vnto his yſſue ſhould be given,
As laſting as the Sunn & Moone,
Or, as the witneſſes of heav'n. *Selah.*
But, now (as if he were abhor'd)
Thou doſt on thyne Anointed frowne;
Thou makeſt voyd thy league, oh Lord,
 And on the ground, haſt hurld his crowne.
12 His Fences, thou didſt rend away,
His warlike forts, thou downe doſt race;
All paſſers-by on him do prey,
His Neighbours flout at his diſgrace.
His foes, thou haſt Victorious made;
Whereat, his haters, ioyfull be;
Thou dull'ſt the ſharpnes of his blade,
 And, in the fight, made faint, was he.
13 Thou haſt obſcur'd his glories raies,
His Throne, thou caſteſt on the ground; *Selah.*
Thou haſt cut ſhort his youthfull daies,
And, him with ſhame thou doſt confound.

M 4 Good

Good Lord, in thy enflamed rage,
Shall still thy face obscur'd remaine?
Oh, minde the shortnes of mine age!
  Why shouldst thy make mankinde in vanie?
14 Who lives, whome Death shall not remove?
Or, who, from Death is ever free? *Selah.*
Oh Lord; where now, is all that Love,
To *David* vow'd, of old, by thee?
  Thy servants great reproach, record,
And, in my breast what scornes I bear,
Among those mightie Nations, Lord,
  Who, likewise, thy blaspheamers are.
15 Oh God! ev'n thy Anointed-one,
They have derided in his waies;
But, Lord, what ever they have done,
  To thee, for evermore, be praise.

Most gratious, God, *thou hast not only promised thy mercifull assistance to all true beleevers; but, with an* Oath *also, confirmed the same for the better strengthning of our weak faith. Grant we pray thee, that we neither become distrustfull of so gratious an* Assurance; *neither discouraged by those Afflictions & persecutions, where withal thou shalt please to purg our corruptions; nor be overcome by those tẽptatiõs, whereby our faith is exercised in the day of triall: but, cause vs to depend on thy promise, & to be couragious & victorious in all our battailes. Give vs wisdome likewise, so to discern who are the true* seed *of* David *(& to whom the performãce of thy* Covenant *doth cheefly appertaine) that wee deceave not our selves by a false application of thy spiritual promises; nor delude our soules with temporarie hopes or fears: But, make vs ever constant both in that which wee ought to beleeve on thy part; & in that which is to be performed on our parts, through* Iesus Christ *our Lord.* Amen.

Pſa. 90.

The prayer of Moſes the man of God. *In this Pſalme the humane Nature, which (as the word* Moſes *ſignifieth) was* Drawne out, *ev'n from the waters of perdition, praiſeth God, for his eternal* decree *of her* Reſtauration ; *&* *confeſſeth her vanity, & mortality &c.* To the ſame purpoſe wee ſhould vſe it.

LOrd, thou art alwaies our abode !
Before the world, beginning had
Thou wer't eternally our God ;
Yea, long, e're heav'n & earth were made.
Thou ſay'ſt, yee ſonns of men, returne ;
And, ſtreight return'd to duſt they be :
As one nights watch, or day outworne,
So, are a thouſand yeares to thee.
2 Thou, like a Floud (as in a dream)
Shalt ſweep them ſuddenly away ;
For, like the flowring graſſe they ſeem,
That ſprings, & fadeth, in a day.
One frowne of thine, conſumes vs quite ;
Thy wrath, our troubles doth renewe ;
Thou ſet'ſt our ſinns before thy ſight,
And, bring'ſt our ſecret faults to vewe.
3 Our tyme, through thy diſpleaſure wears,
And, like a Tale that's told are wee,
Our life is done at ſeaventie years,
Or eighty, when wee ſtrongeſt be.
For, all the reſt wee ſpend in woe,
And, vaniſh e're wee be aware.
Thine Angers force, Lord, who doth knowe !
As is thy wrath, ſuch is thy fear.
4 Inſtruct vs how to count our dayes,
That ſo, our harts may wiſdome learne ;

And, make thou, Lord, no long delaies,
But, pleaſed now, to me returne.
To vs, betimes, thy ſavour daigne,
That wee may all our life be glad,
And, dayes & years, of joye obtaine,
  For thoſe of greef, which wee have had.
5 Thy workings, let thy ſervants vewe,
Thy glories, let their Children ſee.
Oh Lord our God! thy Beautie ſhewe:
Still ſhining on vs, let it bee.
And, all our works (oh God) we pray,
Eſtabliſh thou, & ſo direct;
That, well our labours proſper may,
  And, bleſſed be with good effect.

Inſtruct vs (oh bleſſed God*) ſo to conſider our vanities, our errors, & the vncertainty of our short lives, that wee may redeem the time: & (by true Faith, ioind with Christian prudence) ſo order our Converſations; that thy wrath may be appeaſed, our ſinns blotted away, & all our ſorrowes turned into Ioyes. Moreover, during our short abiding here, vouchſafe vs thy favour; &, ſo aſsiſt our weak endeavours; that wee may, to thy glory, finish the* worke *for which thou haſt placed vs in this world. And, though our works be vnprofitable, or ſuch as like ſtuble will not abide the* Fiery-triall; *yet, let that which we ſhall build vp, be (at leaſt) grounded on the right* Foundation; *that wee our ſelves may be ſafe, through the free mercies, of* Ieſus Chriſt *our Lord.* Amen.

Pſa. 91.

This Pſalme, shewes, that ſuch as abide & beleeve in Chriſt, shal be ſecured from publike & private calamities, (by an eſpeciall protection) of what nature ſoever their perills be; at leaſt, the miſcheef of them shall be prevented, & life

& life eternal vouchſafed, &c. It is vſefull to ſtrengthen Faith in great plagues & general dangers.

WHo, in the Cloſet, & the ſhade
Of God almighty, ſtill reſides;
Is, by his Highnes, fearles made,
And, alway, ſafe with him abides.
For, I confeſſe, the Lord hath binn
A Fortreſſe, & a Rock to mee;
My God, alone, I truſted in,
And, he my truſt ſhall all waies be.
2 He will, no doubt, ſecure thee from
The Fowlers traps, & noyſome Peſt:
His wings, thy ſhelter ſhall become;
Thou ſhalt, beneath his feathers reſt.
Thou, for thy Sheild his Truth ſhalt bear,
And, nothing then ſhall thee diſmay;
Not that, which wee at Midnight fear,
Nor any ſhaft that flies by day.
3 No ſecret plague offend thee ſhall,
Nor what in publike waſts the Land;
Though at thy ſide a thouſand fall,
And tenn tymes more, at thy right-hand.
But, thou ſhalt live to mark & ſee,
The due reward of men vniuſt;
For, God (moſt high) will favour thee,
Becauſe, in him thou putſt thy truſt.
4 No miſcheef, ſhall to thee betide,
Nor any plague thy houſe infect;
For, he doth Angell-gards provide,
Which in thy waies will thee protect.
Their hands, will thee vprightly lead,
And from thy Paths, all harmes expell.
Thou ſhalt on Aſpes, & Lions tread,
On Lions younge, on Dragons fell.

5 For, feeing his delight I am,
I will (faith God) be ftill his garde :
And, fince he knowes my holy Name,
To honours high, he fhall be rear'd.
When he doth call, an ear I'le give,
In troubles, I with him, will be ;
On earth, he longe fhall honor'd live,
And, he my faving-health fhall fee.

Bleffed God; *giue us fuch affured confidence in thee, that wee may be fecured in thofe publike calamities, for which our publike finns have deferved thy fcourge; & be delivered alfo from the mifcheef of thofe perticuler punishments, which our perfonal offences may iuftly bring vpon vs. But (how foever thou dealeft with our bodies in this life) let our foules be faved from the* plauge *of everlafting Death. Let thy holy* Angells, *keep vs in all our waies; & give vs thy grace to keep the waies in which thou, haft appointed vs to walk. VVhatfoever perills or terrors affront vs, give courage to paffe through them, in the execution af our Lawfull Callings, without difmay or diftruft: And, though they bring fome fmart, let them not hinder (but rather further) the accomplishment of our eternal fafety through* Iefus Chrift *our Lord*, Amen.

Another of the fame.

WHo, refteth in the fhade of God moft high,
Within his privy-Chambers is repofed :
And, therfor, in my felfe, thus mufed I ;
Thee, as a Fort, thy God hath round enclofed,
And, is that Rock on which thou fhalt rely.
2 For, he no doubt, wil thy defender be
From fowlers netts, & peftilent infection :
He, with his wings will overfhaddowe thee ;
His Feathers, wil become thy fafe protection ;
And, for thy Sheild, his Truth provideth he.

3 No

3 No fear, that lurks in darknes, thee fhal fright
No arrow, that abrode by day-time flieth :
No fecret plague, that walks about by night,
Nor that which in the ftreet, at noon-day flayeth,
Shal make thee fear, how nigh foe're it light.
4 A thoufand faint, & finck befide thee, fhall,
At thy right-hand, ten thoufand breathles lieng :
And yet, thou fhalt receive no harme at all ;
But, only, fee God's Iuftice, by efpieng
The due reward of finners, in their fall.
5 For, thou doft hope in him ; &, therfore hee
(Ev'n God that is moft hye, & moft excelling)
Wil neither let thee wrong'd, nor harmed be,
Nor fuffer any plague to touch thy dwelling ;
But, place his gard of Angells, over thee.
6 They in thy waies, will thee conduct along,
And in their hands, vphold thee, as thy leaders ;
That not a ftone fhal do thy footing wrong.
Yea, thou vnhurt, fhalt fett thy foot on adders,
On dragons, & on lions, old & yong.
7 For, him, that mee doth love (th' *Almighty* fayes)
I will fecure from forrowes & oppreffion :
That man, likewife, to honour I wil raife,
Who knowes my *Name*, & lives in that profeffion ;
And, I will give an anfwere when he prayes.
8 In troublous times, to him I will be nigh,
And out of all his cares, I will repreeve him ;
Him, I will bleffe, & greatlie dignify ;
His fill of dayes, I will, moreover, give him ;
And, grant him grace, to live eternally.

Pfa. 92.

A Pfalm or fong for the Sabbath. *It feems not vnproper, for that great Sabbath in which wee commemo-rate*

rate our Saviours *resurrection*; *for it magnifieth God, for the exaltation of the* Righteous, *& for the blessednes of his* later end, *&c.*

Right good it is, oh Lord, most hye!
 Thy praises to recite;
Thy Truth & Love to magnifie,
 At morning, & at night.
With tenn-string'd Instruments to sing,
 The praises of thy Name;
And, that wee harpes, & Psalt'ries bring,
 To solemnize the same.
2 For, Lord, thy works reioice my hart,
 Thy Deeds, my soul do chear:
How wonderfull in them thou are!
 How deep thy muzings are!
The Foole & Wordling, nether knowe,
 Nor heed such things at all,
And, though like flowrs, the wicked showe,
 Their prospring, proves their fall.
3 But, Lord, thou allwaies art most hye;
 Mark, therfor; Mark I pray,
How sinnfull men despersed flye,
 And, how thy foes decay.
My horne, the Vnicorne's o're-topps;
 Sweet-oyle is pourd on me;
And, on my Foes, my wished hopes,
 I shall both hear, & see.
4 The Iust, shall flourish as the boughs
 Of Palmes & Cedars do;
Or, as the trees which round God's house,
 Within his Courts do growe.
Yea, they when age on them doth light,
 Growe fruitfull, fatt, & greene;
To prove the Lord my Rock, vpright

And

And blameles, to have beene.

WOnderfull art thou, oh Lord, *in all thy workings: &, though thy purposes are deeper then our imaginations; Yet (by that which thou hast manifested) wee behold in them great cause of much reioicing; & wee desire to praise thee for them, with all our harts. WEe have heretofore, repined at the flourishings of the wicked, & at our owne suffrings; But make vs hereafter, to vnderstand that their prosperities are permitted to encrease their shame; & our humiliations vouchsafed, that they may the more dignify our exaltations: as it befell our blessed* Saviour, *whose infamous* Death, *occasioned that glorious* resurrection, *which we commemorate in our Christian* Sabbath. *Oh! make vs in due time, partakers of his* Rest; *& grant, that our olde age, & our last howres, may be found fruitfull to thy glory, & our salvation, through* Iesus Christ, Amen.

Psa. 93.

This Psalme *prophecied the powre & maiesty of* Christ; *& the perpetuity of his Kingdome, in despight of all their fury who should rage against it. &c.* Wee may sing it to comfort vs, against the rage of the Devill & his members.

THe Lord is King, & weareth
  A Robe of Glory bright;
He cloth'd with strength appeareth,
  And, girt with powrfull might.
The Earth he so hath grounded,
  That, moov'd it cannot be;
His Throne, long since was founded,
  More old then Time, is he.
2 The waters, highly flowed,
  And raisd their voice, oh Lord;
The seas, their furie showed,

And

And. loud their Billowes roar'd :
But, God, in ſtrength excelleth
Strong ſeas, & powrfull deeps ;
With him, ſtill, purenes dwelleth,
And, firm his *T*ruth he keeps.

Oh Lord God, Kings *of* Kings, *incomprehenſible in Maieſtie, and in powre infinite; give us grace ſo to meditate thy vnſpeakable Attributes, that neither the frailties within vs, nor the terrors without, make vs diſtruſtfull of our ſafety in thee: For, thou art our* King, *our* Lord, *& our* God. *Thou haſt* Wiſdome *enough to know what is beſt for vs*; Powre *enough to effect it*; Love *enough to grant it*; *&* Perpetuitie *enough to continue it: Oh! give vs, but* grace *&* faith *enough, to beleeve & apply it*; *& (though the* Waters *rage never ſo horribly) we shall, vndoubtedly be ſafe, for ever and ever.* Amen.

Pſa. 94.

The Church *invokes* Chriſt *to come to* Iudgment, *in regard of the cruelty of her Oppreſſors*; *& shewes the cauſe of their folly, & preſumption. &c.* It ſerves to informe how ignorant carnall men are of the powre & waies of God; & may help to keep vs vndiſcouraged, during their Inſultings. &c.

LOrd God, whoſe claime avengments are!
Thy ſelfe, the Iuſt Avenger, ſhowe;
Thou judge of all, ariſe, drawe near,
And, on the proud, their meed, beſtowe.
For, Lord, how long! alas how long!
Shall Sinners Ioye, in doeng wrong?
2 Deſpightfull words, their tongues have ſpoke,
Great braggs, the wicked have expreſt;
Yea, Lord, thy people they have ſtrook,
And thine Inheritance oppreſt:

They,

They, widdowes, & the ſtranger ſlay,
They, Orphanes vnto death betray.
3 For, God (ſay thoſe) will never knowe;
This, *Iacob's* God ſhall never ſee.
Oh learne, (yee fooles) more wiſe to growe,
Yee people fond, more prudent be.
Cann, hee or deaf, or blinde be made,
From whome, both ears, & eyes you had?
4 He, to the Nations, ev'ry where,
Corrections & Inſtructions gives;
To ſcourg you (then) will hee forbear,
Who, all mens fruitles thoughts perceives?
They bleſſed are, whome Lord, thou chid'ſt,
And, they whome in thy Lawe thou guid'ſt.
5 Thou giv'ſt them reſt, when miſcheevs rage,
Till pitts prepar'd for Sinners be:
And, Lord, thy Flock, & Heritage
Shall never quite be left of thee.
In Iudgment, Iuſtice ſhall be ſhewed;
And, of all faithfull harts perſued.
6 Who will with mee, lew'd men, reſiſt?
Or, take my part againſt the badd?
Sure, God himſelf, doth mee aſſiſt;
My ſoul, had els bene ſilent made.
But, when I ſayd, that fall I ſhould,
Mee, Lord, thy grace did then vphold.
7 When many thoughts, oppreſt me much,
Thy comforts did my ſoul delight:
For, thou partakeſt not with ſuch,
Whoe ſentence give againſt the right;
Or ſuch, as have the Iuſt withſtood,
To death, condemning, guiltles blood.
8 But thou, oh Lord ſhalt me defend.
Thou art my God, my Rock, my Fort,

And, all the harmes my Foes intend,
Thou shalt vpon themselves retort ;
Yea, for the guilt of their offence,
Thou, Lord our God, shalt root them hence.

Oh thou supream Iudge *of the world, & severe* Avenger *of all wrongs; Behold the fury, the despight, & insolent Cruelties of our Adversaries; and deliver the pore, the widdowe, the Fatherles, & all thy Oppressed Children out of their wicked hands. Thy forbearance, hath made the perverters of Iustice, seeme to conceive that thou either see'st not, or els regardest not their impieties: Yea, those oppressers, are growne so powrfull, & so many, that wee scarce finde any to take part with vs against their Iniuries; &, but that wee have assurance of thy assistance, wee should be vtterly without hope. Oh! continue our hopes in thee; Sett thou in order, all that is amisse; destroy all the Favourers of Iniustice; & keep vs alway harmles, both in soul & body, through* Iesus Christ *our Lord,* Amen.

Psa. 95.

This Psalme *exhorts to praise God, and warnes to harken to his voice whilst wee have tyme, lest (like our fore-Fathers) wee be deprived of his Rest, for our obstinancie.* It should be often sung to remember vs, that wee embrace God's free grace, whilst it is offred.

TO God our Saviour, lett's renewe
Our songs, with chearfull voice,
Our thanckfulnes before him shewe ;
With Psalmes, in him rejoice.
For, God, the Lord most powrfull is,
The King of Gods is hee ;
The earth's obscurest vales are his,
And, his, high mountaines be.
2 The seas, he made, they are his owne :

Drie

Drie land, his Creature was;
Come, ſerve him then, & fall wee downe,
Before our Makers face.
He is our God, his flock wee are,
His paſture-ſheep, are wee:
That, you his voice, may therfor heare,
More tender-harted be.
3 Not like your Fathers, when that in
The Deſert, proov'd they were;
And tempted him, though they had ſeene,
His works of wonder, there.
Full forty years, they moov'd his wrath,
And, therfor, thus ſayd hee;
A wandring hart, this people hath,
My waies, they will ſee.
4 And, I to them, in my iuſt rage,
Did by mine Oath proteſt;
That, none of all that froward age,
Should come within my reſt.

Oh God! *the Creator, preſerver, & governour of all things; VVe give thee thancks, for making vs after thine owne* Image, *& for ſending thy* Eternal-word *to regenerate vs, when wee were made worſe then nothing. So far, wee ought to be, from arrogating the powre either of our* Beeing, *or* Well-beeing; *that (wee muſt confeſſe)* to vndoe our ſelves, *is all which wee are able,* of our ſelves do. *Like our fore Fathers, our harts are wandring from thy waies, all our life long; & wee do more & more harden them, by cuſtome in ſinn. Yet, oh Lord, ſeeing wee are the* ſheep of thy paſture; *bring us home to thy Folde: ſeeing we are thy* People, *ſoften our harts; & give us grace, ſo to harken to thy* voice *in this* Day of our Triall; *that, in the* Day of thy Iudgment, *wee may enter into thy* Reſt, *through* Ieſus Chriſt *our Lord,* Amen.

N 2 Pſa. 96.

Pſa. 96.

VVee are herein exhorted, to ſing & preach, the New-ſongs *of the* Goſpell, *to the praiſe of* Chriſt *our King. And (in regard, other Gods are but vanities) all nations are provoked to ioyne in praiſing him. &c.* We ſhould ſing it to glorifie Chriſt, for his powre, & his Truth, &c.

COme now, & in ſome New-indighting,
Bleſſe God (the world's Almightie King)
His Name's due praiſe, in ſongs reciting,
Of his Salvation, daylie ſing.
His Fame, & works of admiration,
Yee people heed, yee Nations hear:
His powre deſerves, high exaltation;
For, all the Gods, leſſe dreadfull are.
2 The Gentiles Gods, are fooliſh fictions,
But our great God, did heav'n creat;
Powr, glory, praiſe, & all perfections,
Attend him, in his holy-ſeat.
To him, due praiſe, yee kindreds render;
Extoll his powre, his glory ſing:
To God's great Name, fitt honours tender,
Approach his Courts; & offrings bring.
3 Within his houſe, with praiſe, profeſſe him.
And, let him be adored there;
Let all the world, their God confeſſe him,
And, ſerve him with a holy feare.
Yea, to the Gentiles let them publiſh.
The Lord their King, & that his might
The wav'ring earth ſhall faſt eſtabliſh;
And, do the wronged people right.
4 Let heav'n & earth, with joy-excelling,
Reioice before him ever more;

The

The feas, & all things in them dwelling,
The feilds, the woods, & all their ftore:
For, lo, the Lord approcheth nearlie,
Behold, to judge the world he comes,
The wicked, he will judge ferverely;
And, give the people righteous doomes.

Honour & wifdome, & powre, & praife, be afcribed vnto thee (oh king of the world) *by all thy Creatures, according to the feverall faculties which thou haft beftowed vpon them. Be thou glorified, in thy felfe alfo; according to that which thy* In comprehenfiblenes *deferveth, beyond what thy creatures are able to afcribe. Let all heathenish* deities, *& all thofe* Idolls, *which carnall men have fet vp in their harts, appear fuch vanities as they are; & let thy* Soveraignty *be acknowledged, (& thy worship truely celebrated) by* Iewes, Gentiles, *& all* Nations *throughout the world. Let vs, efpecially (who are of thy vifible* Church) *performe this duty, & let our harts be fo eftablished, & fo filled with* Holines, *&* filial awe, *that wee may expect thy comming to* Iudgment, *with comefort; & wellcome thy opproach, with shouts of tryvmphs, & fongs of exvltation.* Amen.

Pfa. 97.

The foveraignty of Chrift, *with his comming to* Iudgment; *the Ioy which the faithfull shall conceive thereby, & the confufion which will fall on the wicked, is here foretold, &c. It may be myftically applied alfo, to our Saviours firft comming:* And may be fung, to ftir vp our fpirituall reioicings, in both his *Advents.*

THe Lord is king; be therfor glad
Yee Lands & Iles, now this is known;
With Clouds & darknes, he is cladd,
And Truth & Iuftice, gard his throne,
A burning flame before him goes,

N 3 Where

Wherewith, he ſhall conſume his foes.
2 He, to the world his Glory ſhew'd,
And, earth beheld the ſame with fear;
Like waxe, hills melted, when they vew'd
The Lord (the world's great Lord) appear.
His Righteouſnes, the heav'ns have ſhowne;
His glories, are to all men knowne.
3 All Idoll ſervers, he deſtroies,
And, of all Gods will honor'd be.
It *Syon* gladds, & *Iacob*, ioyes,
His righteous doomes, to hear & ſee.
Above the higheſt hills he dwells:
And, all the Gods, he farr excells.
4 Hate ſinn, yee Lovers of the Lord,
For, he his holie-ones, will ſave:
And, light & Truth, to thoſe afford,
That, harts vpright, & faithfull have.
Yee ſaints therefore, record, confeſſe,
And, praiſe with Ioy, God's holines.

Oh Chriſt *(the everlaſting ſonn of the Father) Thou only art the* Catholick king; *& it is no leſſe then blaſphemy for any other to aſſume that* Title. *Rule thou, therfor, in thine owne Kingdome, & caſt all Vſurpers out of thy Throne. Publish thy glories to the world; Let thy Truth & Iuſtice, terriſy thy Foes, & conſume all Vngodlines out of the land. Root out all Idolatries; that,* Iacob *&* Syon *(thy* Church *& her Children) may reioice. Enthrone thy ſelf alſo in our harts, & let thy preſence conſume thence, the* Mountaines *of our preſumption (with every thing, which there exalts it ſelf, againſt thee) that, the hatred of Sinn, the Love of thy preſence, the light of thy Truth, & the Ioye of the holy-ghoſt, may be there eſtabliſhed, for ever & ever,* Amen.

Pſa. 98.

Pfa. 98.

A Pfalm. *The whole world, is exhorted to fing the new fongs of the* Gofpell, *& the great powre & Victories, of* Chrift. *It shewes alfo, how we ought to praife him.* To thefe ends, we fhould vfe it &c.

NEw fongs vnto the Lord indite ;
For, mighty marvailes he hath done.
His Right-hand, hath prevaild in fight,
His holy Arme, the conqueft wonn.
The Gentiles have in publike vew'd,
How iuft & healpful, he hath beene :
To *Ifr'el*, Truth & Love he fhew'd ;
His Mercies, all the world hath feene.
2 Then, through the world his glory fing ;
Sing praifes, with triumphant voice :
To praife the Lord, the Pfalt'rie bringe,
And on the Harp, with Pfalmes reioice.
The Lord, the King, with mirth adore ;
With Trump & Flute, this Ioye beginn ;
Yee feas, with all your fullnes, roare ;
Thou earth be glad, & all therein.
3 Before the Lord, your ioyes expreffe,
Yee Flouds & hills : for, lo, he comes
To judge the world, with equalnes,
And give the people, righteous doomes.

Almighty Sonn of God, wee bleffe & praife thee for the manifeftation of thy Mercy to the whole world, in the miraculous work of our Redemption. Thou didft come to us in defpifed weaknes; *Yet haft thou therein showne fuch vnrefiftiable powre, that it prevailed againft the wifdome of the worldly-wife ; & magnified thy derided* Croffe, *above all the moft renowned* Deities *of the Gentiles. This thou didft, by appearing in a contemptible eftate : Oh ! how glorious.*

N 4 *& how*

& how powrfull wilt thou be in thy second comming! It now draweth nigh. Oh! let it not come vpon vs, as a theef in the night, *but, as the* Travaile *vpon a woman, who keepeth a iust reconing; & ioyeth in the hopes of her* Birth, *more then shee feares the paines of her Travaile: So, according to the counsell of thy holy spirit, wee may expect, & receive thee, with praises, Triumphs, & reioicings.* Amen.

Pfa. 99.

It magnifieth the royall dignity of Chrift, *& exhorts to feare, serve, & praise him, according to the example of* Mofes, Aron, *&* Samuel. *We may vse this,* to informe vs, that wee & the Patriarks have but one, & the fame, Chrift our faviour.

THe Lord is King, & he doth make
 Betwixt the Cherubins, his throne:
Yee people fear, yee Kingdomes quake.
For, great in *Syon*, he is growne.
Or'e Nations all, himfelf he raif'd:
His Name is fear'd, & holy to.
Oh! let this powrfull king be praif'd,
 For, he vprightly loves to do.
2 His powre delights in righteous waies;
With *Iacob*, he will juftly deal.
The Lord our God, oh therfore praife,
And, at his holy footftool kneel.
His Preift, with *Mofes* A'ron was;
And *Samuel* did invoke his Name:
Thefe humbly fought the Lord for grace,
 And, they from him, obtaind the fame.
3 Hee, from the Cloudie-piller fpake,
And on his words thofe men relide:
They, of his lawes did confcience make,

And,

And, God therfore to them replide.
Yea (though their errors, he did blame)
To them, he did his grace afford;
Oh, serve our God, & praise his Name;
For, sacred is, our God the Lord.

Oh Christ *(who sittest betweene the* Cherubims, *& rulest both in heaven & earth) wee thy subiects, do humbly tender our homage to thy royall Maiestie; magnifieng thy Iustice, thy Mercy, & thy powre. Thou art the same* yesterday, to day, & for ever. *VVee beseech thee therfor, to make vs both followers of the Patriarks thy servants, in their faithfull obedience; & partakers also, of those mercies which thou hast vouchsafed them. Though iustly, thou correctest our errors; yet, in pitty regard our infirmities, accept our penitence, & hear our prayers; even for the sake of thy bitter passion, sweet* Iesus. Amen.

Psa. 100.

A Psalme of praise. *It commemorates two great* Benifits: *our* Creation *(which is common to all) & that Free* Election, *which is peculier to the Chosen Flock of* Christ; *& whereby, they have the Freedom of his pasturage, and of his protection. It is therfore vsefull, to praise God for the same.*

REioyce in God, yee Nations,
In chearfulnes, adore him;
With ioyfull acclamations,
Present your Selves before him:
For, God the Lord, did make vs,
No hand therein, had wee;
He, for his flock doth take vs,
His Pasture-sheep wee be.
2 His Gates & Courts, possesse yee,
To thanck him, goe yee thither;

Iis Name, with gladnes, bleffe yee,
   And fing his praife togither:
For, God is kinde, for ever,
   His grace, he freely daignes;
His Truth, will faile vs never,
   For, endles, it remaines,

Thy hands, oh Lord, did make vs: therfor we praife thee for our Creation, & for all the naturall Faculties, where with it pleafed thee, to endowe our foules & bodies. Thou haft alfo redeemed us: wee therfor likewife, praife thee; & for our Election, Vocation, Iuftification, Sanctification, Illumination, Prefervation, hope of Glorification, & for all the pretious Lincks of that golden Chaine, *wherein are ioyned together the meanes of our* Salvation. *Thou haft, (wee confeffe) done already fo much for vs, that we have almoft nothing to pray for, but thanckfulnes, & the cōtinuatiō of thy free Mercies, hitherto vouchfafed: for which, wee humbly befeech thee; & that wee may truly praife thee for thē, for ever & ever.* Amen.

Another of the fame.

OH! all yee Kingdomes, praife the Lord,
   Before him, let your Ioy be fhowne:
With finging, let him be ador'd;
   And, for your God, let him be knowne.
2 He made vs, & his owne wee be,
His Flock, & pafture-fheep wee are;
His Gates, & Courts, then, enter yee,
   And, give him thancks, & praifes there.
3 Yea, praife him, & his Name confeffe:
For, in the Lord, all good refides;
His Mercies, & his Faithfulnes
   Throughout all Ages, firme abides.

Pfa. 101.

Pſa. 101.

A Pſalme of David. *It perſonates* Chriſt *propoſing the divine, morrall, political, & Oeconomical dutie of good Princes; & promiſing the execution there of, in his Kingdome & Family. This is, indeed, the right ſinging of* Mercy & Iudgmēt, & this Pſalme is vſefull, at the Coronatiō of Kings, or when Magiſtrates, are admitted into their places.

OF Iudgment, & of Love to thee,
Now, Lord, a ſong I will indite;
Oh come! vnite thy ſelfe to me,
And, I will keep my waies vpright.
With perfect hart, my houſe I'le guide,
No wicked thinge, ſhall pleaſe mine eyes;
I'le thoſe deteſt who turne aſide,
And, all their deeds, I will depiſe.
2 No froward hart with me ſhall ſtay,
I will elect no wicked mate;
The ſlandrous tongue I'le cutt away,
High-lookes I ſhun, proude mindes, I hate.
But, through the land, to dwell with mee,
I will equire for men vpright;
And, thoſe men ſhall my ſervants be,
Whoſe harts, in perfect waies delight.
3 No Cheater, ſhall with mee have place,
No Liers, in my ſight ſhall ſtay;
And, from God's Land, I ſoone will chaſe,
And, root all wicked men away.

Oh Lord God! all Authoritie is from thee; and, thou placeſt good Magiſtrates & Governours, *both in* Church & Commōwealth, *for a bleſsinge: or, permitteſt Tirants, Fooles, & corrupt perſons, for the punishment of a wicked people. Defend us, wee pray thee, from this plague; and, grant*

grant, that they whome thou fetteft over vs, may be fuppref-fers of all vices; *protectors of al* virtues; *favourers of true* Pietie; *& be alwaies, good examples (in life & converfa-tion) both to their Equalls & Inferiors. Let us alfo, be the fame in our feverall places & Callings; that (walking with good* confciences, *& vpright* harts, *in an vndefi-led* way) *wee may as well fing of thy* Iudgments, *as of thy mercies.* Amen.

Pfa. 102.

A prayer of the Afflicted, when he is over-whelmed, and poureth out his complaint before the Lord. *The Title shewes,* it may properly be fung by the *pore in fpirit,* who are *afflicted, by the fight of theirowne vnworthines&c. It containes, a confefsion, with a prediction of the benifits of the* Gofpell; *& shewes the eter-nity of* Chrift's *Kingdome.*

LOrd, mark my fuite, receive my crie,
Be prefent at my need:
Thine eares to my complaints apply,
And, hear my fuite with fpeed.
For, fmoke-like, fumes my tyme away,
My bones are parcht with heat;
My wounded hart, dries vp like hay,
And, I forgoe my meat.
2 My panifull groanes, have made me leane,
And nought but skinn & bone;
I fare, ev'n like a Pelicane,
In deferts, left alone.
Yea, like the defert owle, am I;
And, watching, I have fate,
As when alone, on buildings high,
A Sparrow, wants her mate.
3 Mee, all day long, my foes revile,

At

At mee, they frett, & fwear :
And, Afhes are my bread the while ;
My drinck, my Weepings are.
For, thou in wrath advanced'ft me,
That, vile I might be made.
My dayes, like fhades declininge be,
Like new-fprung graffe, I fade.
4 But, Lord, thy tymes, are without end,
All Ages thee record ;
Now then, arife thou, & befreind
Afflicted Sion, Lord.
For, now the tyme to favour her,
Fullfilled is outright,
And, greeved all thy fervants are,
To vewe her wofull plight.
5 That, Earthlie Kings, may ftand in feare,
And, Princes dread thy Fame,
Build *Syon's* wall, & fhew thou, there,
The glorie of thy Name.
Then, thou fhalt hear all thofe that mourne,
Then, thou fhalt healp the pore ;
Which I'le record, that men vn-borne
May praife thee, Lord, therefore.
6 For, from thy holy-place, on high,
The world furvayeng, then,
Thou, Lord, fhalt hear the pris'ners cry,
And fave condemned men :
Thy Name in *Syon* to declare ;
And in Ierufalem ;
(Where Nations all, Affembled are)
To fhewe thy praife to them.
7 Short-liv'd, & weak, & ful of greefe,
Thou mad'ft me, in my way ;
But, Lord, at noonetyde of my life

Remove

Remove me not I pray.
Thy yeares, through ages all extend,
Thy hands, long since, did frame,
Both heav'n and earth ; yet, when they end,
Thou shalt remaine the same.
8 They old shall growe, as garments do,
And, be renew'd by thee :
Yea, thou, oh Lord, shalt change them so,
And, they shall changed.
But, from all Changes thou art free'd,
Thy yeares, for aye endure :
And, all thy servants, & their seed,
Shall bide in thee, secure.

Oh Lord, the sole comforter of all destressed soules! pittie the sighes & complaints of thy pore afflicted Childrē, whome thy displeasure for Sinn, hath worthily defeased, both in minde & Body. Open vnto vs the Armes of thy compassion ; & grant, that what we have lost by our Offenses, *wee may recover by thy Bounty, vpon our true repentance, & amendment of life: which amendment, we beseech thee to hasten ; lest wee be cut short in the midst of our hopes. Repaire alsoe, the Decayes of thy* Church *(in thy tyme appointed) that her children may praise thee for it, before mē, during their short abiding here ; & that, when thou hast changed our Corruption into incorruption, we may glorify thee among thy blessed Angels, world without end.* Amen.

Psa. 103.

A Psalme of David. *The Prophet, praiseth & exhorts to praise God, for many perticuler Benifits, magnifieng his Compassion, longsuffring, Iustice &c. & declares the frailty of man. &c.* It is vsefull to magnify the manifold Mercyes which wee have receaved by Iesus Christ.

Come

COme praiſe the Lord ; come praiſe his Name,
My ſoul, & all that is in mee.
My ſoul, come praiſe his holy Name,
And, of his ſavours mindfull be.
For, all thine errors he forgave ;
He cur'd thy greefs, he clos'd thy wound ;
Thy Life, he ſaved from the grave,
And, thee with tender mercies crown'd.
2 With Goodnes, he, thy mouth doth fill,
He like on Eagle, makes thee younge ;
And, righteous Doomes he giveth ſtill,
To ev'ry one that ſuffers wrong.
His waies to *Moſes* he declar'd,
His deeds to *Iſr'el*, he did ſhowe ;
And, kinde, & gratious is our Lord,
To mercy, prone ; to Anger, ſlowe.
2 He, will not alwaies vs vprayd ;
Nor, evermore diſpleaſd is hee :
Nor, hath he ſoe our ſinns repaid,
As, juſtly they deſerve to be.
For, they that fear him, finde his grace,
Out-reach the ſpreadings of the ſkye ;
And, he from vs, our ſinns doth place,
As farr, as Eaſt from Weſt doth lie.
4 He pitties them who fear his Name,
As fathers pitty their owne ſeed :
For, well he knowes our britle frame,
And, that from duſt, wee did proceed.
Our tyme, is like the feild-bred-flowres,
Which, now doe made a goodly ſhewe ;
Anon, ſome blaſt their forme devours,
And leaves no token where they grewe.
5 But, ſtill there's mercy in the Lord,
For them, that awfull of him bee :

To

To them, that keep, & minde his word,
His righteouſnes, imputeth hee.
His Throne abone the heav'ns is raiſ'd,
And, over all, he beareth ſway:
Of powrfull Angells, he, is praiſ'd;
They hear his voice, & him obay.
6 Let all his hoaſts; his ſervants to,
Performe his will, and praiſe his name:
Yea, ſoe let all his creatures doe,
And oh! my ſoul; do thou the ſame.

Father of all pittie *(who art ſlowe to anger, & ready to forgive) Looke vpon our infirmities; conſider our frailties; in thy abundant compaſsion, forgive our treſpaſſes; and deal not with us according to our deſerts. Cauſe us to be renewed like* Eagles *by caſting of, the* old Man: *Fill our Mouths, with ſongs of thy praiſe; & our harts, with thine owne ſelfe, that vnmatchable ſweetnes! that vnſpeakable goodnos! Cure all our* infirmities; *& healp in all our weakneſſes, by thy* fatherly *care. Preſerve vs in thy* feare; *in the remembrance of thy* Covenant; *and in the wayes of thy Commandements, to our lives end. That, wee honouring thee, by thy* Creatures *here; may glorifie thee among thy* Angells *&* Saints *hereafter, world without end.* Amen.

Pſal. 104.

The Majeſtie, wiſdome, *&* powre *of* God, *in the Creation & preſervation of all his Creatures, is here deſcribed, by excellent* Metaphors. We may ſing it to praiſe him, for making & preſerving all things, to his owne glorie, & for our conſortable vſe. &c. *The Title is*; Halelujah.

NOw, ſhall my ſoul to praiſe the Lord aſſay;
For, Lord my God! vnbounded is thy might:
With glories beames, thy ſelf thou doſt aray,

And

And as with Robes, are cloth'd about, with Light,
Thou curtaine-like, the heav'ns abrode diſplayeſt;
And, in great flouds, thy chābers roofs thou layeſt.
2 The rowling Clouds, thy ſpeedy Charrets are,
And winged windes, thy ſwift-paſd Courſes be;
Thy Meſſages, the glorious Angells beare,
And burning fires, like ſervants, waite on thee.
The Globe of Earth, ſo firmly thou haſt grounded,
That none can ſhake the ſtructur thou haſt fоūded.
3 As with a robe, with flouds thou clothdſt the ſame
And, then, the waves above the hills aſpir'd:
But, at thy Check, ſoone downe againe they came,
And, when thy voice did thunder, back retir'd:
From lofty heights, by winding Vallies, tracinge;
They thither fel, where firſt they had their placing.
4 And, ſtrongly there, thou boundeſt them about,
That they, no more, the world ſhould overflowe;
Among the Dales, clear ſprings, thou ſendeſt out,
Which run between the mountaines to & fro. (eſt
Thou drink from thence, to forreſt heards convai-
And, there, the thirſt of Aſſes wilde, alayeſt.
5 Then by the Bancks of all thoſe running Rills,
Among the boughs the, birdes make melodies:
Thou from above, with ſhewres bedew'ſt the hills,
And giv'ſt enough, all Creatures to ſuffice.
For Cattell, graſſe; for man, thou herbs ordaineſt;
And, him with food, out of the earth ſuſtaineſt,
9 From thence proceeds, the hart-reioicing-wine;
Refreſhing oyle, from thence doth alſo flowe;
That pretious oyle, which makes the face to ſhine;
& bread, wherby man's hart more ſtrōg may grow.
Thy Cedars tall, due moyſture have not wanted;
Not they, which high, on *Libanon*, are planted.
7 The feather'd foules, their neſts on thē do build,

The lofty Firrs, are dwellings for the ſtorke ;
For clyming goats, the mountains, refuge yeald,
In craggy Rocks, the fearfull connies lurke.
The changing Moon, the tymes apointed ſhoweth
The conſtant Sunn, his howr of ſetting knoweth.
8 Thou Darknes cal'ſt ; ſo, night ſhutts vp the day ;
And, then, abrode the Forreſters do roame :
With roarings loud, the Lions hunt theyr prey,
And, vnto thee (oh God) for meat, they come.
The riſing ſunn, anon returneth hither
And, in their denns, they couch againe togither.
9 Then, man till night, afreſh, his labour plies.
How many, be thy wondrous works oh Lord !
In ev'ry thing, thou art exceeding wiſe.
The ſpatious Earth, by thee is fully ſtor'd ;
And, in the ſea are many creatures dwelling,
Both great & ſmall, whoſe number paſſeth telling.
10 There, ſail the ſhipps, &, there thou didſt creat
Leviathan, to ſport vpon the Floud.
Thy Creatures all, from thee expect their meat ;
And, that thou ſhouldſt in ſeaſon, give them food,
Which thou beſtow'ſt, & they (the ſame receiving)
Are filld with Goodnes, of thy bounteous giving.
11 Thou hid'ſt thy face, & loe, they troubled are ;
Thou ſtopt'ſt their breath, & lifeles duſt they bee :
Againe, thou breath'ſt : & they reviv'd appear,
And, all the earth is new arayd by thee.
Oh ! let the Lord, with honour ſtill be named,
And, let him ioy in that which he hath framed.
12 If with his eye, the earth he but ſurvay,
The fearfull earth, doth tremble at his look ;
If on the hills, he but a finger lay,
His very touch, doth make the hills to ſmoke.
And, whil'ſt my Life, or beeing, is enioyed,

To

To praiſe my God my, tongue ſhall be employed.
13 Sweet thoughts of him, conceaved are in me;
And, in the Lord my hart ſhal ever ioye :
For, from his Land, the wicked rooted be ;
And, he, will them, perpetually deſtroy.
Oh let his praiſe, for ever, be confeſſed ;
Praiſe God my ſoul, & ſay : *The Lord be bleſſed.*

Moſt glorious Lord God! *thy admirable powre & wiſdome created the world (which having once overflowed for Sinn, thou didſt againe replenish the ſame) continueng the maine* Fabrick *ever ſince; &, therein mainetaining a ſuccesſion of innumerable different Creatures, by a wonderfull providence (& with a ſpeciall regard vnto mankinde above them all) Give vs therfore, grace, wee beſeech thee, ſo to meditate thy workmanſhip, thy wiſdome, & thy great mercies herein ; that our harts beeing regenerated & revived (by the breathings of thy holy ſpirit) wee may be thanckfull for thy great Favours : & that when our wickednes is rooted out, wee (perceaving all to be good which thou haſt created or ordained) may praiſe thy wiſdome, thy goodnes, & thy bountie, for ever & ever* Amen.

Pſa. 105.

Halelujah. *It typically expreſſeth (by God's deliverances of the Iewes, & his Covenant with them) the ſpiritual League & graces, vouchſafed to us &c.* We ſhould therfor ſing it, not only hiſtorically, but with a reſpect alſo, to the Covenant of grace, & his mercies, by *Chriſt Ieſus.*

COme praiſe the Lord, invoke his Name ;
To all men make his actions knowne :
In Pſalmes of praiſe, ſing forth his fame,
And, ſpeak what wonders he hath done.
Let them, who ſeek the Lord, be glad,

Let of his Name, their boaft be made.
2 Oh fearch God's powre, & feek his face;
Still, minde what wonders he hath done:
Let all, that are of *Abraham's* race,
And *Iacob's*, his elected-one,
God's wondrous works, record with heed,
And, minde what he hath fore-decreed.
3 He, is our God, our mighty Lord;
His Iudgments through the world are fpread:
He beares in minde his promif'd word,
Vnto a thoufand Ages made:
Ev'n that, which he to *Abr'ham* fwore;
And vow'd to *Ifa'ck* heretofore.
4 To *Iacob*, came the fame decree,
In *Ifr'el* to continue ftill;
To thee, & all thy feed, fayd hee,
The Land of *Can'an* give I will.
Yea, thus he fpake, when fewe they were,
And, they themfelves, meer ftrangers there.
5 When forraigners, they liv'd among,
(And, oft from place to place remoov'd)
He fuffred none to do them wrong;
But, for their fakes ev'n kings reprov'd.
My prophets, harme yee not, fayd hee,
Vntouch'd let my Anointed be.
6 Then, he by dearth, their Land made pore,
And, did the ftaff of bread withhold;
But, *Iofeph*, he, firft fent before,
Eu'n him, whome for a Slave they folde.
With fetters, there, his feet they pain'd;
And, him, in irons, they detain'd.
7 But, when his Triall was decreed,
God's word, his innocence difclof'd;
The king did fend, to have him freed,

And

And by the Prince, he was vnloſ'd.
His cheef commander he was made,
To rule his houſe, & all he had.
8 Of all his Lords, he did command;
That he his Counſellers might guide.
Then, *Iſr'el* came to Egipts land,
And, *Iacob* did with *Cham* reſide:
And, ſo his Children thrived there,
That, ſtronger then his foes they were.
9 Whoſe hate, & fraudulent intent
When to his Folk, he well made knowne,
His ſervant *Moſes* then he ſent,
And *A'ron* his Elected-one,
Who wrought great marvailes in his Name,
And wonders in the Land of *Ham*.
10 He darknes cal'd; & dark it grewe;
(For his commands were not withſtood)
Throughout their Coaſt, their fiſh he ſlewe,
And chang'd their waters into bloud.
Vpon their land he froggs did bring
Which climb'd the chambers of the king.
11 He ſpake, & flies of divers formes,
And, lice through ev'ry quarter craw'ld;
Inſteed of raine, he gave them ſtormes,
And, hayle, & lightnings forth he cald.
Which, downe, their vines, & figtrees brake,
And in their groves, great ſpoile did make.
12 The Locuſt came at his command;
And Caterpillers did abound:
The graſſe they waſted from the land,
And ev'ry fruite, vpon the ground.
Then, he their Eldeſt borne did ſmite,
The very prime of all their might.
13 His people, rich from thence he brought:

O 3 Among

Among his Tribes, no weaklings were :
All *Egipt* ioy'd when they went out ;
For why? of them, they ftood in feare.
  A Canopy of Clouds they had ;
  To give them light, a fire he made.
14 The people askt, & quailes he gave,
With heav'nly bread, he filled them :
The Rocks likewife, for them he clave,
And through dry Lands he fent a Streame :
  Becaufe, to minde that promife came,
  Which he had made to Abraham.
16 His people, & his chofen bands,
He brought away with Ioyfulnes,
To them, he gave the Gentiles lands,
And, they their labours did poffeffe :
  That they might mark what he decreed,
  And keep his lawes, with carefull heed.

Preferve us oh Lord, *from that hardnes of hart for which thou fendeft thy dreadfull iudgments into the world; & withhold alfoe thy plaugues from our Kingdome: But, efpecially, that fpirituall* Darknes *& thofe* Iudgments, *which are miftically fignifiied, by* Lice, froggs, Locufts, *& the reft of the* Egiptiā *plagues: And as a meanes of this favour, make us mindfull of that* Covenant, *which thou haft made vnto vs, & wee vnto thee, in* Chrift Iefus. *VVee confeffe thou didft gratioufly lead our Fore-fathers in the* wildernes; *feeding, guiding & preferving them, by thy miraculous powre; Be thou alfo, we pray thee, our Affiftance & protecter in this our Pilgrimage; feeding us with that heavenly* Manna, *& refrefhing us out of that fpirituall* Rock, *whereof, they had the type; that wee may followe them who are gone before into the* Land of the living, *& there praife thee, world without end.* Amen.

Pfa. 106

Pſa. 106.

Halelujah. *It commemorates the perverſenes of the* Iewes, *in whome the* humane Nature, *was typified: therefore (changing the* perſons, *to our ſelves.)* We may ſing it to ſet forth, God's Grace & long-ſuffring toward vs; Who have enioyed the ſame favours, & are guilty of the ſame perverſenes.

COme praiſe the Lord; for wondrous good is he;
And, without end, his tender mercies are.
His powrfull Acts, by none cann vttred be:
His praiſes due, none fully cann declare.
They bleſſed are, that have true judgment heeded,
And in the paths of righteouſnes prooceeded.
2 With ſuch reſpect, let me remembred be,
As that, which to thy choſen thou doſt bear:
Thy ſaving-health, vouchſafe thou vnto me;
And place me there, where thyne Elected are.
That, I may taſt, the pleaſures of thy Nation,
And partner be in all their exvltation:
3 Wee have amiſſe, like our fore-fathers done,
God's wondrous works, in Egipt moov'd not thē,
His mercies great, they never thought vpon,
But, at the Sea (the red-ſea) vexed him.
Who, naitheles, them (for his nameſake) ſpared;
That, his great powr, might be by them declared.
4 The Red-ſea, then, was dride, at his command,
And, there, as through the deſert, they do goe,
He, ſaved them from their oppreſſors hand,
And, them redeemd, from their ſtronghanded foe,
For, in the floud he overwhelmd their haters,
And, non of them, eſcaped from the waters.
5 Then, they beleev'd, & praiſd him in a ſong;
But, ſoone his words, & works forgotten were:

For flesh, ev'n in the Deserts, they did long,
And much provok'd the Lord's displeasure there.
Their brutish lust, with flesh, indeed, he serv'd;
But therewithal, their lustful souls were sterved.
6 Their Campe, at *Moses* grudgd; & with despight
God's holy-one, ev'n *Aron*, did persue:
For which, the Earth did Swallow *Dathan* quite,
And, quick-devour'd, *Abiram*, & his crewe.
A sudden flame, their Congregation fired;
And, made an end of those that had conspired.
7 An Idoll then, in *Horeb*, they did raise;
A molten Calfe, as God, adored they:
And gave to God (their *Glory* & their *Praise*)
An Oxes forme, that eateth grasse, & hay.
For God their Garde, nor for his powre they cared
In *Egyipt*, *Cham*, or at the sea declared.
8 God, therefore sayd, he quite had ruin'd them,
But that, his wrath by *Moses* was alayd.
The pleasant Land, likewise, they did contemn,
Beleeving not the words that he had sayd.
And, in their tents, their murmurs were a token,
They did not hear, nor heed, what God had spokē.
9 Another tyme, his hand advanced was,
Them, in the Desert, to have overthrowne;
To mixe their seed, among the gentile-race,
And, scatter them, through many lands vnknowne.
Because, vnto *Baal-peor*, they had bowed;
And, fedd on meats, to lifeles Idolls vowed.
10 Yea, then, the Plague did fast among thē run,
Because their fault God's anger had encreast.
But, Iustice was by *Phineas*, timely done;
And, there vpon, that mischeef quickly ceast.
His righteousnes, therefore, shall be commended
Through Ages all, till Ages all are ended.

11 At

11 At *Meribath*, they made him angry, to,
And, wrath likewiſe, with *Moſes*, for their ſake;
For, they provokt his humble ſpirit ſoe,
That, he, ſome words without adviſement ſpake.
They did not ſlay their foes, as God forewarned,
But, mixt with ſuch, and their ill cuſtoms learned.
12 Their Idol-Gods they ſerv'd; which proov'd a
To Devills, they did ſacrifize their ſeed: (ſnare,
They ſpilt the bloud of thoſe that guiltles were;
Ev'n their owne ſonns, & Daughters blood, they
To *Canans* God, for offrings, thē they killed; (ſhed
And all the Land with bloody ſinns defiled.
13 Thus, by their works, poluted they became,
And, whoriſhlie, perſude what they deviz'd:
Which did Gods wrath againſt them ſo inflame,
That he therefore his heritage deſpiz'd
For, them to ſerve the Nations he conſtrained,
And, over them, their Adverſaries raigned.
14 Their Foes, oppreſt & brought thē verie lowe;
And then (though him their Courſes did provoke)
He helped them, when they did helples growe;
And, when they cride, compaſſion on them tooke.
His Cov'nant, & his grace, to minde he called,
And ſuccour'd thē, by thoſe, who them enthralled.
15 Oh Lord our God! ſtill, ſend vs healp frō thee,
That wee therfore may laud thy holy Name,
Divided from the Gentiles, let vs be,
To ſing thy praiſe & trivmph in the ſame.
Let Iſre'ls God, with praiſe be ſtill confeſſed;
And, let al people ſay; *The Lord be bleſſed.*

VVee confeſſe, oh Lord God, that wee have ſinned according to all the tranſgreſsions of our forefathers; & added many Offences vnto theirs. VVee confeſſe alſo, that (as to them) thou haſt multiplied thy mercies towards us; Inſomuch

ſomuch that our enimies, yea our Afflictions, have beene made comfortable: And in ſteed of Plagues (whoſe encreaſe & continuance wee rather deſerved) thou haſt alured vs vnto thy love, by many extraordinario bleſsings. Oh God! let us no longer abuſe thy patience; but make us now, ſoe to mind our part of the covenant *which is betwixt us; that wee may be ſeperated from our* heatheniſh converſations; *be remembrend among thy* people; *behold the good of thy* Choſen; *reioice in the gladnes of thy* Nation; *& be pertakers in the glory of thine* Inheritance, *for ever & ever.* Amen.

Pſa. 107.

Halelujah. *It exhorts, to praiſe God, for his vniverſall Grace; Acknowledgeth him, the deliverer of all men, in all places, and in all troubles; Confeſſeth him the Corrector, Orderer, and diſpoſer of kingdomes, perſons, & famelies, &c.* It is vſefull both for temporall & ſpirituall bleſſings; *for, by bodiey ſuffrings; ſpirituall miſeries, are myſtically ſignified.*

COme praiſe the Lord, & thanckfully confeſſe,
That he is good, & gratious, without end,
Let thoſe whom God redeem'd, his praiſe expers,
Ev'n thoſe whome he did from their foes defend;
Collecting them, from Eaſt, & weſterne Nations,
From Northern Clymes, & ſouthern habitations.
2 In deſerts wilde, & where no dwellings were,
They wandred on, with drought, & hunger, faint:
And, them he freed, from all deſtreſſes there,
When they to him, had vttred their complaint.
He ledd them on, in paths directly guiding
To Citties faire, whear they had ſafe abiding.
3 Oh! let men praiſe the goodnes of the Lord,
And publiſh out, his wonders to their ſeed:

For,

For, he to hungry men doth meat afford;
And, with good things, the longing soul doth feed.
He, those vnbinds, that are in fetters chained;
And in the bands, & shades of death detained.
4 The word, of God most high, they did reject,
And small account, of his advise they made;
With heat, & toile, he therfor did afflict
And cast them downe, when they no helper had.
But, in their need (when they againe complained)
He tooke away the greef, which they sustained.
5 Frō deaths black shades, he shew'd thē light some
And, all their bands, did quite asunder break; (wais
Let all mankinde, therfore, his wonders praise,
And of his works, among their Children speake.
The brazen Gates, he crakt, & open sett them:
Their yron barrs he broke, & forth he sett them.
6 He plaugeth fooles, because they have transgrest;
And, for their sinns, they much afflicted are:
Their fainting soules, doe pleasant meats detest,
They to the gates of death approached near:
But, seeking God (when they were so oppressed)
From all their paines, & feares, he them releafed.
7 He sent his word, which did their greevāce heal,
Preventing so, their fall, which hastned on.
Oh let all men! God's goodnes, therfore tell,
And shewe their seed, what wonders he hath done.
Let them declare his works, with joyfull singing,
The sacrifize, of thanckfull praises, bringing.
8 They that in shipps at sea employed are,
(And for their gaine to crosse the waves are bold)
May vewe the works of God-almighty there,
And in the deepes his wondrous deeds behold.
For, he but breaths, & streight a storm appeareth
Which vp aloft, the rowling billowes beareth.

9 Now

9 Now mounts to heav'n ; anon, defcēds the keel,
And they grow faint, with labour & with fear :
As druncken men, they ftagger, & they reel ;
And of their skill, they quite deprived are,
Then, to the Lord they cry, who them releafes,
From all their feares, their dangers, & deftreffes.
10 For, he, the ftormes, to gentle calmes cōvarts,
And, quiet then the raging fea, becomes ;
Then they are joy'd ; Then eafed are their harts,
And, them he brings, to their defired homes.
Of thefe his works, let all men make relations,
And fhewe his deeds, to future generations.
11 Oh fing his praife, where great Affemblies are,
And him, among your elders, glorify ;
He deferts makes, where once great waters were ;
He draines the fprings of mighty Rivers drie.
And, from rich Lands, their fatnes, oft he taketh ;
When by their finn, her dwellers, him forfaketh.
12 The Deferts vaft, he turnes to ftanding Lakes ;
And fprings convaies, to lands which barren were :
For hungry foules, a dwelling there he makes,
Who, for themfelues do build a Citty there.
They fowe & plant, & reap the hoped bleffing,
Both of their feed, & of their Vines encreafing.
13 He profpers them ; & lo, they are encreaft,
Their flocks & heards, do fatt & fruitfull grow.
Yet, otherwhile, he letts them be oppreft, (low,
And with great plagues, he, fometime, brings thē
He takes from kings, their princely eftimation ;
And, makes them ftray, in pathles defolation.
14 But frō all greefs, the meek he ftill doth raife,
And, makes like flocks, his houfholds to appear ;
At fight thereof, the Iuft will fing his praife,
And they fhall dumbe be ftrook, that wicked are.

All

All this, they mark; that have true wisdom learned:
And, God's great love, by them is well discerned.

Most Mercifull God! what Affliction is there, from which wee are not howrely delivered, or preserved, by thee? Nay, what necessarie benifitts are there, which wee have not in the best seasons receaved from thee; in what place soever, or of what Nation, or condition soever wee are? In our wandrings, in our poverty, in our sicknesses, in our imprisonments; in our Iournyes at sea & land, in our labours, in our goods, in our children, in our sorrowes, in our prosperities, in our persons, in our famelies, in life, in death, yea in everie thing, wee have continuall experience of thy Mercies, insomuch, that we may confesse thou delightest in nothing, but in shewing Mercy; vnles our sinns compel thy Iustice to afflict us, that thy Mercies may not be despised: and, there is great Mercy, even in that, also. Oh good God! make us ever mindful hereof; & give us wisdome so to mark & consider these things, that both wee & our posteritie, may magnifie thy vnspeakable bounty, & declare thy wonderful workings, for ever & ever. Amen.

Psa 108.

A song or Psalme of David. *This is composed of the later parts of the* 57. *&* 60 Psalmes; *yet differs from both: for, those beginn with lamentations, & end with reioicings; but, this is wholy triumphant, & personates the Church praising God for her enlargment: &c.* Wee may sing it, when the Church is released from some persecution, or her limitts extended farther &c.

MY hart is fixed; & I, oh Lord,
Will in my songs, thy fame record,
And, with my tongue, sing praise to thee:
My Harp & Psaltry, are awake;
And, I, my selfe, will readie make

To

To praiſe thee, where Aſſemblies be.
2 For, through the heav'ns thy Truth doth ſtretch;
Above the Sphears thy mercies reach.
Oh God! be ſtill exalted high.
Thy praiſe, through heav'n & earth extend;
Let thy righthand, thy Dear deſend,
And, ſtill vouchſafe me thy replie.
3 For, as thy holy Voice declard,
With trivmphs, *Shechem* I have ſharde;
And, I have meaſur'd *Succoth* Vale.
Mine, *Gilead* & *Manaſſeth* are,
My head, mount *Ephraim* high doth bear,
In *Iudah*, ſtands my judgment Stall.
4 Proud *Moab* is my drugding ſlave,
My foot in *Edom*, fixt I have;
And *Paleſtine* doth ioye in me.
For, who to *Edom* was my guide?
Or, to the Citty fortifide?
But, God of whome deſpiſd were wee.
5 Oh God! who didſt our hoaſt forſake,
From vs, our greefs, thus, alwaies take;
For, man's vaine ſuccours we contemn.
Through God, wee valiant Acts have done;
Our foes, by him, are overthrowne:
And, he ſhall ſett his feet on them.

Oh Lord God of Hoaſts! true in thy word, & powerful in thy performances. According to thy auncient promiſes, thy Church is wonderfully enlarged; & thou haſt now thy lot of Inheritance in thoſe places, where they have bene enimies to thy Truth. Wee beſeech thee, more & more, to enlarge thy Kingdome, & to be continually preſent with us, in all our ſpiritual conflicts: that, by thy powre we may tread vnder foot, the world, *the* fleſh, *& the* Devill; *making ſervants vnto us (in the execution of thy* will*) thoſe affections, which have*

have heretofore prevailed againſt us. VVee rely on thee only: On thee only, our harts are fixed: And, for thy goodnes; we deſire, with all our faculties, to praiſe & magniſy thy Name, for evermore. Amen.

Pſa. 109.

To the cheef Muſition a Pſalme of David. *It is applied unto* Iudas *Acts* 1, 20. *and* is it vſefull to terriſy Gods foes, & all Hypocrites, by ſhewing the Judgments pronounced by the holy-ghoſt, againſt all ſuch. *But, let none abuſe this, or any ſuch like* Pſalmes, *by repeating them in their owne quarrells; leſt the* Curſes *fall on themſelves.*

OH God my praiſe! now ſilence breake;
  For, wicked men that guileful be,
With open Iawes, againſt me ſpeake,
And, with falſe tongues, have ſlandred mee.
With hatefull words they mee encloſe;
Without all Cauſe, with mee they warr,
And for my Love, they are my foes:
  Yet, for their weal, my prayers are.
2 For my goodworks, ill deeds I gett;
My love with hate, they do requite:
Or'e them therefore, ſome Tyrant ſet;
At his right-hand, let Sathan waite.
Let Iuſtice, them to death perſue;
Account it ſinn for them to pray:
Cutt ſhort their dayes; & make them fewe:
  Let others take their place away.
3 Keep fatherles, their Orphane-breed,
And, husbandles, their widdow'd wives;
Yea, Cauſe thou their accurſed ſeed,
To begg & wander all their lives.
Their vncouth denns, let then forſake;

To

To begg, what muft their life fuftaine :
Their labors, let oppreffors take,
And, Strangers rob them of their gaine.
4 Let none regard, though they lament,
Nor pitty take on fuch a race :
But, quite away (in one defcent)
Their of-fpring, & their Name deface.
Let God, ftill, minde the guilt they drewe,
From both their parents, at their birth,
And, keep it allway's in his vewe,
Till they are nam'd no more, on earth.
5 For why, they no compaffion fhew'd,
To him that greev'd & pained lay.
But, they the needy foul perfu'de :
The broken hart, they fought, to flay.
They Curfings Lov'd : let them be made
The part, therefore, of their juft lot.
In Bleffings, they no pleafures had ;
And, therfor, they poffeffe them not.
6 With curfes, they, themfelves did clothe,
As with a gowne, or with a cloke ;
Therefore, as oyle or water doth,
Through bones & bowells, let them foke ;
Let Curfes, them like Belts, inclofe ;
And, as their clothes, fuch men aray :
Ev'n thus, oh Lord, requite my Foes
Who of my foul, amiffe do fay.
7 But, (for thy Name fake) fave thou mee ;
Deal wel with me, & mercy daigne :
For, wounded is my hart in mee ;
And, I am pore, & full of paine.
I vanifh like an Evening fhade,
I, Locuft like, am toft about :
My knees, are weake through fafting made ;

My fleſh is leane, & waſted out.
8 They, mee deſpiſe ev'n to my face,
And, ſcornfull nods, at mee they make.
Oh Lord my God ! of thy meer grace,
To bring me help, now vndertake,
Make them to ſee, & then confeſſe,
That by thy hand I helped am ;
Lord, though they Curſe, yet do thou bleſſe.
And, let them riſe, to ſee their ſhame.
9 But, make oh Lord, thy Servants glad ;
Whilſt they, that my illwillers are,
With ſhame (ev'n their owne ſhame) are clad,
As if with Robes arayd they were.
My tongue ſhall praiſe thee then, therſore,
Confeſſing, where Aſſemblies be,
That God is Patron of the pore ;
And, from falſe doomes, their ſoules doth free.

Oh God ! terrible art thou in thoſe iudgments, which thou doſt pronounce againſt all malitious & vnrepẽtãt Sinners. VVee beſeech thee therfore grant us grace, to repent all our tranſgreſsions, & to shewe compaſsion to all thy pore members in their Aſſlictions ; that wee may finde Mercy in our ſorrowes. VVee often ſee thy iudgments ; but. wee neither know whome thou correcteſt in love to amendment, nor whome in fury to their deſtruction : For, thou reſerveſt that ſecret vnto thy ſelf (To keep vs, both in our dealings & Cenſures, alway charitable to thoſe whome thou ſmiteſt) Oh teach vs, therefore, true Charity; & let vs never doe, or wish evill to any man, in our owne Cauſes: But, let us apply thy iudgmẽts, to ſinn in generall; & imprecate that they may fall only, on the enimies of our Lord and ſaviour Ieſus Chriſt. Amen.

Pſa. 110.

A Pſalme of David. *It is literally of Chriſt, Math.* 22.

& it mentioneth, the Deity, Humanity, Soveraignety, Preiſthood, Powre, Conqueſts, Paſſion, & Reſurrection of the Meſſiah. Wee may ſing it with reſpect to thoſe perticulers.

VNto my Lord, the Lord, thus ſpake,
  Sitt downe at my right hand ;
And, of thy foes, I'le footſtooles make,
  Whereon thy feet ſhall ſtand.
The Lord, ſhall out of *Syon* bring,
  The ſcepter of thy might ;
And, over them thou ſhalt be king,
  Who now reſiſt thy right.
2 On thy great Day, in ſerving thee,
  Men, willing mindes will ſhewe ;
And, from the wombe, thy birth ſhall be,
  As is the morninge dewe.
The Lord, hath ſworne, (& will nor check,
  Nor change the word he ſwore)
Thou art, (as was Melchizedek)
  A preiſt, for evermore.
3 The Lord, ſhall ſmite when wroth he growes
  Great kings, at thy righthand.
The Gentiles judge, &, ſlay his foes
  Which are in ev'ry land.
The heads of kingdomes he ſhall ſlay ;
  And, as he paſſeth-by,
Shall drinck the Torrent in the way,
  And, raiſe his head on high.

Almighty God, who haſt given thy eternal Sonn (with whome thou art the ſame in Eſſence) to be in an vnſpeakable manner conceaved in the Virgines wombe : *To be made an everlaſting* preiſt, *for us, after the Order of Melchizedek. And in his Paſſage through this life, to drinck*

drinck the bitter Torrent *of his* Passion : *Grant wee beseech thee, that by virtue of his blessed* Incarnation, *our nature may be sanctified & prepared for Grace; that by his* Death, *we may dye to sinn ; that by the powre of his* Resurrection *wee may arise to righteousnes ; & by his glorious* Ascention, *be victorious over all our enimies, both spiritual & temporall, for ever & ever.* Amen.

Psa. 111.

Halelujah. *It praiseth God for his miraculous works, his wisdome, Mercy, Iustice, & for the Covenant of his Grace &c. It may be sung to continue in vs, the fear of God, & to praise him for his benifits; especially, for our Redemption.*

WIth all my hart, God's praise I'le sing,
Where saints assembled are.
For, they, God's works to minde will bring,
Who, love to them doe bear.
Most famous deeds, the Lord hath done,
His Iustice, hath no ends :
His works are worthy to be knowne,
His bounty, farr extends.
2 All them that feare his Name, he feeds ;
His League he thinks vpon ;
And, for his folke, by wondrous deeds,
The Gentiles Realmes he wonn.
His hands, have Truth & Iustice, wrought ;
His precepts, all, are sure ;
With Truth & Iudgment, fully fraught,
For ever to endure.
3 God sent, and hath his Flock redeemd ;
His Leagues eternall are :
His Name is rev'rently esteem'd ;
And, full of holy-feare.

The feare of God, is Wifdome's gate ;
  And, therefore wife is he,
Who feekes to enter in thereat :
  His praifes, endles be.

Moft mercifull Father (wōderfull in thy workings, dreadfull in thy iudgments, vnfallable in thy Truth, & vnfpeakable in thy Mercies) fill us wee pray thee with that fanctified Feare which is the beginning of true VVifdome; So manifeft vnto us thy eternal Truth; fo remember vs of thy Covenant; & fo feede us with fpirituall nourishments, that we may be ftrengthned to walk in thy wayes; & at the laft, enter the Gates of eternall bleffednes, through the mediation of Iefus Chrift *our Lord* Amen.

Another of the fame.

AL praife to God, my hart now render fhall.
Before the Iuft ; of him I'le mention make,
Confeffing that his wond'rous Actions, all,
Deferve that wee fhould pleafure in them take.
Exceeding great, his glorious deeds appear,
From age to Age, his Iuftice doth extend ;
Growne famous, all his glorious workings are,
His Bounties, & his Mercies have no end.
In feeding fuch as feare him, he is free ;
Kept firme, his promife is, from age to age.
Long fince, that fo, his Folk his powr might fee,
Made were, the Gentiles lands their heritage.
Nor Truth nor Iuftice paffe, but from his hand.
Of all his lawes, the firme fulfillings, be,
Provided foe ; that, they fhall ever ftand
Quit, from all wrongs, & from all falfhoods, free.
Redeemer of his people, he became.
So firme a League likewife, he did ordaine,
That, he hath fixt, & fortifide the fame,

Vnchan-

Vnchangably, for ever to remaine.
With holines & feare, he clothes his Name:
Yea Wisdome's first foundation is his fear.
Right wise are they, that well observe the same:
And such, from Age to age, commended are.

Psa. 112.

Halelujah. *It mentions many priviledges & properties of the* Elect; *& shewes, that the wicked (for their greater vexation) shall behold their happines &c.* It is a consolatory Hymne; and serves to keep vndiscouraged, those whoe are exercised by the skoffs & prosperities of worldlings.

WHo on Gods lawe his love doth place,
And, feareth him, right blest is hee:
God, will on earth advance his race,
And, blest his faithfull seed shall be.
His house with plenty shall be dight,
His Iustice, shall not be confinde;
In darknes, he shall still have light,
For, he is meek, & just, & kinde.
2 The righteous lends, & helps the pore,
His dealings, he discreetly weighes;
His fame, abides for evermore,
And in a state vnchangd, he staies.
He starts not, evill Newes to heare.
On God, his hopes & muzings be.
His hart is fixt, & will not fear
Till on his foes, his wish he see.
3 He, on the pore, doth Almes bestowe,
And, alway just, he doth abide.
For which, his horne shall powrfull growe,
And, with renowne be dignifide.
Which, when vngodly men perceave,

They ſhall, through envy & deſpight.
Growe furious, gnaſh their teeth, & greeve.
And, looſe thir hopes, & longings quite.

WE humbly beſeech thee oh mercifull God, to infuſe into our harts, ſuch a filial fear of thee; Such a firme truſt in thy Mercies; Such a prudent regard to all things which are neceſſarily pertinent to our ſelves; So charitable a reſpect vnto the neceſsities of our pore brethren: & ſoe conſtant a willingnes, to performe all the duties in which we are obliged to any of thy Creatures: That, being without ſlaviſh terrors, we may be couragious, what rumors ſoever we hear; & enioy the commodities of this life, to the vexation of our ſpiritual foes; & eternall Bleſſednes *hereafter to thy glory.* Amen.

Another of the ſame.

ALl they that fear the Lord, attaine to bliſſe;
Becauſe, that, ſuch delight God's will to doe.
Conferd on them, ſhall honors be, for this,
Deriving to their ſeed, great bleſſings to.
Encreaſing wealth, their houſes, full ſhall fill.
For aye, the Iuſtman's righteouſnes remaines.
Great light, on him, in darknes beameth ſtill.
He righteous is, & kinde, & Mercy daignes.
If need reqnire he lends, & gives beſides.
Kept ſtreight are all his waies, by prudent care.
Layd faſt his groundworke are; & firme he bides.
Made endles, his memorialls (likewiſe) are.
No fears he feels, though evill Newes there be;
On God with fixed heart he doth relie:
Puts truſt in him; not ſhrincking, till that hee
Quite overthrowne doth all his foes eſpie.
Releef among the pore beſtoweth he;
So keeping, ſtill, his dealings, all, vpright,

That,

That, him advanc'd, Vngodly men fhall fee;
Vex, gnafh their teeth, & loofe their lõgings quite.

Pfa. 113.

Halelujah. *It magnifieth God for his great love to mankinde both in generall & in perticuler. But, cheefly for extending his* Church *fo vniverfally; for raifing us from the dunghills of corrupted* Nature, *to the thrones of* Grace; *& for taking away our fpiritual fterrillity. &c.* The vfe appears.

YEe fervants of the Lord,
With praife, God's Name, adore;
The Name of God the Lord,
Bleffe, now & evermore.
Oh fing his praife!
Through ev'ry place, which in his race,
The Sunn, furvaies.
2 All nations, fear his powres,
His glory mounts the fky.
There is no God like ours:
No other Lord, fo high.
Yet, he doth bowe,
All things to fee, that in heavn be,
Or Earth belowe.
3 The pore, from ground he fetts,
From dyrt, the meek, he brings;
And, them with kings he fetts,
Ev'n with his peoples kings,
And, her that had
A barren wombe; he, made become
A mother glad.

Glorious Lord God! who (to the confufion of the proud & hauty) haft made choife of the vile & defpifed things of this world, thereby to magnify thy Name. Raife us, we pray thee, from the Dunghill of our Corrupted Nature; *that by thy* Grace, *wee may become* Rulers *over our owne Affections: And make us also (who have bene heretofore barren in all Goodnes) so fruitfull, hereafter, in Faith & good works, that our soules, may be saved, & thy Name glorified, throughout the whole world, for ever & ever.* Amen.

Another of the same.

PRaise yee the Lord, & blesse his Name;
Yea, now & ever blesse the same,
Yee servants, of the Lord our God.
For, from the Sunns ascending place,
Ev'n to the vtmost of his race,
His Name's due praise, is fam'd abrode.
Or'e Nations all, yea, or'e the Sphears,
The Lord our God, his glory rears,
And, never was his equall found.
For, though his dwelling be on high,
He doth beholde with humbled eye,
All things in heav'n, & on the ground.
2 The pore, from dust & mire he brings,
To sit with Princes, & with Kings;
Ev'n of his people to be King.
And, he, a joyfull mother made
Of her, that erst no children had.
Vnto the Lord, oh therefor sing.
To *God* the *Father*, To the *Sonn*,
And *holy-Ghost*, (those, *three in one*
And, that eternall *One in three*)
All *glory* bee, for ever more;
All *powre* & *praise*, as heretofore,
Ascribed, now & ever be.

Pſa. 114.

By alluding to the deliverance from Egipt, *to the driving back of* Iordan *&* *the* Redſea, *to the trembling of* Sinay, *& forcing waters from the hard rocks; our ſpirituall deliverances, & reformations, are typified.* Therefore, our Church vſeth this Pſalme, as proper for *Eaſterday.*

WHen *Iſr'el,* brought from Egipt was
 And, *Iacob* from a forraigne tongue;
In *Iudah* was his holy place,
To him, did *Iſr'els* rule belong.
The Sea ſaw that, & fledd away,
Ev'n *Iordan* alſo, backward ſlipt.
The mountaines then, like Rams did play;
 Like Lambes, the leſſer hillocks tript.
2 Thou ſea, what made thee ſo to fly?
Why did'ſt thou, *Iordan,* backward goe?
Why daunc't like Rams the mountaines hye?
Yee hills, like Lambs, why tript yee ſo?
Shake earth, at preſence of the Lord,
When *Iacob's* God is preſent, ſhake;
For, he, from Rocks, a ſtanding Ford,
 And, fountaines, in the flints doth make.

Almighty God, the deliverer of all pore deſtreſſed Captives; wee are by Nature the ſlaves of Sinn, Death *& the* Devill, *who do labour to hold us in eternall bondage: But, wee praiſe thee, thou haſt made a miraculous paſſage for our eſcape: Oh! grant therfor that thy preſēce, may ſo ſtartle us out of our ſecuritie, & ſoe mollifie our flintie nature, that the teares of true penitence may flowe plentifully from vs; & that, we (thanckfully walking in that way which thou haſt prepared for our entrance into the* Land of the living) *may be quite freed from our ſervitude; & enioy peace & reſt in thy Kingdome, for ever & ever.* Amen.

Pſal. 115.

The Faithfull deſire that al honor may be aſcribed to God alone, & that their foes may not blaſpheamouſly queſtion his powre. Then, in the name of heathen Idolls, *& their worshippers, reprooves the vanity of all thoſe aſsiſtances whereon carnall men rely &c.* It is vſefull when falſe worſhippers blaſpheame God, by reaſon of our aſ-fliction &c.

NOt ours the glory make,
Lord, give not vs the ſame:
But, for thy Truth & Mercy ſake,
Aſcribe it, to thy Name.
2 To ſay, where is their God!
Why ſhould the Gentiles dare?
Since he in heav'n hath his abode,
And, works his pleaſure there?
3 Men's hands, their Idolls make;
They, gold & ſilver be:
Poſſeſſing mouthes that cannot ſpeake
And, eyes that cannot ſee.
4 Their eares are ſenſeles to;
Their noſtril ſmelleth not:
Their hands & feet, nor feel, nor goe;
No breath is in their throte.
5 All they, whoe thoſe adore,
(Or forme them) like them be:
In God, let *Iſr'el* truſt therefore,
For, their defence is he.
6 On God, preſerving them,
Let *Aron's* houſe depend:
Let thoſe, who feare him, truſt in him;
For, he will ſuch defend,
7 God, will remember vs,

And,

And, on vs, Mercy ſhowe.
On *Iſr'el*, & on *Aron's* houſe,
He, bleſſings will beſtowe.
8 He proſpers great & ſmall,
That, fear of him profeſſe:
You & your ſeed, likewiſe, he ſhall
Still, more & more, encreaſe.
9 Of God, you bleſſed be
Who made both earth & heav'n:
The heav'n of heav'ns, inhabits, he,
And, earth to men hath given.
10 Lord, none cann thee adore,
Who dead, & ſilenc't are:
But, I, both now & evermore,
Thy praiſes will declare.

Not for our owne deſervings, cann wee claime any thing (oh Lord God) neither for our owne ſakes, or our owne glorie, ought wee to deſire any deliverances, or benifits from thy Maieſtie. As much, therfor, as our ſelf-love *will permit, wee deſire, meerly for thine owne honour ſake, that publike Idolaters, & carnall minded men (who ſerve Gods of their owne making) may not ſcandalize thee, or thy Truth, by occaſion of ſuch Miſeries or Diſgraces, as fall on vs, who profeſſe the ſame. But, make vs (oh God) to love thee & thy glory, ſo farr above our owne lives & reputations; That, whether wee be delivered or no, wee may ſubmit our ſelves to thy pleaſure; & be truly comforted, hartely pleaſed, & reioyce vnfainedly, that wee are counted worthie to ſuffer for thy glorie.* Amen.

Pſa. 116.

The Faithfull profeſſe affection to Chriſt; *Acknowledg their condition, both by* Nature *&* Grace; *encourage others to truſt in Gods favour; & reſolve the ſame in them ſelves.*

We

We may ſing it, when, after ſome great Affliction or temptation, wee are comforted, & ſenſible of our preſent, & paſſed eſtate &c.

I love the Lord; for, hee an eare
  To my complaints doth give:
And, ſince he pleaſeth me to hear,
  I'le ſeek him, whil'ſt I live.
The feares of death, encloſd me round;
  Hell torments, mee enthrald.
But, ſtill, when paind my ſelf I found,
  On God's great Name, I cal'd.
2 Preſerve my ſoul, oh Lord, I ſayd;
  For, thou art full of grace.
Iuſt, kinde, & ev'ry pore man's ayde.
  My healp, when greev'd I was.
My ſoul, to this thy refuge fly;
  For, God is thy larg meed.
From death my ſoul; from teares, mine eye;
  From falls, my feet he freed.
3 I ſhall, with God, enioy my life
  Where livinge men abide.
This I profeſſe, with firme beleif,
  Though I was terrifide.
Yea, though in raſhnes I did ſay,
  That all men liers were;
What for thy guifts I ſhould repay,
  Now, Lord, my queſtions are.
4 Thy Cupp of ſaving-health I'le take.
  Vpon thy name, I'le call;
And, of my vowes, I'le payment make
  Before thy ſervants all.
Thy ſaints, their deaths, & ſuffrings, be
  Right pretious in thine eye.
Oh Lord, thy ſervant ſerving thee,

Thy

Thy handmayds Childe, am I.
5 My fetters all, thou brak'ſt away,
And, I, oh Lord, therefore,
The ſacrifize of thancks will pay;
And, thy great Name adore.
To thee, oh Lord, I'le pay my vowes,
Where thy Aſſemblies be;
Ev'n in the Courts of Gods owne houſe
Ieruſalem, in thee. *Haleluiah.*

Hear our prayers oh Lord God, *& deliver our ſoules from the Death of Sinn. For, we are compaſſed with many perills & fearfull Temptations; Inſomuch that wee are ſometime almoſt ready to deſpaire, & diſtruſt that there is noe Truth in any of our hopes. Oh keep us (by thy ſpeciall grace) from falling into thoſe whirlpooles, out of which there is no returning. VVhen the guilt of Sinn, the fears of Death, the torments of hell, & the ſugeſtions of the Devill (conſpiring with our frailties) have once encloſed vs. VVee have then, no powre of reſiſtance in our ſelves; & it is thy great Mercy, if the little ſpark of our faith be not wholy quenched. Help vs therfore in our extremityes. Break the chaines of our Sinns, unloſe the ſnares of Sathan, & give us grace to praiſe thee in thy* Ieruſalem, *& to magnify thy Mercy in the Land of the living, world without end.* Amen.

Pſa. 117.

This is the leaſt Pſalme; *but it hath reſpect vnto the greateſt* Myſterie. *For it provokes all Nations to praiſe God, for extending his grace to the whole world; as appears Rom.* 15. We ſhould ſing it to praiſe God for his *Univerſal Grace.*

GOd's praiſe, yee Nations all declare;
The Lord, yee people all adore:

For

For, large to vs, his Mercies are,
His Truth endures for evermore. *Haleluiah.*

VVee praiſe thee oh Father of Mercy, for that Vniverſall Grace *which thou haſt vouchſafed, in offring thy ſalvation (without reſpect of perſons) vnto all mankinde, forſaking none vntill they have firſt forſaken thee. Make effectuall vnto vs, wee beſeech thee, this generall favour; That wee embracing the ſame, by the* Will *(which thou firſt makeſt capable of what thou preſenteſt thereunto) and that co-operating with thy* Spirit *(according to the powre which thou ſhalt give vs) we may be pertakers of that* ſpeciall grace, *which makes vs the Obiects of thy* eternall Election; *& from which there is no falling away. Grant this, even for* Ieſus Chriſt *his ſake.* Amen.

Pſa. 118.

This Pſalme Chriſt *applied vnto himſelf. Math* 24. *For, he is that Corner-ſtone here mentioned. Here alſo are miſtically touched vpon, his* Paſſion, Reſurrection, *& ſonne other Evangelicall Verities. It is therefore vſed by our* Church, *as proper for* Eaſterday.

THe Lord is good, him therfor bleſſe;
And, for his Grace that faileth never,
Let Iſr'el alſo, now confeſſe,
His Mercy doth abide for ever.
Yea, let the houſe of *Aron* ſay,
His Mercies have no ending day.
2 Let all, who fear him, publiſh out,
His Mercies, that eternal be:
For, when at need, his healp I ſought,
Hee, heard my plaint, & ſett me free:
And, ſince the Lord, is thus mine Aide
Of man, I cannot be afraid.
3 My helpers, God's aſſiſtance have;

And,

And, I perceave it on my Foes.
More safe it is God's help to crave,
Then on man's healping to repose,
Yea, faith in God, more safety brings,
Then to rely on mighty kings.
4 All Nations, seige to mee did lay,
But, in God's Name, I them destroyd:
They me beleaguer'd ev'ry way,
But, in God's Name, I them destroy'd.
As Bees, they compast me about,
Like fire in thornes, soone in, soone out.
5 I soone destroy'd them in Gods Name,
For, when they sought to do, me wrong,
The Lord, my gratious ayde became,
My strength, my health, my ioyfull song.
And, in his house, the Iust may sing,
What God's right-hand to passe did bring.
6 For, God's right-hand is lifted high,
Greats things the Lords right-hand hath wrought;
And, from the Grave escap'd am I
To tell, what God to passe hath brought,
For, though he sore afflicted me,
Yet, he from death did sett me free.
7 Of Righteousnes vnclose the gate,
That, I God's praises may expresse:
This Gate is God's; yea, this is that,
By which the Righteous have accesse,
And, him I'le praise; for it is hee,
That heares, & healps, & saveth me.
8 That's now the cheefest Corner-stone,
Which once the builders did despise;
It was the work of God, alone,
And, seemeth wondrous in our eyes.
This is the day the Lord hath made;

Come,

Come, let vs all, therein be glad.
9 Save Lord ; oh ſave vs, Lord, wee pray ;
Bleſſe him, that commeth in thy Name.
That from his houſe God bleſſe vs may,
We pray, & much deſire the ſame.
For, God's the Lord, by whome our ſight
Obtaines the Viſion of his Light.
13 With Cords the Sacrifices binde ;
Them, to the Aulters Corners, tye.
Thou art my God, whoſe praiſe I'le minde ;
My God, whome I will glorify.
Oh ! praiſe the Lord, for, great is he,
And, without end his Mercies be.

Oh Lord Chriſt our ſaviour ! *Thou art that pretious* corner-ſtone *which vnites, not* Iewes *&* Gentiles *only, but even the* Godhead *and the* Manhood *into one ſpirituall Buildinge. Thou, art he by whome all our Enimies are deſtroyed. Thou, art hee, by whome wee eſcape the* grave *of ſinn, & the terrors of everlaſting Death. Thou, only, art that* Gate of Righteouſnes, *by which wee enter into life eternal ; And, thou only, art that Light, in whoſe bleſſed* Viſion, *our happines doth conſiſt. Oh give vs part in all that, which thy* Incarnation, Paſſion, Death, Buriall, Reſurrection, *&* Aſcention, *hath merrited & conquered for vs ; & (if it pleaſe thee) let this be the Day, which thou haſt made to fill vs with ſuch a gladnes, as shall make vs ioyfull, for ever more.* Amen.

Pſa. 119.

This Pſalme *conſiſteth of many exhortations, promiſes, prayers, complaints, conſolations, directions, Reſolutions, & thancksgivings ; varciouſly intermixt, according to the* Churches *various Occaſions : &* principally informes, that God's word is the Rule of Life. &c.

Alaph. 1.

Alaph. 1.

HEe's bleſt, that in the perfect way
  Of God's pure *Lawe* hath trod
Who doth his *Teſtaments* obay,
  And, wholy ſeeketh God.
For, ſuch will take no ill in hand,
  Nor, from his *Pathway* ſwarve,
But, Lord, as thou doſt give command,
  Thy *Precepts*, they obſerve.
2 Would God! my waies were ſo direct
  That keep thy *Lawes* I might.
For, whilſt I thy *Commandes* reſpect
  On mee, no ſhame cann light.
With vpright hart, thee praiſe I will,
  When, learn'd thy *Iudgments* be;
And, then I will thy *Lawes* fullfill;
  Therefore, forſake not mee.

Another of the ſame.

ALl thoſe are bleſt that in a blameles way,
    Have by the *Lawe* of God their feet confinde,
  As bleſt are thoſe, that his *Decrees* obay,
  With all their harts, deſiring him to finde.
An evill act, they never take in hand,
  Nor frō Gods *Pathway*, ſhall their footing ſwarve
  Wee, likewiſe, are inioyn'd by thy Command,
  That wee, thy *Precepts*, duely ſhould obſerve.
Ah! therefor, would my wayes were guided ſo,
  That, all thy *Statutes*, well obſerve I might.
  For, if thy *Lawes*, I have regard vnto,
  No ſhame at all, on mee ſhall then alight.
And, when thy righteous *Iudgments* I have learn'd
  With hart ſincere, I'le ſing thy praiſe therefore.
  To keep thy *Lawes*, I will moreover learne.

Oh! then, forſake me not for ever more.

Give us, oh Lord, ſuch perfect knowledge of thy Lawe; *ſuch regard of thy* Teſtimonies; *ſuch practiſe in thy* Waies; *ſuch obedience to thy* Precepts; *ſuch love to thy* Statutes; *Such diligence in thy commands, & ſuch awe of thy* Iudgments: *that our vnderſtanding may be freed from* error, *our* Converſations *from* polution, *our* Affections *from vanity: & that thou mayſt ever be glorified by us; & wee, never be forſaken of thee. Even for* Ieſus Chriſt *his ſake.* Amen.

Beth. 2.

HOw cann youth's pathway cleanſed be
  But by thy *word*, oh Lord?
With all my hart, I ſeek to thee,
  Oh! guide mee by thy *word*.
I'le keep thy *Lawe*, with all my hart,
  That I diſpleaſe not thee.
Oh Lord (that alway bleſſed art)
  Thy *Statutes*, teach to mee.
2 To preach the *Iudgments* of thy Mouth,
  My lipps I will employ.
For, in thy *Teſtimonies*, truth;
  As, in great wealth, I ioye.
Vpon thy *Lawes*, & *VVaies*, alone,
  My thoughts, & Love are ſett.
Thy *Statutes*, my delight is on:
  Thy *VVord*, I'le not forget.

Another of the ſame.

BY what, may yongmẽs wayes made blameles be;
  But, by their taking heed vnto thy *VVord*?
With all my hart, I have deſired thee,
From thy *Commands*, let me not wander, Lord.
By layeng vp thy *VVord* within my hart,

To

To keep me from offending thee I thought.
Oh Lord my God, thou alwaies bleſſed art,
Vouchſafe to me thy *Statutes* may be taught.
Betweene my lipps, I oft have ſounded forth
The *Iudgments* of thy mouth ; and I have deem'd
Thy *Teſtimonies* path of greater worth
Then riches are, (by others moſt eſteem'd)
Both on thy ſacred *Precepts* I do muſe,
And, ever, to thy *VVaies* have borne reſpect.
Thy *Statutes*, as my pleaſures I will vſe ;
And, Lord, *word*, I never will neglect.

Su , to deferr the amendment of our li we be decrepit with age; but let thy word reform in our youth ; at leaſt, from this preſent howre, let us beginn the cleanſing of our waies with our whole harts. Let us ſeek, thee, bleſſe thee, ſpeak of thee, Muſe on thee, & ſo delight in thee; that thou maiſt delight in us, & keep us in the way of thy Commandements, for ever & ever. Amen.

Gimel. 3.

LOrd, grace thy ſervant ſo, that he
May live, & keep thy *VVord.*
The wonders of thy *Lawe* to ſee,
Enlight mine eyes oh Lord.
A ſtranger here on earth, I, am ;
Thy *Precepts*, let me knowe.
My ſoul, with longings, ſaint became,
Thy *Iudgments*, love I ſo.
2 Their Curſed pride thou haſt contrould,
Who from thy *Lawes* do ſwarve :
But, ſhame & ſcorne, from mee withhold,
For, I thy *Truth* obſerve.
Enthroned Princes mee reproov'd,

Yet, on thy *Lawes* I thought.
Thy *Teſtimonies* I have lov'd :
To mee they Counfell taught.

Another of the fame.

COnfer fuch Bountie on thy fervant Lord,
That to fulfill thy *Lawe*, furvive I may :
That, I may fee the wonders of thy *VVord*
Vnclofe, likewife (oh Lord) mine eyes I pray.
Confid'ring that on earth I am a ftranger,
Hide not from me the knowledge of thy *Truth.*
My foul, to leave the body is
Shee fo defires the *Iudgments* of thy
Controld thou haft, the Curfed pride of them
Who from thy iuft *Commandements* have fwarved.
Remoove away their fcornes who mee contemn ;
For, I thy *Teſtimonies* have obferved.
Contefted with, by Princes, I have binn :
Yet, I thy fervant, on thy *Statutes* mufe.
Thy *Teſtimonies*, my delights are in,
And, them to be my Counfellers I chufe.

Almighty God (*feeing wee are but* Pilgrims *here on earth (fubiect to many wants, many Infirmities, & many oppreſsions) gratiouſly vouchſafe us, that which is outwardly neceſſary for the body ; Supply that which is defective in our ſoules ; & let thy* Lawe *arme us againſt the oppoſition of all our Adverſaries, through* Iefus Chrift *our Lord.* Amen.

Daleth, 4.

ACcording to thy *word*, now chear,
My foul, which lowe is brought.
My life's Confeffion, thou fhalt heare,
Let mee thy *Lawe*, be taught.
Mee, in thy *way* appointed, fet :

And,

And, I'le they works record.
Greef tires my ſoul, oh comfort it,
According to thy *word.*
2 Me, from the path of Lies, remoove,
And, by thy *Lawe*, direct.
For, I the waies of Truth do love;
Thy *Iudgments*, I affect.
Diſgrace me not, for, firme I ſtand,
To what thou haſt *decreed:*
And, I will runn at thy *Command*,
When thou my hart haſt freed.

Another of the ſame.

DEclined is my ſoul, ev'n to the ground;
Oh quicken mee, according to thy word.
My waies I ſhew'd, & I thine anſwere found;
Thy *Statutes*, alſo, teach to mee oh Lord.
Diſcloſe to me thy *Teſtimonies* path,
And, of thy wondrous works my talke ſhall be.
My life conſumes, becauſe much greef it hath;
According to thy *VVord*, eſtabliſh mee.
Divide mee from that Path which liers love,
And gratiouſly vouchſafe to mee thy *Lawe.*
The way of *Truth*, is that which I approve;
And, of thy *Iudgments*, I do ſtand in awe.
Diſtruſtfull of thy *word* I never grewe,
Permit me not, oh Lord, to be diſgrac't.
The way of thy *Commands* I will perſue,
As ſoone at thou my hart enlarged haſt.

Indowe our harts oh God! with ſuch vnfained humiliation, *with ſuch true* Confeſſion, *with ſuch harty* contrition, *with ſuch love to thy Truth, with hatred of error, & with a renewing of the whole man; that wee may be more & more enlarged from our ſinns & Corruptions, vntill wee be perfectly restored to the full liberty of the* Sonns of God, *through* Iesus Christ *our Lord.* Amen.

He. 5.

SHewe mee thy *Truth*, & from that way,
I never will depart.
Teach mee thy *Lawes*; & them, for aye,
I'le keep with all my hart.
Thy *Statutes* Paths, to mee declare;
For, I delight theron.
To love thy *Word*, my hart prepare,
And, Avarice to shunn.
2 From folly, turne my eyes, oh Lord,
And, keep mee in thy *way*.
Confirm thy Servant in thy *Word*,
That, so, I fear thee may.
Because thy *Iudgments* gratious be,
My feared shame remove.
And, in thy *Statutes* quicken me,
For, Lord thy *Lawes* I love.

Another of the same.

ETernall God, thy *Statutes* teach to mee,
That til their end, I may fulfill them all.
To keep thy *Lawe* let me instructed be,
And, I with all my hart, observe it shall.
Enable me, to keep each *Lawe* of thine,
Because, that in their path, I pleasure take.
My hart vnto thy *Testaments*, incline,
That so, all Avarice I may forsake.
Estrange mine eye, from Obiects that are vaine,
And, let mee be revived in thy *Path*.
Thy *word*, to mee thy servant, now make plaine
Who, to thy fear, him self devoted hath.
Expell thou far away, the shame I fear:

For

For, juſt, & good (oh Lord) thy *Judgments* be.
See, what my longings for thy *Precepts* are,
And, in thy righteouſnes, revive thou mee.

Oh Lord! Ignorance of thy Lawe, *is the Cauſe that wee neither love nor beleeve it; & want of* Love & Beleef, *are the occaſions of all our errors. Give us therfor, wee pray thee, that Love, that knowledge, & that beleef of thy* word, *which may keep us in thy Paths. Root* Covetuoſnes, *out of our harts; let no folly allure our eyes to wander aſide, hereafter: & (becauſe there is Mercy in all thy Judgments) keep us from the ſhame which wee fear, & have already deſerved: Even for* Ieſus Chriſt *his ſake.* Amen.

Vau. 6

THy loving ayde, vouchſafe mee ſtill,
As thou haſt *promis'd*, Lord:
So, I my ſcorners anſwere will;
For, I beleeve thy *word.*
Since, on thy *Judgments* I rely,
Oh! do not, Lord, with drawe
Thy *VVord of Truth*; & then, ſhall I
For ever keepe thy *Lawe.*
2 Now I to ſeek thy *way*, am bent,
I cann with freedome walke
And, I will of thy *Teſtament*,
To Kings, with boldnes talke.
In thy *Commands*, I will delight:
For, I have them approov'd.
I'le minde thy *word*, & keep aright
Thy *Lawes*, which I have lov'd.

Another of the ſame.

FVlfill thy promiſd *word*, & favour daigne;
Yea, grãt thou mee thy ſaving-health oh Lord!

So, I shall make replies to them, againe,
Who flout at me, because I trust thy *word.*
Firme trust, vnto thy *Iudgments*, Lord I have,
Therefor, to leave thy *Truth* permit me never:
But, make me to thyne *Ordinances* cleave;
And, keep thy *Lawes*, for ever & for ever.
Free, shall my walkings be, & vncontrould;
Because thy *precepts* are belov'd of me.
Thy *Testaments*, to kings I will vnfold,
And, of the same, no whit ashamed be.
Full dearly, I have loved thy *commands*;
And, they my most affected pleasures prove.
I'le in thy *precepte*, exercise my hands,
And, muse vpon thy *Lawes*; for, them I love.

VVrite thy Lawes in our harts, oh Lord, & engrave them in our minds wee humbly beseech thee. Soe regenerate us, that wee may become a Lawe *vnto our selves; & have no desires in us, but those which are agreable to thy* Will. *So, wee shall neither slavishly fear, the powre of any Authority; nor be made ashamed by any bitter Censurers, or scornfull reproovers: but, maytake confidently, & vse conscionably our liberty in* Christ Iesus. Amen.

Zain. 7.

THat *promise* keep, which thou hast made,
Thy servant's hope to be.
From thence (in greefs) I comforts had:
Thy *word*, revived mee.
Though my disgrace, the proud have sought,
Vnto thy *Lawe* I clave.
Vpon thy *Iudgments* past, I thought:
And, ear to them I gave.
2 Of sinners, who thy *Lawe* forsake,
I am in greevous feare.

Yet,

Yet, where my Pilgrim-Inn, I take,
  My songs, thy *Precepts* are.
I kept thy *Lawe*, & on thy Name,
  I mus'd when many slept.
And, thus to passe, oh Lord, it came,
  Because thy *Lawe* I kept.

Another of the same.

GIve heed vnto that *VVord*, which thou hast sayd;
  That *VVord* which thou didst make my hope to (be.
  For, thence in my Afflictions I have ayde:
  It is thy *VVord* that still reviveth mee.
Growne quite despis'd I was, in proudmens eyes,
  And, yet, I from thy *Lawe*, declined not.
  Thy *Iudgments*, past, did in my thought arise;
  And Lord, from them, I consolation got.
Great horrors have surprized me, because,
  The wicked from thy *precepts* have gone wrong.
  And, in my house of Pilgrimage, thy *Lawes*,
  And thy *Commandements*, have beene my song.
Good Lord! I mention of thy Name have made,
  Ev'n in the night; & I thy *Lawe* have kept.
  And, ev'ry profitable thing I had;
  Because, I from thy *Precepts*, have not stept.

Oh Lord! there is no better comforter in trouble, then a faithfull remembrance of thy gratious promises; nor any meanes to prevent the feare, the disgraces, or the mischeevous practises of the proud oppressor, then by the Meditation, *&* practise *of thy* Lawes. *Grant therfore, wee may soe* minde *the One, & so* performe *the other; That wee may reioyce in this house of our Pilgrimage, all our life long.* Amen.

Chith. 8.

I Vow'd oh Lord, to keep thy *VVord*,
  For, thou my portion art.

Thy *promis'd Mercies* now afford ;
  I begg them with my hart.
I turned to thy *Teſtaments*,
  When I had ſcann'd my waies ;
In keeping thy *Commandements*,
  I vſed no delaies.
2 By troups of ſinners, robd I was :
  Thy *Lawes*, yet, minde I ſtill.
And, that thy *Iuſtice* I may praiſe,
  At midnight, riſe I will.
Whoe e're dreads thee, & keeps thy *word*,
  Shall my Compainon be.
Thy Mercy fills the world, oh Lord,
  Oh ! teach thy *Lawes* to mee.

Another of the ſame.

HOw that thou art my portion, Lord, I ſayd,
  And, I to keep thy *Lawe* have made a vowe.
With all my hart, I for thy grace have prayd,
  According to thy *VVord*, have mercy now.
Here, I have called vnto minde thy *waies*,
  And, turn'd my feet vnto thy *Teſtaments*.
Yea, I have ready bene, without delayes,
  In executing thy *Commandements*.
Huge Troupes of wicked men have robbed mee :
  Yet, ſtill thy *Precepts*, in my hart I bear.
At midnight, I will riſe, & ſing to thee,
  Becauſe thy *Iudgments*, true & righteous are.
Here, I have gain'd the fellowſhip of thoſe,
  Who ſtand in fear of thee, & keep thy *VVord*.
Throughout the world, thy *tender-Mercy* flowes,
  Let me be train'd in all thy *Statutes*, Lord.

Grant us Grace oh God! ſoe to examine the Courſe of our life paſt, & what waies wee intend to walk hereafter ; that
wee

wee may returne to thee with ſpeedy repētance: & ſo reſolve to keep thy commandements during the tyme to come; that wee may enioye thee for our Portion; *& (both in the* Night *of our afflictions, & among the troups of our* perſecutors) *be comforted in the remembrance of thy abundant Mercyes, through* Ieſus Chriſt. Amen.

Teth. 9.

THy ſervant, Favour hath receiv'd
According to thy *word.*
And, thy *Commands* I have beleev'd,
Therfore inſtruct me, Lord.
Though till my troubles, I mis-trod,
Thy *VVord,* I follow now.
Thy *Precepts,* teach to mee, oh God:
For, Good, & kinde, art thou.
2 Thy *Lawe,* with all my hart I ſeek;
Though, mee the proud belye.
Their harts are fatt, (ev'n Brawner-like)
But, lov'd thy *Lawes,* have I.
Now, I have learn'd thy *Statute's* Truth,
My Cares, I bleſſings deem:
And, I the Precepts of thy Mouth,
Above all wealth eſteem.

Another of the ſame.

IN all things, to thy Servant thou art juſt,
According as thy *VVord,* oh Lord, hath ſhowne.
Since therefor, to thy *Covenant,* I truſt,
Thy *Judgmēts,* & thy Truth, to mee make knowe.
If that, I had not bene, by ſorrowes croſt,
I, ſtill had err'd: But, now I keep thy *VVord.*
Moſt Good thou art, & all is well thou doſt:
Therefore, thy *Statutes* teach to mee, oh Lord.
I, by the proud, have greatly bene belide;

Yet,

Yet, still, I keep thy *Lawe* within my brest:
Their hart (with fat) like brawne is stupifide;
But, with delight, thy *Lawe* hath mee possest.
It is my weal, that I afflicted was;
For, by that meanes, thy *Statutes*, now, I heed.
That *Lawe* of thine, which from thy mouth did (passe,
Great sums of gold, & silver doth exceed.

Sanctifie vnto us (oh Lord, all our Afflictions; that, being by them purified from our Corruptions, wee may become vpright in all our wayes. Suffer vs not to be so fatted in our prosperities as to become insensible of thy Mercies *or* Iudgments. *Let our experience in thy word, teach us, to see & acknowledge, that our Afflictions are blessings; And whatsoever Scandalls do arise, let us continue in Obedience to thy* Lawe, *& thanckfully esteeme the same as wee ought, for ever & ever,* Amen.

Iod. 10.

TO learne thy *Lawe*, instruct mee, Lord,
For, mee thy hands have made:
So, when they see mee trust thy *word*,
Thy servants will be glad.
I knowe thy *Iudgments* righteous are;
And all thy Stripes are Love.
Now, let thy grace, thy servant chear
And, true, thy *VVord* approve.
2 I love thy *Lawe*, grant mee therefore,
Thy grace, that live I may,
Defame the proud, who wrong mee sore;
For, I thy *VVord* obay.
Who knowes thy *VVill*, & searcth thee,
All such to mee convart:
And, in thy *Lawes*, lest sham'd I bee,
Lord, rectify my hart.

Another

Anather of the same.

KIndle the knowledge of thy *Lawe* in mee.
For, by thy hands, I fashion'd was, oh Lord,
Thy servants will reioice, my face to see,
Because I have relied on thy *word.*
Knowne, well, thy *Iudgments* are, to be vpright.
And, Lord, on mee thy stripes in love thou laydst.
Oh, make thy *Tender-mercies* my delight,
And comfort mee, as in thy *VVord* thou saydst.
Kinde, let mee finde thee Lord ; that I may live :
Because contentement in thy *Lawe* I finde.
Defame the *Proud,* who mee vniustly greeve ;
For on thy *Precepts,* I employ my minde.
Keepe those who thee do feare, & know thy *VVill,*
That they may be converted vnto mee.
And in thy *Lawes,* my hart confirme thou, still,
That from disgrace, I may preserved bee.

Lord, wee are the workmanship of thy hands: Soe instruct vs therfor, in the vnderstanding and performance of thy Lawe, *that wee may accomplish the end of our Creation. Make our knowledge of thy* Statutes, *our Faith in thee, & our conformity to thy* Will, *soe evident ; that thy Servants may reioice, our foes become ashamed, our corrections appear tokens of thy Love ; our shame be prevented, our harts cheared, & life eternal obtayned.* Amen.

Caph. II.

MY soul, for succour panting lies.
Yet, is thy *word* my stay.
I seek thy *Truth* with longing eyes,
Oh Comfort mee, they say.
I, like a smoke-dride botle seeme ;
Yet, on thy *Lawe,* I thought :
Summ vp my dayes, & *iudge* all them,

That

That have my ruine fought.
2 For mee, the Proud funck pitts, which be
Forbidden by thy *Lawes:*
Thy *VVords* are true, oh fave thou mee,
Perfu'de without a Caufe.
Quite from the Land, they drove me nigh,
Yet, to thy *Lawes* I cleave.
Oh chear mee, by thy grace, that I
Thy *VVord* may never leave.

Another of the fame.

LOrd, for thy healp my longing foul doth pant,
And, on thy *Promife* al my hopes do lye.
Mynes eies do faile, becaufe thy *VVord* I want,
Come comfort mee, with fpeaking looks, they crie.
Like botles in the fmoke I do appear,
Yet, ftill, thy *Statutes* minded are of mee.
How long fhall I thy fervant fuffer hece!
Thy *Iudgments*, on my foes, oh, let mee fee.
Lo, for my life, the proud deep pitts have made,
Such as thy *Lawe* forbiddeth to prepare.
They mee perfued, though no caufe they had;
Oh helpe; for all thy *Precepts*, faithfull are.
Long fince, my ruine they had nigh contriv'd:
I, naitheles, thy *Statutes* did not leave.
Let mee by thy compaffion be reviv'd,
And, to thy Teftimonies, I will cleave.

Oh Lord, *wee have Adverfaries, continually digging pitts for our foules. VVee are fenfible of great Afflictions, & our life daylie wears out by vnperceaved infirmities. Yet, wee feel not that longing to obtaine an incorruptible eftate, as to continue our prefent vanities. Oh let that* experience, *which wee have of miferies here; & that* Faith *which wee ought to have of what thou haft promifed hereafter, make*
our

our harts pant with longing after the accompliſhment of thy Truth, & for our full fruition of thee, through Ieſus Chriſt *our Lord.* Amen.

Lamed. 12.

THy *VVord*, in heav'n remaines for aye;
 Thy *Truth* ſhall ſtill abide.
The earth, ſo firmely thou didſt lay,
 It cannot ſwarve aſide.
Thy *Lawes* keep ev'ry thing vpright;
 For, all, thy ſervants be.
But that thy *VVorde* was my delight,
 My Cares had ruin'de mee.
2 I will not from thy *Truth* decline;
 For, life to mee it brought.
Oh ſave thou mee; for I am thine;
 And, thy *Decrees*, have ſought.
Though ſinners do my ſpoile intend,
 Thy *VVord*, in minde I bear.
Of all good works I ſee an end;
 But, large thy precepts are.

Another of the ſame.

MAde firme in heav'n, thy *promiſe* is, oh Lord,
 And, ſhall for ever, & for ever, laſt.
 Thy *Faith fullnes*, all ages will record,
 For as earths globe, the ſame thou fixed haſt.
Moſt firme to thy *Decrees* thy works do ſtand,
 And, all things as thy ſervants, wait on thee.
 But, that I pleaſure take in thy *Command*,
 My ſorowes, long er'e this, had ruin'd mee.
My hart ſhall never from thy *Lawes* decline;
 For, I, by them, to life againe, was brought.
 Vouchſafe to ſuccour mee, for I am thine:
 And, after thy *Commandements* have ſought.

Much

Much waiting, hath among the wicked bene,
My fall to ſee; but, I thy *Statutes* minde.
Of all perfections, I an end have ſeene,
Save of thy *Lawe*; which cannot be confinde.

Almighty God, by being obedient vnto the Lawe of their Creation, thy other Creatures are preſerved in order, & cōtinue thy faithfull ſervants. Man-kinde only is rebellious; & yet, wee have had often experience that a litle delight in thy Lawe, is rewarded with great Bleſsings. Soe encreaſe therfor, our beleef of thy Truth, *& our love to thy* Lawe; *that wee may be more & more conformable to thy* Will, *& at laſt be ſaved, through* Ieſus Chriſt, *our Lord.* Amen.

Mem. 13.

IN thy *Commands* I pleaſure take,
My dayly thoughts they bee;
Mee, wiſer then my foes *they* make,
And, ſtill, remaine with mee.
More, learne I from thy *Statutes*, then,
My Teachers vnderſtand.
And, wiſer am, then aged men,
By keeping thy *Command*.
2 My feet, from evill waies I kept,
That keep thy *Lawe* I might.
I, from thy *Iudgments* have not ſtept,
For, mee thou holdſt vpright.
Though hony to the mouth be ſweet,
Thy *VVord* more ſweetnes hath.
Through thy *Commands* I grewe diſcreet,
And ſhun'd the Liers Path.

Another of the ſame.

NO parte of all the day I cann forbear
To minde thy *Lawe*; becauſe I love the ſame.
It makes me wiſer then my haters are,

For

For my companion still thy *Lawe* became.
Nay, more then all my teachers I conceave;
Because, my Musings are vpon thy *VVill.*
And, more then aged men I do perceave;
Because they *Testimonies* I fulfill.
No wicked pase, or Path, my feet shall vse,
That so, thy *VVord* the better keep I might.
And, I thy *Iudgments* never will refuse,
Because thou hast instructed mee aright.
Not halfe so sweet is honie to my mouth,
As are thy *VVords:* for, perfect sweet are they.
Thou hast encreast my knowledge, by thy *Truth*:
And, therfor, I abhorr each evill way.

*The wisdome (*oh Lord) *of this world, is but foolishnes, in respect of that which is learned by thy* Word: *For, nothing is soe profitable or pleasant, as that; if it be meditated aright. Give us grace, therfor, wee pray thee, so to love it, & so to meditate thereon; that wee may crack the shell which hides the sweet kernell thereof, from the world; &, by help of thy spirit, thereby attaine that wisdome which (our Ordinary Teacher) the bare Letter hath not powre to discover; & let it guide us out of all error, both in life & doctrine, though* Iesus Christ. Amen.

Nun. 14.

THy *word* is to, my feet a light:
A Lampe, my way to showe.
I vow'd thy *doomes* to keep aright,
And I will keep my Vowe.
I, sore am greev'd; Lord, me revive,
According to thy *Truth.*
Teach mee thy *Iudgments*; & receive
The Praises of my mouth.
2 Although my soul in danger be

Thy *Statutes* I obay;
And keep thy *Lawes*, although for mee,
The wicked, snares do lay.
Thy *Cov'nants* are mine Heritage;
They much reioice my minde;
And, thy *Decrees*, from age to age,
To keep, I am inclinde.

Another of the same.

OH God, thy *VVord* like Lāps my way doth show,
And, to my feet, it is a shining flame.
To keep thy righteous *Iudgments*, I did vowe;
And, I resolve that I will keep the same.
Opprest I am; Me, therefor Lord revive
As by thy *VVord*, thy promise is to do.
Accept that praise which I shall freely give;
And, in thy *Iudgments* Lord, instruct me to.
On thy *Commands*, my thoughts are alway sett,
And, lo, my soul is alwaies in my hands.
Vngodly men, for mee have laid a nett;
Yet walk I not astray from thy *Commands*.
Of all my Ioyes thy *VVord*, alone, is cause:
Thy Testaments I make mine heritage.
My hart resolves, to love & keep thy *Lawes*
While time endures, & throughout evry Age.

Many waies (oh Lord) is thy Lawe *healpfull vnto vs. It is a* Schoolmaster, *to teach us*; *A* Rule, *whereby to square our Actions*; A glasse, *to shew us our deformities*; A light, *to guide us out of error*; *& a* Remembrancer, *to shewe vs what we are liable vnto by* Nature; *That so, the terrors thereof may make the flesh more obedient to the spirit (& their harts the more thanckfull, whome* Grace *hath freed from the Curse & condemning powre thereof) yea, it is alwaies vsefull in some kinde or other. Oh, write it therfor*

therfor in our harts & engrave it in our mindes, for ever & ever. Amen.

Samech. 15.

THy *Lawe* I love with all my hart,
And wicked thoughts detest.
The place of my defence thou art;
And, on thy *Word*, I rest.
Lewd men avoyd; for I would faine
My God's *Commands* obay.
According to thy *Word*, maintaine
My life, & hopes, I pray.
2 Support mee, & I nought shall dread:
For, to thy word I cleave.
Vpon thy *Lawes* transgressers tread:
For, guile shall them deceive.
Purgd out like drosse, the wicked be:
I therefore love thy *Lawe.*
And, of thy *Iudgments*, & of thee,
My flesh doth stand in awe.

Another of the same.

PRroud thoughts I hate, and such as cause offence
But, with much love thy *Lawe* I do embrace.
Thou art my sheild, oh Lord, and my defence;
And in thy *Word*, my confidence I place.
Pack hence, all yee, that evill doers be;
For, all my God's *Commands*, I will obay.
According to thy *Word*, vphold thou mee;
That both my life & hopes, enioy I may.
Protect me, & no dangers I shall fear:
For, in thy *Statutes*, I will then delight.
Suppresse all those that from thy *Precepts* err:
For why, they muse on nothing but deceit.
Purg'd out by thee, like drosse, thee wicked are;
And, I thy *Testimonies* love therefore.

My flesh doth dread thee with a trembling fear;
And, by thy *Iudgments*, I am frighted sore.

Oh Lord, let the consideration of thy Iudgmēts *purge out all our wickednes, & so terrify our wanton flesh, that it may tremble to offend thee. Let the Meditation of thy* Lawe of Love, *so work vpō our harts, that our verie thinckings may be sanctified. And let us be continually supported by thy assisting* Grace, *that in thought, word, & deed, wee may persevere in obedience to thy* Will, *& be safe vnder thy protection, for ever & ever.* Amen.

Aijn. 16.

IN Iudgment, I vprightly deal;
Let no man mee oppresse.
Be suretie, for thy servants weal;
From Tyrants, me release.
Mine eyes, are dimm'd since for thy *VVord*,
And saving-health I sought.
Deal well with mee thy servant, Lord,
Let me thy *Lawe* be taught.
2 Since, thee I serve, Lord, grant I may
Thy *Testimonies* knowe.
Now, is the time to work; for they,
Thy *Law* would overthrowe.
Far more then gold, (then finest gold)
Thy *Statutes* I affect.
Thy *Lawe*, in all things, I vphold,
And, errors way, reject.

Another of the same.

QUit me from such as doe my harme assay;
For, I according to thy *Lawe* have wrought.
Be suretie, for thy Servants weal, I pray,
That, to the proud, in thrall I be not brought.
Quite wasted are mine eyes, & almost blinde,
Since thy just *VVord*, & healp I did expect.

Accor-

According to Mercie, be thou kinde;
And, me thy ſervant, by thy *Law* direct.
Quench not that Light by which thy *Truth* is known
But, give thy ſervant knowledg in thy *VVord:*
For, they thy bleſſed *Lawe* have overthrowne,
And, it is time that thou thy healp afford.
Quick therfore be: For, I above all gold,
Yea more then gold refinde, thy *VVord* affect.
Thy *Statutes* all, to be vpright I holde;
And all erroneous waies, I diſreſpect.

Preſerve us, oh God, from their wickednes, who pretending a Chriſtian Libertie, *ſeek to overthrowe, & make voyd thy* Lawe *(to the quenching of the ſpirit, & to the fullfilling of their fleshly* Will*) Grant rather, that the more wee are freed, from the* Bondage of the Lawe *(& the leſſe obliged to the works thereof, for our* Juſtification*) the more we may labour to fullfill the ſame; even for the love of* Righteouſnes *in* Ieſus Chriſt, Amen.

Pe. 17.

RAre things, thy *Teſtaments* compriſe,
And are my ſoules delight.
Thy *Statutes* make the ſimple wiſe,
Their knowledg giveth light.
Through longing for thy *Lawe*, I drewe
My breath with panting Mouth.
Veiwe mee in Love, as thou doſt veiwe
The Lovers of thy *Truth*.
2 So guide my goengs by thy *VVord*,
No ſinn in mee may raigne.
From ſpoile of men, preſerve me Lord,
For I thy *Truth* retaine.
Teach mee thy *Lawes*, & let thy face,
Vpon thy ſervant ſhine.

For, Streames I weep, when men tranfgreffe,
Or break a *Lawe*, of thine.

Another of the fame.

RIght wonderfull thy *Teftimonies* are :
And, therfor Lord my foul to keep thē ftrives.
Thy *VVord's* approching, makes great light ap-
And, Vnderftanding to the fimple gives. (pear,
Refpire & pant I did, with mouth vnclo'fd ;
So greedy of thy *Precepts*, I became.
Oh look on mee, as when thou art difpofd,
To look vpon the Lovers of thy *Name.*
Reftraine my ftepps according to thy *VVord* ;
And let no finn, in me domion gaine.
From Cruel men, defend thou mee oh Lord,
So, I thy facred *Precepts* will retaine.
Reflect on mee the brightnes of thy face,
And, fhewe thy *Teftimonies* vnto mee.
For, downe my cheeks the teares do flow apace,
Becaufe, thy *Lawes* defpifd & broken be.

Sweet Iefus, though we defire to feeme wife; wee are very fimple in the beft knowledge: Oh encreafe our vnderftanding. Though vvee profeffe great Affection to thee & thy Lawe; *yet vvee foone deny (yea forfvvear) both, if vvee are in danger to partake of thy fuffrings. Oh look vpon vs therfor, vvith fuch an afpect, as thou didft caft on thy* Apoftle *St.* Peter, *that vveeping bitterly for our Sinns & vnkindeneffes as he did; vve may obtaine the fame forgivenes.* Amen.

Zade 18.

THou juft in all thy doengs, Lord,
And in thy *Iudgments* art.
Thy *Teftimonies*, & thy *VVord*,
Are true in ev'ry part.
I burne with zeal, becaufe I fee

My

My foes, thy *Truth* neglect.
Thy *VVord* is pure, which cauſeth mee
That I the ſame affect.
2 Thy precepts, I will ſtill retaine,
Though I deſpiſd am growne.
Thy *Iuſtice*, alway ſhall remaine;
Thy *Lavve*, & Truth, are one.
In thy *Commands*, my pleaſures are,
Though troubles on mee fall.
Thy juſt eternall *VVill* declare,
And, thereby, live I ſhall.

Another of the ſame.

SIncere thou art, oh Lord, in all thou doſt:
A true, & righteous *Iudgment* thou haſt paſt.
Thy *Teſtimonies* are exceeding juſt:
And, ſo is all that thou *Commanded* haſt.
Spent, through my zeal I am, & almoſt pin'de,
Since of thy *Truth* my foes regardles growe.
Thy *VVord*, is to the vttermoſt refin'de;
And, for that cauſe, thy ſervant loves it ſoe.
Scorn'd & deſpiſ'd I am; yet cannot this,
My thoughts from thy *Commandements* withdrawe.
Thy *Iuſtice* an eternall *Iuſtice*, is;
And, *Truth* it ſelf, thou giveſt for thy *Lavve*.
Sore paines & ſorrowes, have layd hold on mee:
Yet, I from thy *Commands* content receive.
Thy righteous *Teſtimonies* endles be:
Oh let me know them, Lord, that I may live.

It is true oh Lord, that vvhat ever thou willeſt *is* Juſt, *& needs no other reaſon thereof, but that thou* Willeſt *it, becauſe thy* Will *is* Truth *&* Juſtice *it ſelf. Keep us therfor, from queſtioning the* Juſtice *of any thing vvhich thou haſt* Willed *or Decreed: & preſerue us, alſo, from* *their madnes, vvho fancie* Decrees *vvhich thou never mad'ſt; & ſuch as doe not make thee iuſtifiable by humane Reaſon. Teach us to knovve, that, though thy* Juſtice *is incomprehenſible, yet ſo much as thy vvord hath expreſſed of it, is ſuch a* Juſtice, *as makes thee (even in our capacities)* Juſtifiable, when thou art iudged; *& ſuch, as may encourage us, to endeavour, to be* juſt as thou art juſt, & holie as thou art holy, *by thy example. This grant, for* Iesus Chriſt *his ſake.* Amen.

Coph. 19.

LOrd hear; for, in my hart I crie,
And, I thy *VVord* obay.
To hear my call, thine ear apply,
That keep thy *Lavves* I may.
Relieng on thy *VVord,* I call'd,
Before the Morning-light;
To mark thy *VVords* mine eyes foreſtald,
The Watches of the night.
2 As *iuſt* & *loving,* Lord, thou art,
So, hear & quicken mee.
Lo, ſuch as from thy *Lavve* depart
For miſcheeſe, comming be.
Oh Lord, to mee, now nearer drawe:
Thy *VVord* all truth containes,
And, long agoe, I knewe thy *Lavve,*
Eternally remaines.

Another of the ſame.

THey, healp oh Lord, with all my hart I crave,
Thy juſt *Commands* reſolving to obay.
To thee I call aloud; mee daigne to ſave,
That ſo, thy *Teſtimonies,* keep I may.
To thee, before the break of day, I call,
And, for my certaine ayde, thy *VVord* I take.

The

The watches of the night mine eyes forestall,
  That on thy *Lawe*, my muzings I may make.
Thine ear, vnto my voice, in mercy, bowe;
  That, mee, thy *Iudgments* may revive, oh Lord.
  They fast approach, who seek my overthrowe,
  Ev'n they, who strangers are vnto thy *VVord.*
To mee, oh Lord, at all tymes, be thou nigh.
  Thy *Statutes*, all perfection do containe.
  And, many daies agoe, informed was I,
  That thy *Commands*, for ever shall remaine.

VVee rise early, (oh Lord) & cann sit vp late at night, to prosecute our common affaires, or to prevent the mischeevous purposes of any temporall Adversary. Cause us, vvee pray thee, to be as vigilant, in seeking thee; in Meditating the deep Misteries of thy Lawe; *& in foreseeing what spirituall enimies are approching to endanger our soules. Vouchsafe this, oh Lord: & in all our endeavours, assist us; in all our prayers, hear us; & in all our necessities be present with us, in* Iesus Christ *our Lord*, Amen.

Resh. 20.

REgard my greef, & save me Lord,
  For, I obaie thy *Lawes.*
Hear me, according to thy *VVord,*
  Oh save, & plead my Cause.
Because thy *VVord* they muse not on,
  From health are sinners far.
Revive mee Lord, as thou hast done,
  For, great thy *Mercies* are.
2 My foes, & spoilers many be;
  Yet, I thy *VVord* professe,
And greeve when I the wicked see,
  Thy *Statutes* to transgresse.
Thy *Lawe* I love; oh quicken mee,

As thou hast promis'd Lord.
For, endles thy just *Judgments* be;
And, ever true, thy *VVord.*

Another of the same.

VEwe Lord, what sorrowes have oppressed mee:
For, to observe *Lawe*, My minde I give.
Let mee adiudged, & deliver'd be;
And, mee according to thy *vvord* revive.
Vngodly men from saving health are far,
Because they do not seek thy *Statutes*, Lord;
Exceding great thy *Tender-mercies* are;
Revive thou mee according to thy *vvord.*
Vext & persude, by many, I have beene;
And, yet, I from thy *Precepts*, have not straid.
I greeved was when sinners I had seene;
Because, thy holy-*vvord*, they disobayd.
Vnto thy *Lawe*, observe what love I shew;
And, of thy tender mercie, quicken mee.
Thy *vvord*, through all eternitie is true;
And, everlasting thy just *Judgments be.*

Oh Christ the Mediatour; in our minds wee are lovers & observers of thy Lawe; *but in our mẽbers wee are captivated vnto the* Lawe *of* Sinn: *for which, our greeved spirits do complaine with sighes & groanes, that are neither vtterable by the voice, nor sensible to the flesh. Oh deliver us from this bondage; Plead thou our cause to thy Father; Comfort our deiected soules; & let our love & practise of thy* Lawe, *quicken us, in the way of Righteousnes, & make us partakers of thy* Tender-Mercies, *for ever more.* Amen.

Schin. 21.

THough Princes, causeles, wrong'd mee much,
Thy *Lawe* I sleighted not:
But, in thy *word*, my ioies were such

As

As his that Spoiles hath got.
The lienge lipps I do abhorr;
But I affect thy *word*.
Seav'n times a day, I praiſe thee, for
Thy righteous *Doomes*, oh Lord.
2 The Lovers of thy *Lawe* have peace;
And, harme they ſhall have none.
Lord, on thine aide my hopes I place;
And, thy *Commands* have done.
My ſoul thy *Teſtimonie* kept;
In love therewith I grewe.
I, from thy *Precepts* have not ſtept;
For, thou my waies doſt veiwe.

Another of the ſame.

WHē cauſe was none, ev'n Princes wronged mee;
But, of thy *word* alone, my hart had feare.
And, in that *word*, my Ioies, moreover, be
As great as their's that ſharing booties are.
With much diſlike, all falſhood I deteſt:
And, I thy *Lawe*, vnfainedlie affect.
Sev'n times a day, thy praiſe I have expreſt;
Becauſe thy righteous *Iudgments* I reſpect.
What perfect peace have they that love thy *word?*
Ev'n ſuch, that nothing cana their quiet marr.
For thy ſalvation, I have hoped, Lord;
And, thy *Commands* by mee performed are.
Well pleas'd, & with exceeding much delight,
My ſoul thy *Teſtimonies* keepeth ſtill;
Thou know'ſt: for all my waies are in thy ſight;
That I, thy *Precepts*, & thy *Lawes*, fulfill.

Oh bleſſed Redeemer, who wert perſecuted by Princes, *for my ſake, without a Cauſe; Thy many* Prayers, *daylie offred to thy* Father; *thy true delight in his* Word; *thy deteſtation*

deteſtation of falshood, & thy perfect fulfilling of the Lawe, *have obtained, that thy righteouſnes may be aſcribed vnto us. Oh grant, that by performing what thou haſt enabled us to do, wee may retaine & encreaſe the* Talent *freely given; & enioy thy* Peace, *which paſſeth all vnderſtanding; for ever & ever.* Amen.

Tau. 22.

REceive my cry, & guide thou mee
 As thou haſt promiſd, Lord,
Give ear, & ſaved let mee be;
 According to thy *vvord.*
When thou to me haſt ſhowne thy *vvaies,*
 My lipps thy praiſe will ſhewe.
My tongue thy bleſſed *vvord* ſhall praiſe;
 For, all thy *Lawes* are true.
2 Mee, let thy powrfull hand protect;
 For, I thy *Lawe* approove.
Thy *Saving-health* I do affect,
 Thy *Precepts* I do love.
Oh, let mee live to ſing thy praiſe;
 In *Judgment,* mee preſerve.
Thy ſervant ſeek, who ſheep-like ſtraies;
 For, I thy *Lawe* obſerve.

Another of the ſame.

YEald my Complaint, oh Lord, thy graitious ear,
 And, knowledge of thy *Lawe,* to me afford.
 My humble ſuite, vouchſafe, I pray, to hear;
 And, ſave thou mee, according to thy *vvord.*
Yea, ſave thou mee; & I thy praiſe will preach,
 When thou ſhalt thy *Commands* to mee declare.
 Thy *vvord* likewiſe, to others I will teach;
 For, all thy *Precepts,* true & righteous are.
Yeald me thy hand, my ſaftie to aſſure;

For,

For, thy *Commands* my chosen part, I make.
Thy Saving-health, I labour to procure,
And, in thy *Lavve*, oh Lord, I pleasure take.
Yet, longer let me live, to sing thy praise;
And, let thy *Judgments* Lord, my helpers be.
Now, mee thy servāt seek, who sheep-like straies,
For, never is thy *Lawe* forgot of mee.

Most mercifull Father, wee have all erred & strayed from thy waies like lost sheep; give us therefore that Lawe of Faith, *by which wee may be brought home to thy* Folde. *VVhen wee have obtained this Grace; let us truely esteeme it, hartly praise thee for it, & diligently preach it to others. Oh spare our lives, vntill the* New-man *shall be fully perfected in vs; that wee may accomplish the work for which wee were created, & glorify thy Name, world without end.* Amen.

Psa. 120.

A song of Degrees. *VVhy these* Psalmes *are so called, it is vncertaine (for, Iewish fancies are not worth heeding) but, perhaps, our* Degrees *tovvard the spirituall* Temple, *are here mystically included: for, the first* degree *thitherwvard, is to have a sight of our misery, & a detestatiõ of the worlds vanities (figured by* Mesech & Kedar, *in this Psalme.* It is vsefull, when wee are constrained to live among false worshippers, or wearied by our owne corruptions &c.

I Call'd on God in my destresse,
Who heard mee when I prayd:
From lieng & deceitfulnes,
Lord, save my Soul; I said.
What hire, oh thou deceitfull tongue!
Prepared is for thee?
But, arrowes that are sharp & strong,

And

And coales that burning be?
2 Ah! woe is mee, that I so long,
In *Mesech* must reside!
And, that, perforce, I must among
The Tents of *Kedar* bide.
My soul hath beene too long, alas!
With such as wranglers are:
For, when I speake to them of peace,
For warr, they do prepare.

Father of Mercie; *Keep vs from the lieng deceits of the* Devill, *&* *his* Members; *& reward them according to their malice. Vouchsafe to us, also, such a sight, & loathing, of our naturall estate; that wee may have an earnest longinge to be translated from the* Tents *of Vngodlines, & be incorporated into thy heavenly* Ierusalem *through* Iesus Christ, *our Lord.* Amen.

Psa. 121.

A song of Degrees. *Another* Degree, *is to fixe the eye of our soul on God, acknowledging him only, the meanes of our deliverance, & our defence &c.* It directs vs, to whome wee should seek; & encourageth to depend on God in all our waies.

MIne eyes above the hills, I reare,
And, thence, of healp, I hopefull am;
For, from the Lord my succours are,
From him, that heav'n & earth did frame.
My feet vnmoov'd, he alway keeps;
He, is my garde, that ever wakes:
For, he nor slumbers, neither sleeps,
Who charge of *Isr'el* vndertakes.
2 The Lord, ev'n as thy shade, will stay
On thy righthand, for thy defence.
Nor Moone by night, nor Sunne by day,

Shall

Shall harme thee by their Influence :
For, God will ſave thee from all woe,
Hee, will thy ſoul from dangers free ;
And (whether in, or out, thou goe)
Thy gard, at all times, he will bee.

Gratious Protector ; *Cauſe us, to expect all our deliverances from thee, with a conſtant dependance vpon thy ſavegard, in all proceedings. Keep us without ſlavish fear, or wavering, in our* Faith*: And, be thou allway ſoe watchfull over vs, & ſo near vnto vs; that neither thoſe dangers whereto wee are commonly ſubiect, nor the extraordinarie* Influences *of the heavens, nor any other vnexpectede Evẽts, harme our bodies, endanger our ſoules, or interrupt our lawfull callings, either now, or hereafter.* Amen.

Pſa. 122.

A ſong of Degrees. *Another* Stepp, *is a delight in the pietie of others, ioined with love to God's worship, & accompanied with harty wellwishing to his* Church. *The* Elect *are here perſonated reioicing on this* Degree. Wee ſhould vſe it to provoke vs vnto the ſame.

I Ioyed, when they ſaid to mee,
God's houſe let vs aſcend vnto :
For, now *Ieruſalem*, to thee
And, through thy Ports, our feet ſhall goe.
Ieruſalem is fairly Scited ;
A Towne well-built, & well-vnited.
2 There meet the Tribes (God's Tribes alone)
Hus name in Iſr'el, to declare.
There, placed is, the *Judgment* Throne ;
The Thrones of *Davids* houſe are there.
Oh ſeek her peare, for, they are bleſſed ;
That have to *Salem*, love expreſſed.

3 Let

3 Let Peace, a Bullworke round her make,
Let Plenties in her Turrets be:
This Peace wee wiſh, ev'n for their ſake,
Who, mates, & Brethren are to mee.
Yea, God our Lord's faire habitation,
Thus, makes mee pray for thy Salvation.

Inſpire us, oh Lord, with a delight, & mutuall deſires, to further each other in thy ſervice. Let us take pleaſure in thy Sanctuarie: *&, be alwaies, to our powre, helpfull & zealous, to effect & continue the Peace of* Syon; *even for the ſakes of our brethren, for our owne ſakes, & for thy glory ſake (oh* Father*) that, wee may reap the benifit of her Peace & Plenties, through* Ieſus Chriſt, *our Lord.* Amen.

Pſa. 123.

A ſong of Degrees. *Another* Stepp *is obedient attendance of God's will, in all ſuffrings, with aſſured faith in him; which is here profeſſed by the faithfull ſoul.* It is vſefull, to advance vs to this Degree.

OH Lord, that in the heav'ns remaineſt,
Lo, wee advance our eyes to thee:
And, Lord our God, till healp thou daigneſt,
They ſhall on the affixed bee,
As men or Maides, that waiting ſtand,
Vpon their Lord, or Ladie's hand.
2 Oh, grant vs Lord, thy dear compaſſion;
For, wee extream contempts have borne.
Vouchſafe vs, Lord, thy Conſolation,
For why? our harts are greev'd with ſcorne,
Ev'n by the ſcornes, & pride of them,
Who live at eaſe, & vs contemn.

How ever thou shalt pleaſe to afflict vs, oh Lord (or how long ſoever thou deferr any deſired Bleſsing) let vs be con-

contented to attend thy Pleaſure; & watchfull, to performe what thou shalt require further at our hands; ſoe our ſuffrings, shall the ſooner, be redreſſed, & our dutifull obedience, be rewarded through Ieſus Chriſt *our Lord.* Amen.

Pſa. 124.

A ſong of Degrees. *Another* Staire, *is acknowledgment of former deliverances, & of the beginnings of Gods graces already obtained, as in this* Pſalme. Wee may vſe it after any Deliverance, but eſpecially, ſuch as are moſt publike.

BUt, that the Lord, our part did pleaſe to take,
But that God holpe vs, *(Iſr'el* now may ſay)
When men did their Aſſaults againſt vs make,
Wee to their throtes had bene a living-prey;
For, wroth at vs, with ſpighfull rage were they.
2 Wee by the Flouds, had then bene cloſed round;
Ev'n quite above our ſoul, the ſtreames had gone:
The ſwelling flouds, our ſoul had ſurely drownd.
Wee, therſor, bleſſe & praiſe the Lord, alone,
That, by their teeth wee were not ceaz'd vpon.
3 For, as a bird, out of a fouling ſnare,
Ev'n ſo, our ſoul eſcaped from the ginn:
The nett is broke, & wee deliver'd are; (binn)
And, God, (whoſe work, the heav'ns & earth have
Is hee, whoſe Name, our healp conſiſteth in.

Many times oh Lord, wee are delivered, by thy Mercy, from evident & vnavoidable perills: But, there is no moment in which wee are not compaſſed about with inviſible foes (& vnthought of Dangers) far more fearfull & more impoſſible to be avoyded; vnles thou didſt gratiouſly defēd us. Grāt therfor, that a filiall awe of thy Iudgmēts *& a true eſteeme of thy* Mercies, *may make us hartily thanckfull*

S *vnto*

vnto thee, for them, now & for ever. Amen.

Pſa. 125.

A ſong of Degrees. *Another* Aſcent, *is firme Beleef in God. The ſafetie of ſuch, is here alluded to the impregnability of* Mount-Syon, & Ieruſalem : *& the puniſhment of wavering* Apoſtates *is threatned &c.* It is vſefull to raiſe vs to this *Degree &c.*

M*Ount-Syon* like, for ever fixt are thoſe
Whoſe hopeſull truſt vpon the Lord is founded
For, he his faithfull People will encloſe
(Ev'n as with hills *Ieruſalem* is rounded)
As long as Time's perpetuall motion goes.
2 The Rod of wicked men ſhall not alight,
Where God the Lot of righteouſnes beſtoweth.
Leſt righteous men pertake in evill might.
For, to the Good, the Lord his mercy ſhoweth
And, favours all that are in hart vpright.
3 But, Sliders-back, & ſuch as wander wide,
In their owne crooked paths, & waies vneven,
Shall by the Lord, be thither ledd aſide,
Where, portion due to hypocrites, are given :
But, *Iſr'el* ſhall in endles peace abide.

Oh God, many ignorances & errors, both in Iudgment, & Manners, *wee are naturally ſubiect vnto. Teach us therfore what wee ought to* Beleeve, *or practiſe; & then preſerve vs vnwavering in our* Faith, *& ſo ſincerely conſtant in a holy* Life; *That wee may not have our portion, with* Apoſtates, *or* Hypocrites, *but, be pertakers in the true* Peace *of* Iſr'el, *through* Ieſus Chriſt *our Lord.* Amen.

Pſa. 126.

A ſong of Degrees. *another* Degree *is a reioicing in our* Electiō *& ſpirituall freedome; which is here typically expreſ-*

preſſed, with a prophetical prayer for that ioye promiſed by Chriſt *vnto the true* Mourners. *Ioh.* 16, 20. Wee may ſing it as a thanckſgiving for our Redemption ; & to comfort in ſpiritual mournings.

WHen God made *Syon* free ;
And her from thrall did bring,
It ſeemed as a Dreame to be ;
And, wee did laugh & ſing.
2 The Lord (the heathen ſedd)
Great Marvailes wrought, for vs.
Great marvailes he hath, wrought, indeed,
And, therfor, ſing wee thus.
3 Lord, back our Captives bringe,
As Flouds to ſea-ward flowe,
So, they ſhall then reioice & ſing,
Who did in ſorrowe ſowe.
4 Who, outward-bound, doth mourne,
If he good ſeed employ,
Shall doubtles, back againe returne,
And, bring home ſheaves with ioy.

Let our greateſt reioicings (oh Lord) be in thy redeeming us from the Bondage of Sinn; & that our Names are in the Book of Life: for, marvailous was this deliverance. Let our greateſt ſorrowes be for our Offences, and for the loſſe of thy favour; which are, indeed, Cauſes of the greateſt Lamentation: ſoe, our short ſorrowe shall be turned in to everlaſting Ioyes, & glorious Trivmphs, world without end. Amen.

Pſa. 127.

A ſong of Degrees for Solomon. *Another* Staire *is to aſcribe our* beeing & well-being *to the* Mercie & providence *of God.* It may be ſung to acknowledge the ſame, in all our works, & endeavours, &c.

IF God the Pallace build not,
The workmen loofe their paine,
If God the Cittie fheild not,
The watchman wakes in vaine.
In vaine is early ftirring,
In vaine, late watch wee keep,
Or eat the bread of caringe,
But, thofe God loves, may fleep.
2 A fruithfull wombes poffeffing,
At God's difpofing ftands:
And, Chrildren are a bleffing,
Like fhafts in Giants hands.
Right bleft is he, that beareth
His Quiver ful of thofe;
For, in the Gate, he dareth,
To meet, & fmite his foes.

Grant almighty God; that whether wee endeavour for our foules or bodies, we never glory or truft in our owne workings; *For, thou muft bleffe the* beginning, proceeding, *&* conlufion *of every endeavour, or all our induftry is loft. Nay, wee have not, fo much as powre over our bodie, or the fruite therof. Let us therfor, neither forget thee in the vfe of the meanes, nor neglect the meanes which thou haft appointed. That, (what ever the events be) our vndertakings may, bring profit to us, & glory to thy holy Name.* So be it.

Pfa. 128.

A fong of Degrees. *Another* Stepp, *is filiall feare of God; to which, many temporall blefsings are here promifed.* It is vfed at the folemnization of mariages; & ferves to encreafe in vs, the feare of God.

IF God thou feare, & keep his way,
He, bleffings will beftowe:

Thy

Thy labour shall thy food purvay,
  And, happie thou shalt growe.
Like fruit-full vines vpon thy house,
  Thy wise shall proove to thee;
Thy Children, like faire olive-boughes,
  Shall round thy Table be.
2 Thus, thou that fearest God shalt thrive;
  From *Syon* he shall blesse:
And, thou shalt see (whilst thou dost live)
  Ierusalem in peace.
He shall prolong thy life, till thou
  Thy Childrens Children see;
And, that thy ioye may greater growe,
  In *Isr'ell*, rest shall bee.

Oh Lord; of thy abundant Mercy, thou hast promised, not only the blessings of the next life; but alsoe, all those which are most comfortable in this world, so far forth as shall conduce to their happines, who truly serve & feare thee. Oh teach us that filiall fear, & that obedience, for which thou hast made those promises, that wee may performe what thou requirest. Yet, not for the outward blessing sake; but meerly for the love of Iesus Christ *our Lord.* Amen.

Psa. 129.

A song of Degrees. *Another* Step, *is a patient sustaining of the Crosse. VVhich patience of the saints, is here mentioned; & both the tiranny & condition of their oppressors, breefly illustrated.* Wee may, vse it to increase & continue Christian Patience.

FUll often since my youth, may *Isr'el* say,
  Full often since my youth, they mee assailed;
And, still, without successe they went away: (trailed,
Yea on my back, their ploughs, the ploughers
  And, on the same, long furrowes ploughed they.

2 The Lord, (who is a perfect Righteous-one)
The Cords of wicked men in peeces breaketh.
And, *Syons* foes, shall quite be overthrowne,
Ev'n like that grasse, which root on houses taketh,
 And, fades away, before it ripe is growne.
3 For, nor his Armefull, nor his handful, there,
Remaines for him that bindes, or him that mo-
Nor is there any high-way Passenger, (weth.
Who, there, is blessing, in God's Name bestoweth.
 Or, doth so much, as, bidd them well to fare.

Sweet Iesu, (*who wert persecuted, even from thy cradle, to thy grave; & on whose back, the sharpe stripes, ploughed long furrowes for our Sinns) worthelie have wee deserved to be whipped with reproches to our face; to be furrowed with slanders behinde our backs, and to suffer all other indignities. Nevertheles, since by thy suffrings, thou hast as well prevailed for us, as for thy self; make voyd the attempts of our Adversaries; & enable us to sustaine with Christian patience, that part of thy* Crosse *which thou appointest us to bear: that being chearfull partakers of thy suffrings, we may partake also, thy victorious Triumphs in the Kingdome of heaven.* Amen.

Psa. 130.

A song of Degrees. *Another* Ascent, *is earnest prayer: Which the Faithfull soul here powreth forth for assistance, &c.* It may serve as a forme of prayer in great extremities.

LOrd, from the depths, to thee I sue;
 My vocall prayer hear.
And, when my Voice, my wants doth shewe
 Encline to mee thine ear.
Lord, who cann bear it, if severe,
 To mark our faults thou be?
But, that wee faint not in thy fear,

Com-

Compaſſion waites on thee.
2 On God I waite, & on his word,
My ſoul her hopes doth lay:
My ſoul, more waiteth for the Lord,
Then watchmen, for the day.
Oh Iſr'ell, truſt in God; for, hee;
Hath gratious help, in ſtore.
And, from thy ſinns delivers thee,
Both now & evermore.

Gratiouſly hear our prayers, oh Lord, in all our troubles & enter not into iudgment with us thy ſervants, vnles thou overshaddowe us by the wings of thy Mercie; for, our iuſtice is vnrighteouſnes in thy ſight. Give us grace to hope in thee, with patient expectation of thy good pleaſure; & ſoe enable vs (at leaſt in our true deſire) to fulfill our promiſes to thee, that without infringment of thy Juſtice, *we may be delivered both from the guilt & punishment of our ſinns, through thy* Mercie *in* Ieſus Chriſt *our Lord.* Amen.

Pſa. 131.

A ſong of Degrees. *Another* Degree *is vnfained* humilitie: *For,* ſuch as humble them ſelves ſhall be exalted. *Here, all arrogance, ambition, & ſelſtruſt is diſclaimed, a ſole dependance on God profeſſed, and others exhorted to the ſame.* It is vſefull, to beget humility.

OH Lord, I have no ſcornfull eie,
Nor proud nor loftie minde.
I ſeek not things that are too high,
But, humbly am inclinde.
My ſoul is like an infant wean'd,
(Ev'n from his mothers breſt)
And, Iſr'el, ſo (to be ſuſtaind)
On God, ſhould alway reſt.

None of thy Creatures, oh God, have made them ſelves

to be so vile as wee; yet, none are more proud or selfeconceited; none more presumptiously inquisitive into thy forbidden Seacrets. *Oh give us more* humility; *& lesse desire to those curiosities which are above vs, & pertinent to advance the* Kingdome *of* Sathan, *rather then the* Kingdome *of* Heaven; *which is to be entred which a* Childlike *Obedience &* humiliation. *This* Humiliation, *wee againe beseech thee to grant vs, for* Iesus Christ *his sake* Amen.

Psa. 132.

A song of Degrees. *Another* Degree, *is a hartie purpose to prepare a* Temple *for God, in our harts; & to endeavour the setling of his outward* worship, *which is here mystically applied.* It is vsefull to stirr vs to this Degree.

REmember Lord, what *David's* troubles be,
And, what to *Iacob's* mightie God, he swore.
In house or bedd, I will not rest, said he,
Nor shall mine eyes, or sleep, or slumber more;
Vntill a place be found, of my providing,
For, *Iacob's* God, the mighty Lord's abiding.
2 Lo, *Ephrata*, wee heard, the place should be,
And, in the forrest-feilds, wee found the same.
Thy house therefore, to enter, purpose wee,
And, at thy footstoole, will adore thy Name.
Arise, oh Lord, ascend thy resting bowre;
Thou, & the *Arck*, of thy Almightie powre.
3 Let Righteousnes, thy sacred Preists aray,
And, let thy saints a ioyfull tryvmph make:
Oh turne not thy *Messiah's* face away,
For, thy beloved Servant *David's* sake,
To whome thou swar'st thy promise, vnrecalled,
That on his Throne, his Seed should be installed.

4 If

4 If they, ſaidſt thou, my League & word reſpect;
Thy Children, on thy Throne ſhall ever ſitt:
For, I the Lord, did *Syon* hill, elect;
And, for my dwelling, I have choſen it.
My ſetled reſt is there, & I'le poſſeſſe it;
I love it, & with plenties, I will bleſſe it.
5 The pore thereof, with bread I will ſuſtaine,
Her Preiſts I'le clothe with health, her ſaints ſhal
A Lamp for mine Anointed, I'le ordaine, (ſing,
And, I will make the horne of *David* ſpring:
I, thoſe will ſhame, that for is harme endeavor;
But, on himſelf, his Crowne ſhall flouriſh ever.

Suffer vs not, oh Lord, to take reſt in any thing, vntill wee have provided thee a dwelling in our ſoules; & then, let vs entertaine there, nought els, but that which may be ſerviceable vnto thee. Take thou poſſeſsion of vs, & furnish vs, as becommeth Temples for thy preſence. Remember all thy promiſes to the Faithfull; *for they only are that ſeed of* David, *to whome thy Covenants belong; they are thoſe* Elect-ones *whome thou haſt promiſed never to forſake. Give vs, all outward meanes, of this inviſible grace; Continue among vs the* ſucceſſion, *of holy & faithful* Paſtors; *The* Bread *of thy* Word; *the* Clothings *of* Righteouſnes; *the* Lampe *of Illumination*; *the* Horne *of good* Goverment; *& the* Ioye *of the* Holy-ghoſt; *that the enimies of thy* Church, *may be aſhamed, & shee crowned, with honour & bleſſednes, for ever.* Amen.

Pſa 133.

A ſong of Degrees. *Another* Step, *is that, which the prepoſterous Zeal of* Schiſmaticks *hath much defaced. (to wit)* Charitie, *& brotherly* Vnitie; *which is here, excellenly Illuſtrated, to moove vs to aſcend it.* Wee ſhould ſing it, to encreaſe *Vnitie* & *Love.*

SEe Breth'ren, see, how sweet a blisse
It is our lives in love to lead.
It like that pretious Oyntment is,
Which once anointed *Aron's* head;
And, on his beard, from thence did flowe,
Ev'n to his garment skirts belowe.
2 It like refreshing dewe doth prove,
Which downe on *Hermon's* topp distills;
Ev'n like the dewe, which from above
Descendeth downe on *Syon* hills.
For, there, God promisd, heretofore,
To blesse with life, for ever more.

Oh God! so deare to thee, is brotherly Love, that all Faith, *(yea, &* Martirdome*) wanting that Virtue, is of no esteeme: So profitable is it vnto vs; That (like pretious oyntment on the head, or like shewres falling on high mountaines) it descends & spreads vntill every member be refreshed therewith. Encrease therfor, wee beseech thee, this* Virtue *amongvs (without which, all others are counterfeits) & let vs so preserve Vnity &* brotherly kindnes *in this life, that wee may enioy thy eternall* Love *&* Vniõ, *in the life to come, through* Iesus Christ *our Lord.* Amen.

Psa 134.

A song of Degrees. *This is the last* Degree*: For the highest* Ascent, *is,* the glorifieng of God. *Note, that the first & last* Degrees *only, are placed according to their* Order; *because, necessarily, our first step to Godward, must be* the sight of our Misery; *The highest, is,* to praise him: *The rest are not ascended by all, in one and the same order; & therefore no precise order is observed in their placing.* Wee should sing it to provoke to this Dutie.

COme now, & praise the Lord, all yee,
That his attendants are;

Ev'n

Ev'n you, that in God's temple be;
  And praiſe him, nightly, there.
Your hands, within Gods holy-place,
  Advance, & praiſe his Name;
And, yov, from *Syon*, he ſhall bleſſe,
  That heav'n & earth did frame.

Lord, wee were created for thy Glorie; All the time of our Pilgrimage on earth is to fill vs for thy praiſe; & the higheſt Degree *which wee cann attaine to, either in that life, or the next, is to ſing* Halelujah *vnto thy* Name. *Oh grant wee may ſo honour thee in theſe* Temples *of our* Bodies *(here, vpon the* Way*) on whome the* Nights *of affliction, & the* Dayes *of conſolation, doe interchangably ſucceed; that in thy* Ieruſalem *wee may ſing praiſes vnto thee, in that ſpirituall Temple, wherein, the preſence of the* Lambe, *maketh a continuation of Day, of Ioy, & of all happines, for ever more.* Amen.

Pſa. 135.

Halelujah. *It exhorts to praiſe God, in regard of his greatnes; for our election; for his omnipotency, Mercy, Iuſtice, eternitie; & becauſe other Gods are but ridiculous fictions, &c.* To this end, wee (who are miſtically the Sonns of *Aron* & *Levy*) ſhould ſing it &c.

OH all yee ſervants of the Lord,
  His Name with praiſe confeſſe;
Ev'n you, that of our God the Lord,
  The houſe & Courts poſſeſſe.
Oh praiſe God's Name; for, ſweet it is,
  To ſing of his renowne.
For, *Iacob*, he hath choſe for his,
  And *Iſr'el*, for his owne.
2 God is, (I knowe) a powrfull one;
  He doth all Gods excell:

In

In heav'n, his pleaſure he hath done ;
  In earth, in ſea, in hell.
He maketh vapours to ariſe,
  Ev'n from Earth's fartheſt ends :
And, he out of his Treaſuries,
  Winde, raine, & lighting, ſends.
3 The firſt-borne, through the *Egiptian* coaſt,
  Of man, & beaſt he ſlewe.
And, on king *Pharoh*, & his hoaſt,
  Rare wonders, hee did ſhewe.
Great kings & kingdomes, downe he brought,
  Ev'n *Sihon*, *Heshbon's* king,
And, *Og*, of *Bashan* ; yea, to nought
  All *Can'an's* Realmes, did bring.
4 Then, for his *Iſr'els* heritage
  Their lands, he did beſtowe :
For which, hee's fam'd, from age to age,
  And, ſtill ſhall famous growe.
When he to judge them doth appeare,
  His people, ſhall be ſav'd :
But, heathen God's, man's makings were,
  Of gold & ſilver grav'd.
5 Their carved mouthes are ſpeachles found,
  Their eyes, no light cann ſee :
Though they have eares, they heare no ſound ;
  Their throates, quite breathles be.
Much like to theſe, their Makers are ;
  And they, that ſerve them, toe.
The Lord, therefore, let *Iſr'el* fear ;
  And, ſo, let *Aron* doe.
6 The Lord, let *Levie's* houſhould bleſſe ;
  In *Syon*, let all them
Who fear the Lord, the Lord confeſſe
  That keeps *Ieruſalem*. *Haleluiah.*

Oh

Oh Lord *our* God, *wee hartely thanck thee, for our creation & preservation. VVee magnify thy wisdom, thy powre, thy providence, thy Iudgments, & thy Mercies; and wee acknowledge that the Deities of heathenish and carnall men) yea & all other things in which wee trust (are but vanities, & false Gods, fashioned by our owne wicked fancies. Grant therfore, that all of us (even preist & people) who in* Word *professe thee; may in* hart, *fear thee; & in* deed, *faithfully serve thee; now & for ever.* Amen.

Psa. 136.

This Psalme, *exhorts to praise God both for generall and perticuler benifits; & shewes, that all are bestowed for his meer mercy-sake, which is eternall.* It may be sung, literally to commemorate, what God did for the Patriarks: or, mistically, as a thancksgivinge for the spirituall deliverances, which these typified.

THe Lord is Good; him therfore blesse:
And, for his Grace, *that lasteth ever.*
The God of Gods, let vs confesse;
Because, his Mercie *faileth never.*
The Lord of Lords, with praise extoll;
For, where he loves, *he alway* loveth.
His Acts, alone, are wonderfull;
Because, his Favour *endles proveth.*
2 His Wisdome, did creat the sphceares,
(*For, to all times, his* Kindnes *lasteth*)
And, earth above the seas he rears;
Because, his Pittie *never wasteth.*
He, did the greater Lights provide;
For, through each Age, his Grace *extendeth,*
He made the Sunn, the day to guide;
Because, his Goodnes *never endeth.*
3 He fram'd the Moone & starrs, for night;
For, without bound, is his Compassion.

And,

And, *Egipts* eldeſt-borne did ſmite,
Becauſe, his grace *hath no ceſſation.*
He brought forth *Iſr'el* from their land;
(For, ſoe his endles grace *procured)*
With ſtretcht-out Arme, & powrfull hand;
Becauſe, his Mercie *ſtill endured.*
4 Hee did the Red ſea, then divide;
(For, ſtill, his Kindnes, *he retaineth)*
And, *Iſr'el* through the ſame did guide;
Becauſe, his Favour, *ſtill, remaineth.*
There, he did *Pharoh's* Army drowne;
(For, Love, *hee freely, ſtill, beſtoweth)*
And through the Deſerts brought his owne;
Becauſe, eternall Grace *he showeth.*
5 Both huge, & powrfull kings he ſlewe;
(*For, everlaſting are his* Graces)
Yea, famous kings he overthrewe;
Becauſe, his Love, *times date ſurpaſſes.*
Great *Sehon,* king of th' *Amorites,*
For, his Affection *never faileth*
And, *Og* that ruld the *Bashamites,*
Becauſe, his Mercy, *ſtill prevaileth.*
6 Their heritage beſtow'd hath he,
(For, ſo, his endles Love, *required)*
His *Iſr'el's* heritage to be;
Becauſe, his Grace *is vnexpired.*
He did exalt vs, from belowe;
(For, he to Pittie, *ſtill, enclineth)*
And, hee redeem'd vs from our foe;
Becauſe, no time his Grace *confineth.*
7 Hee to all fleſh their food hath given;
For, his great Mercy *faileth never.*
Oh glorify, the God of heav'n:
Becauſe his Grace *abideth ever.*

VVhen

VVhen wee looke back, oh Lord, vnto the beginning of thy viſible workings (pondering, the never interrupted ſucceſsion of thy Mercies, vnto this day) & therewithall obſerve the performance of all thy promiſes to thy Church *heretofore; & the continuance of thy abundant* Loving-kindnes, *to us at this preſent: VVee are aſſured that thy* Goodnes & Compaſſion *is* eternall. *VVee therfore, beſeech thee to give vs true thanckfulnes, for the ſame; that wee may confeſſe it aſwell in* deed, *as* word; *& praiſe & magnify thy* Name *for ever & ever.* Amen.

Pſa. 137.

This Elegiacal Hymne, *miſtically expreſſeth the Zeal, & love of the Faithfull, to the* Citty of God: *And Propheceis, the fall of the ſpirituall* Babilon. Wee may ſing it to comfort vs during the continuance of our Naturall bondage, & the tirranies of *Antichriſt.*

AS wee nigh *Babel* River ſate,
Wee, overcharg'd with weepings were,
To thinck on *Syon's* pore eſtate;
And hung our harpes, on willowes there:
For, they to whome wee were inthralled,
On vs, for ſongs of *Syon*, called.
2 Come ſing, they ſayd, a *Syon-hymne.*
Lord! cann wee ſing thy ſongs in thrall?
Vnles (oh dear *Ieruſalem*)
Thee, in my mirth, preferr I ſhall;
Or, if the thought of thee forgoe mee,
Let hand & tongue, prove vſeles to me.
3 Oh Lord, remember *Edom's* brood,
And, how, whilſt thy *Ieruſalem*,
Vnſackt, & vndefaced ſtood,
Her ſpoile was haſt'ned on, by them.

For,

For, loud thy cryed, race it, race it;
And, to the groundwork, downe deface it.
4 Oh daughter of proud *Babilon*,
Thou ſhalt, likewiſe, deſtroyed be;
And, he will prove a bleſſed-one,
Who ſhall avenge our Cauſe on thee:
Ev'n hee, that payes thee our diſgraces;
And, braines thy babes, in ſtony-places.

Oh Lord, *many of thy people, ſuffer the ſcornes, & inſultings, of that* Babilon *which was typified, by the* Chaldean *Citty; And the Myſticall* Edomites, *labour the vtter defacing of thy* Church. *But, deliver us oh Lord, & reward them according to their intentions againſt us. Let us take no pleaſure in any temporall thing, till wee have prevailed againſt the fury of our ſpiritual deſtroyers: & give vs grace, ſo to crush all ſinns, & hereſies, in their firſt birth; that we may be made eternally ſafe & happy, through* Ieſus Chriſt, *our Lord.* Amen.

Another of the ſame.

AS nigh *Babel* ſtreames wee ſate,
(Full of greefs, & vnbefreinded)
Minding *Syon's* pore eſtate,
From our eyes, the teares deſcended;
And, our Harps wee hanged, by,
On the willowes, growing nigh.
2 For, (inſulting on our woe)
They, that vs had there inthralled,
(Their imperious powre to ſhowe)
For a ſong of *Syon*, called.
Come yee Captives, come, ſaid they;
Sing vs now, an Hebrewe Lay.
3 But, oh Lord, what hart had wee?
In a forraigne habitation,

To

To repeat our ſongs of thee,
For our ſpoiler's recreation?
  Ah, alas! wee cannot, yet,
  Thee, *Ieruſalem*, forget.
4 Oh *Ieruſalem*! if I
Do not mourne (all pleaſure ſhunninge)
Whilſt thy walls defaced lie;
Let my right-hand, looſe his cunninge:
  And, for ever, let my tounge
  To my Pallet, faſt be Clung.
5 Oh remember, bleſſed Lord,
E're *Ieruſalem* was waſted,
How the ſonns of *Edom* roar'd;
And, her totall ruine haſted:
  Till, they levell, all had laid,
  Raſe it, raſe it quite, they ſaid.
6 But, thou ſhalt be ſpoiled thus;
And, be vſ'd (oh *Babels* daughter)
Iuſt as thou haſt vſed vs,
And, that man, who in thy ſlaughter,
  On the ſtones, thy Child'ren braines,
  Shall be bleſſed, for his paines.

Pſa. 138.

A Pſalme of David. *God is here praiſed for the truth of his* Word; *for glorifieng his* Sonn Chriſt; *for confirming his* Elect; *& for the* Common grace *vouchſafed to all, &c.* It may be ſung for any Deliverance; But, eſpecially for our Redemption.

WIth all my hart, I'le ſing abrode thy ſame,
  And praiſe thee, where the Gods aſſẽbled are;
Ev'n in thy houſe, I'le magniſy thy Name,
And, for thy Truth, & Love, thy praiſe declare:
  For, thou thy Name, & word, o're all, doſt rear.

T When

2 When I did call, thou mad'ſt replie to mee,
And, ſtrength vnto my ſoul, thou didſt afford,
All kings of earth, ſhall, therfor honour thee,
As ſoone (oh God) as they have heard thy word ;
  And, ſing thy praiſe, in thine own Paths, oh Lord.
3 For, thou art great, & thou oh Lord, art high,
Yet, haſt regard of humble men, belowe.
Thou vew'ſt the proude, but, with a ſleighting eye.
Therefore, altho through many greefs I goe,
  I certaine am, thou comforts wilt beſtowe.
4 Thy righthand Lord ; ſhall my ſalvation bee,
My foes ſeirce rage, thy ſtretcht-out hād ſhal ſtay.
Thou ſhalt performe all things concerning mee.
Thy mercies, Lord, abide the ſame, for aye ;
  Reiect not then, thy handy-work, I pray.

Oh Lord our Creator, *thou cauſleſly reiecteſt none whome thou haſt made; neither art thou ſuch an accepter of Perſōs, as, too many fancie thee bee: But impartially accepteſt in every Perſon that which is the Obiect of thy eternall Election*; *&* (*where ſoever thou findeſt the ſame*) *loveſt that, vnto the end. Therefore, thou extendeſt thy Truth and Mercy to all*; *vouchſafing, alſo, thy Aſsiſting powre, to perfect that work which thy* free-grace *hath begunn*; *yea & thou effectually perfecteſt that worke, in ſoe many as do humbly ſubmit them ſelves to thy will, & reſiſt not proudly the motions of thy ſpirit: And* (*though they paſſe through many temptations & hazards*) *thy hand ſtill reacheth vnto thē comforts, & meanes of ſafe perſeverance vnto the end. Oh give us wiſdome to perceave, & grace humbly to acknowledge this great* Mercie (*which who ſoever denies*; *Denies thy greateſt glory*) *& make thou, our endeavours anſwereable to the grace & powre which wee have receaved through* Ieſus Chriſt, *our Lord.* Amen.

Pſa. 139.

Pſa. 139.

To the cheef Muſitian a Pſalme of David. *It confeſſeth, the all-ſeeing providence, powre, wiſdome, and Mercy of God; And expreſſeth a deſire of the* Faithfull, *to be ſerched, & rectified, by him, &c.* It warnes vs, not to live Hypocriticallie; in regard, God beholds vs, at all times, & in all places &c.

OH Lord, thy all-beholdinge eies,
Have ſerch'd, & well obſerved mee.
Thou, ſee'ſt me ſitt, thou ſee'ſt mee riſe;
Thou, know'ſt my thoughts e're thought they be.
Thou, vew'ſt my wayes & walkings Lord;
Thou ſee'ſt what in my bedd I doe;
And, I do never ſpeak a word,
But, lo, thyne ears do hear it to.
2 Thou ſtandſt before me, & behinde;
Thy hand, on mee, doth alwaies lie:
Thy wiſdome cannot be confinde,
And, for my reach it is too high.
Then, from thy ſpirit, & from thee,
Oh whither cann I fly, or goe?
If heav'n I clime, thou there wilt be;
If hell I dive, there art thou to.
3 If on the Mornings wings I ride,
And, thinck to fly beyond the ſeas;
Thy hand, ev'n there, cann be my guide,
They right-hand, there, on mee cann ceaze.
Or, if I ſay, the Duſkie night
Shall hide mee; Night ſhall me bewray;
For, darknes, is to thee as light;
The day like night, the night like day.
4 My Reines, to thee apparant are;
For, in the wombe, thou cloſedſt mee:

T 2 I, ſtran-

I, ſtrangely was compoſed there,
And, therefore, I will honour thee.
Thy wondrous works, my ſoul doth knowe;
And, that my ſubſtance thou didſt marke,
Ev'n when (as in the earth belowe)
 I was compoſed in the darke.
5 Before I perfect Beeing, tooke,
Or, Forme, or Matter, for this frame;
My Members all, were in thy booke,
And, thou foreſaw'ſt what now I am.
Therefore, thy thoughts of vs; how dear!
And, Lord, how infinite they bee!
As num'rous as the Sands they are;
 And, wake mee, ſtill to muze on thee.
6 Vngodly men, & men of blood,
Deſtroy, & cauſe them to be gone;
For, they ſpeak ill of thee, oh God,
And, vainely proude, thy foes are growne.
Thy haters, I have hated, Lord,
And, greev'd at ſuch as thee oppoſe;
With perfect hate, I them abhord,
 And, thoſe accounted as my foes.
7 Oh God! a ſtrict enquiry make;
My hart, & ev'ry thought ſurvay:
Search, if an evill Courſe I take;
 And, ſhowe mee thy eternall way.

There is nothing, oh Lord, in the ſtructure of our bodies or in the diſpoſition of our mindes, but it is knowne to thee, with every Cauſe & effect thereof. Neither darknes nor diſtance of place cann ſo hide us from thee, but, that, thou ſeeſt our Actions, heareſt our words, & perceaveſt our thoughtes; Yea, & what they are enclinable vnto, before wee thinck them. Give us grace therefor, to behave our ſelves, alwaies, as in thy ſight. Let our ſecret intentions be vpright,

vpright; & cauſe us to love and hate, as thou doſt. Purge away all that which is evill in us; & infuſe into our harts all those graces, which may make us acceptable to thee in Chriſt Ieſus. Amen.

Pſa. 140.

To the cheef Muſitian a Pſalme of David. *It perſonates* Chriſt's *myſticall body, deſiring deliverance, from Oppreſſors; And deſcribing their malice, pride, & Trechery &c.* It is vſefull, when any *Congregation* is greeved by the bitter ſcandalls, lieng doctrines, or miſcheevous inſinuations, of Atheiſts, & falſe brethren &c.

LEt me, oh God, from ſinners be defended.
From thoſe that are to violence inclined:
For, in their harts, they miſcheef have intended,
And in malitious Leagues, are faſt combined.
Their ſtinging tōgs the vipers teeth have matched
Between their lipps, is Adders poyſon hatched.
2 Lord, frō the hands of wicked men releaſe mee;
From Cruel-men, vouchaſe ſecure to make me:
For, to ſupplant my goengs, they oppreſſe me;
And lo, the proud prepareth ſnares to take mee.
Yea, they have netts, & ginns, & trapps prepared.
In al my waies that I might be inſnared.
3 Lord, hear I pray, & mark my ſupplication;
Thee, for my God, oh Lord, I have profeſſed:
And, thou (Lord God, the ſtrength of my Salvation)
Did'ſt gard mee, when in Fight I was oppreſſed.
Oh, grant not, what the wicked man deſireth,
But, croſſe his plotts, leſt hee too high aſpireth.
4 The Miſcheef of their lipps will fal vpon them
Ev'n on their heads, that mee have circumvented.
Coales burning-hot; ſhall downe be hurled on thē.
They ſhal with flames, in dung'ons be tormented;

And, in thoſe Pitts infernall, be detained,
From whence, Redemption never cann be gained.
5 On earth, hee ſhall not thrive, that's evill tõgued,
For, wicked men, Reveng, to death perſueth.
But, God (I knowe) doth patronize the wronged
And, in the pore man's cauſe, his judgmet ſheweth.
For which, the juſt, within his preſence living,
Shall glorify his name with praiſes-giving.

Deliver us, oh Mercifull God, *from the cruel purpoſes, ſtinging ſlanders, & miſcheevous practiſes of our wicked & proud Adverſaries, who ſeek the ruine of our ſoules. Arme us againſt them, as hither to thou haſt bene pleaſed: Fruſtrate their deviſes; bring on them, their owne wickednes; & inflict on them that vengance which is prepared for impenitent Perſecutors: That wee being ſaved by thee, thou mayſt be glorified by us, for ever & ever.* Amen.

Pſa. 141.

A Pſalme of David. *It perſonates* Chriſt, (*the lifting vp of whoſe hands on the Croſſe, is accepted, inſtead of the legall ſacrifice) prayeng in the behalfe of his Members.* And it is vſefull for vs, to deſire God's acceptation of our Prayers; to give us the Goverment of our tongues, & to rectify our thoughts &c.

LOrd, hear with ſpeed my voices lamentation;
Vouchſafe to give my mournfull clamors hea-
As incenſe, or an Afternoones Oblation, (ring.
Accept my Prayers, & my hands vprearing.
Lord, let my mouth, as with a watch, be warded;
And, let the Portalls of my lipps be garded.
2 Leſt I to ſinn, with ſinners, may be trained,
Preſerve my hart, oh Lord, from ſinns infection
Who, rather then, their pleaſures to have gained,
Deſire in Love, the righteous man's correction.

As

As curing balme, the fame fhould be received ;
And, I would pray for thē, whē they were greeved.
3 Whē frō the Roks, their judges down are heved,
The reft wil hear : for, I fweet words have fpoken :
As on the Land, where blocks are hew'd & cleaved
Our bones before the Grave, lie ftrow'd, & brokē.
Yet, ftill, mine eye on thee oh Lord attendeth,
And, ftill, my foul on thee alone, dependeth.
4 Then, fuffer not my foul to be reiected.
And, (that I be not by their wiles enfnared)
Let me from thofe clofe engines be directed,
Which for my foul, the wicked have prepared. (thē,
Let their own fnares, which they have layd, intrap
And, let me, Lord, for evermore, efcape them.

Accept oh Lord, our petitions, in the mediation of Chrift Iefus. *Make us watchfull over our tongues, & fo purify our harts from all evil affections; that the pleafant baites of the wicked alure vs not to be partners in their finns. To that end, teach us to bear patiently, & accept thanckfully, the reproofs & Corrections of thy Children; yea, let us pray for them, who shall charitably reforme us. And, though by perfecution wee should be fcattred like bones among graves, (or chipps vpon the face of the earth) yet, let us alway truft in thee; & at laft be gathered vp, revive, & be made bleffed everlaftingly, through* Iefus Chrift. Amen.

Pfa. 142.

Mafchil of David, when he was in the Cave. *It feemeth miftically to perfonate* Iefus Chrift, *expreffing the agony of his foul in the Garden; Or his being forfaken at his Paffion.* It may be fung when wee are left comfortles of the world.

MY voice to thee, Oh God, I reare,
To thee, oh Lord, I fue ;

T 4 To

To thee, my troubles, I declare,
My greefs, to thee I shew.
For, when o're whelm'd my spirit was,
My Path was knowne to thee:
Ev'n when they hidd, where I should passe,
A seacret snare for mee.
2 I looked on my right-hand side,
But, noe man knew mee there.
All succours faild; not one I spide,
That of my soul had care.
Then, Lord, thou art my hope said I,
My Lot, whilst life I have.
In my destresse, observe my crye;
From spoile, thy servant save.
3 Yea, since for mee they are too strong,
To praise thee, sett mee free:
So, righteous men to mee shall throng,
When thy great Love, they see.

Sweet Iesu, *in thy bitter Agony, thou hadst not any one (no not among thyne owne desciples) so sensible thereof, as* to watch with thee one howre. *A secret snare was layd for thee in that* Garden, *whither thou went'st to pray for consolation; And, when they ledd thee to thy* Passion; *None would knowe thee; None assist thee; Neither had any one, care of thy soul.* *Oh* Dearest Redeemer, *this, is often the Case of us thy* Members *in some Degree; And, when our Spirits are most overwhelmed with sorrowes, it so happens; That no man pitties it; No eye beholds it, but thyne. For, thy Passion sake, do thou behold us with commiseration in these extremities, that wee may be comforted; & that wee & others, may magnify thy great mercie, for ever & ever.* Amen.

Psa. 143.

A Psalme of David. *It expresseth with much fervencie,*

venie, many conflicts of the spirit; imploreth God's free Mercy; in regard of our vniversall impurity, of the malice of our foes, & disability of our nature &c. The vse is manifest.

LOrd, my humble supplication,
Heed, & heare with acceptation,
In thy Doomes, of Truth & Right.
Iudge, but judge thou not severely;
For, if thou observe vs nearly,
None are blameles in thy sight.
2 By the foe, my soul is chased,
Wounded, & in darknes placed,
As one buried, long agoe.
I, am inwardly, perplexed,
Yea, my spirit sore is vexed;
And, my hart is full of woe,
3 On the times, now past, I ponder,
And, on all the works of wonder,
Which were framed by thy hands.
Thee, I seek, with due submission;
And, my soul, for thy fruition
Longeth, as the thirstie Lands. *Selah.*
4 Lord, with speed, give ear vnto me,
And, thy face divart not fro me;
For, my spirits, feeble growe.
Since, on thee I have depended,
Let mee timely be defended,
Lest, into the grave I goe.
5 Guide my feet by thy direction,
For, thou hast my hart's affection.
Me from all my foes release.
Lord my God (my safe abidinge)
Bring mee, by thy spirits guiding,
To the Land of Righteousnes

6 Grace, to do thy pleaſure give mee :
For, thy Nameſake, Lord, revive me ;
  Let thy Iuſtice be my gard.
Yea, deſtroy (of thy compaſſion)
Thoſe that ſeek my ſoules vexation :
  For, I am thy ſervant Lord.

Oh Lord God ; *if thou shouldſt iudg us according to our deſervings, wee & all fleſh, should everlaſtingly periſh. VVee appeal therefore, to thy Mercie ; &, with a thirſty longing, deſire ſpeedy aſsiſtance, according to thy accuſtomed* Loving-kindnes ; *leſt wee be ſwallowed vp by Deſpaire, or devoured by our foes. For thine* owne ſake *(even for thy* Iuſtice, *for thy* Mercy, *& for thy* Name ſake*) direct us in thy waies ; Inſtruct us in thy VVill ; protect us from all evills ; & bring vs into the* Land of the Living, *through* Ieſus Chriſt *our Lord.* Amen.

Another of the ſame.

LOrd, mark my ſuite ; my ſad complaining hear ;
And, in thy Truth & Juſtice, anſwear give.
Iudg not thy ſervant, with a doome ſevere,
For, in thy ſight, not one doth blameles live.
The foe hath chas'd my ſoul, of life nigh reſt mee.
And in the dark, as one long dead hath left mee.
2 In mee, therfore, my ſpirits downe are caſt ;
My hart is fill'd with many a heavie thought :
I muſe vpon the dayes, that now are paſt,
And on thy works, (ev'n al thy hãds have wrought)
With ſtretchtout hands, & with ſoul-thirſty pãting
I thirſt for thee, as Land, when raine is wanting.
3 My ſpirit faints (oh God) with ſpeed give ear,
If longer, thou thy face obſcure, I dye.
Oh let thy Love to mee betimes appear ;
For, I on thee ; on thee alone, relye.
Yea, let me Lord, within thy Paths be trained ;

For,

For, vnto thee, I lift a ſoul vnfained.
4 Protect mee, Lord; in thee is my abode:
Keep off my foes, & teach thy will to mee.
Let thy good ſp'rite, (becauſe thou art my God)
My guide vnto the Land of Iuſtice be.
Yea, mee, oh Lord, for thy Nameſake, revive thou,
My ſoul, ev'n for thy Iuſtice ſake, reprive thou,
And, of thy grace, all thoſe that mee oppreſſed,
Deſtroy thou Lord, for, I am thine profeſſed.

Pſa. 144.

A Pſalme of David. *It bleſſeth God, for his regard of the humane Nature; Deſires* Chriſt's *approch to Iudgment; And requeſteth to be delivered from worldlings &c.* It is vſefull to theſe purpoſes, & to inform vs, that to be God's choſē-ones, is the greateſt happines &c.

OH praiſe the Lord, for, he is all my Powre,
My hands & Armes, in warlike feats directing;
My grace, my gard, my ſheild, my healp, my Towre,
My truſty freind, my foes to me ſubiecting.
Lord, what is mā that thou art pleaſd to know him?
Or what his *child* that thou ſholdſt ſavor ſhow him?
2 Mā is as nought, his ioys like ſhades forſake him.
The heavn's, oh Lord, decline, & down deſcēd thou
But touch, the Hils, & thou to ſmoke, ſhalt mak thē;
To ſcatter them, thy dreadfull lighting, ſend thou:
Shoot out thy ſhafts, vntill they be deſtroyed;
Let thy ſtrong hand, to healp mee, be employed.
3 Oh ſave mee, from the water's over-ſwelling;
Let mee from forraigne Children be ſecured,
Whoſe mouthes, are alwaies lies & folly, telling,
And, whoſe righthands, to falſhood, are envred.
Then, to thy praiſe, new ſongs, I will be ſinging,

On

On harp, & Psalt'ry of a tennfold stringing.
4 Let him, who doth on kings bestow salvation,
(And, from the sword, his servant *David* saveth)
Protect me frō that sorraine generation, (ceaveth
Whose mouth speakes lies, & whose right-hand de-
Who beg for sonns & daughters, in their prayer,
Like plants & pretious stones, welshap'd, & faire.
5 Who pray for Granards, fully stored ever,
Whos floks yong breed, evn in their streets aboun-
Whose wellsed Oxe, in labour, faileth never ; (deth :
&, in whose Townes, nor cry, nor tumult soundeth,
For, tho such men a blessing have possessed ; (sed.
Yet, they whose *God's* the *Lord*, are much more bles-

Father of Mercy & God of all Consolation; thou art alwaies, our powrefull deliverer, & becommest every thing vnto vs, which our harts cann desire. Oh, make vs thanckfull vnto thee, for thy great regard of soe vnworthy Creatures: And, though meer worldlings, *& Carnall* Professors, *seeke thee for temporall Blessings; Let vs, love, serve, & praise thee, meerly for thine owne sake. Keep vs from their falshood, Hypocrisie, & selfelove, with all their otherwicked conditions; And, though they boast of thy transitorie Blessings, which wee enioy not: Let us be contented that thou art our God. Let that be our portion of happines, & let vs enioye it, (oh Lord) for ever & ever.* Amen.

Psa. 145.

Davids Psalme of Praise. *It may be vsed as a Patterne wherby to glorify God, according to his principal Attributes, such, as his* Infinitenes, Omnipotencie, Majesty, Justice, Mercie, Goodnes, Providence &c. *VVhich are mentioned in this Psalme.*

I'Le honour thee oh God my king,
And, laud thy Name for aye :

Ev'n

Ev'n to thy Name, I'le alway ſing,
  And praiſe thee ev'ry day.
For, thou art great, beyond all bounds,
  And, great, thy praiſes are:
Through Ages all, thy glory ſounds,
  Thy wonders they declare.
2 I'le, alſo, ſhew thy royall ſtate,
  And thy rare works vnfolde;
That men thy wonders may relate,
  When I thy powre have tolde:
That, they thy Righteouſnes may ſhow,
  And, much, thy glorie minde;
For, thou to anger, Lord, art ſlowe,
  Right gratious, meek, & kinde.
3 Thy goodnes, & thy mercies, be
  In all thy workes expreſt;
Ev'n all thy works, Lord, honour thee,
  And, thee, thy Saints have bleſt.
Thy kingdomes glory they will ſhowe,
  And, ſing thy greatnes forth;
That, all mankinde thy powre may knowe,
  And, ſee thy Kingdomes worth.
4 For, thou for evermore ſhalt raigne,
  And, rule through Ages all.
The weak, oh Lord, thou wilt ſuſtaine
  And, lift vp thoſe, that fall.
On God, all creatures fixe their eyes,
  And, fedd, in ſeaſon be;
For, all things living to ſuffice,
  An open hand hath hee.
5 The Lord is juſt in all his waies;
  His works, are ſacred all.
Nigh them who call on him, he ſtaies;
  Nigh thoſe, who truly call.

Their

Their hopes, who fear him, he effects;
Ands, hears, & faves all thofe:
Ev'n thofe who love him, God protects;
But, finners overthrowes.
6 Oh let my mouth due praife, therefore,
Vnto the Lord expreffe;
And, let all flefh, for evermore,
His holy Name confeffe.

Great oh Lord, is thy Kingdome, thy Powre & thy glory, great are thy VVorks, thy VVonders & thy Praifes: Great alfo, is thy VVifdome, thy Goodnes, thy Iuftice, & thy Mercy: Yea, fo infinite art thou in thefe, & all other excellencies; That no attributes, are fufficient to expreffe thee. Neverthelcs, wee thy Creatures, being partakers of thy Abundance, & witneffes of thy Bounty, towards all whome thou haft made; Do (according to the meafure of our Capacities) bleffe thee for the fame: And defire, to praife and magnify thy Name, *for ever & ever.* Amen.

Another of the fame.

ADvance I will, thy Name, oh God my king;
For evermore, I will extoll the fame.
Bleffe thee, I will, oh Lord, & alway fing,
A daylie fong of praifes, to thy Name.
Confid'ring, that thy, Greatneffe, bound hath none
(And, how thine honor fhould as boundles be)
Declare I will, thofe wonders thou haft done;
That, men from age to age, may fpeak of thee.
Ev'n of thy Fame, & glories, I will treat,
And, fhewe how rare, thy wondrous workings (are:
For, when thy dreadfull Acts I fhall repeat,
Then, other men their largnes will declare.
Great fpeach, of thy great goodnes, they fhal make,
And, (finging of thy Iuftice) they fhalt fhowe,

How

How apt thou art, compaffion ftill to take ;
How prone to pitty ; &, to wrath, how flowe,
In doeng good ; to all, thou Lord, art free.
Thy Mercies are, vpon thy Creatures all.
Kept glorious, by thy deeds, thy praifes bee
And, therfor, all thy Saints, confeffe thee fhall.
Lord, of thy kingdome's glorie, they fhall tell,
And (fhewing ev'ry where, what powre, thou haft)
Make knowne how much thy mighty Acts excell ;
And, with what ftate, thy royall Throne is plac't.
Not as a king that's only temporall ;
For, endles & eternall, is thy throne.
On thee, who e're depends, though he fhould fall,
Thou, Lord, wilt lift him vp, when he is down.
Plac't are on thee, all creatures eyes, oh God !
And, thou doft give them food, in feafon, ftill.
Quite open, thou doft reach thy hand abrode,
Each living Creatures longing, to fulfill.
Right juft, thou art, oh Lord, in all thy wayes ;
And (as in all thy works thou holy art)
So, thou art near to ev'ry one that praies ;
To all, that feek to thee, with honeft hart.
To thē, that fear thy Name, their wifh thou giv'ft ;
And, fuch as call vpon thee, thou wilt fave.
Vngodly men, of fafety thou depriv'ft
But, all thy Lovers, thy protection have.
Wherefore, oh Lord to publifh out thy fame,
In praifefull wife, my mouth fhall ftill endeaver
Yea, & all flefh, fhall bleffe thy holy Name,
And praife the fame, for ever, & for ever.

Oh Lord thy fpirit hath faid, thou art good to all, *& that* thy Mercy is over all thy Works. *Stop the mouthes therfore of all thofe perverters of thy Truth (and blafpheamers of thy moft glorious* Attribute) *who dare af-firme,*

firme, that thou haſt eternally Dereed, *purpoſſely* Created, *& irrevocably* neceſſitated, *that the greateſt number of ſoules, should be veſſells of wrath & condemnation, without any reſpect vnto Sinn; Good God, let this damnable blaſphemy, ſpread no further. Give all men grace to perceave, that they who pretend to honour thee by this doctrine, do (conſequently & vnavoydably) impute vnto thy ſacred* Majeſtie, *all the wickednes both of men, & Devills; contrary to all piety, contrarie to thy expreſſe* Word (*which is perverted to maintaine this hereſy*) *& contrarie to that which naturall Reaſon, hath written in our harts. Lord, theſe are they, which have made thouſands hide their Talent, by ſayeng, that* thou expecteſt to reap where thou ſowedſt not: *& they have ſoe corrupted their owne iudgments (& moſt of their hearers) that there is no meanes to prevent this, peſtilence of the ſoul but by prayer. Vnto thee, therfor wee pray. Oh hear us; even for thine owne honor ſake, & for thy* Mercie *ſake, in* Ieſus Chriſt *our Lord* Amen.

Pſa. 146.

Halelujah. *It ſtirreth vp the ſoul to perpetuall thankſgiving, & to depēdance vpon God alone; giving reaſons for the ſame &c.* Wee may ſing it to minde vs of thoſe duties.

MY ſoul, praiſe thou the Lord;
(As long as thou haſt breath)
In ſong his praiſe record,
And, honour him till death.
No credit place
In earthlie kings, or ſuch vaine things
As humane race.
2 Breath failes, & duſt they be;
One day, their pompe deſtroies:
Right bleſt therefore, is hee

That

That *Iacob's* God enioyes;
And hopes in him,
Who framed these, heav'n earth, & seas,
And all in them.
3 For, God is Faithfull, still,
Men wrong'd, assist will hee,
The hungry he doth fill,
And, setts the pris'ner free.
He, Sight bestowes,
Loves men vpright, & maketh streight
What crooked growes.
4 The stranger he receives,
To Orphanes, help imparts:
The widdowe he releives,
And Sinners paths subvarts.
The Lord, therefore,
Oh *Syon*, shall be king of all
For evermore. *Haleluiah.*

Almightie God, Creator of heav'n & earth, & the sure healper of all who trust in thee; pitty our oppressions; satisfy our spirituall hunger; free vs from the bondage of sinn; cure the blindnes of our Vnderstandings, & be mercifull to vs in all the rest of our necessities & infirmities. Grant, also, that (renouncinge all other Confidence, & depending only, on thy favour) wee may praise thee, for these, & all thy Mercies, in Christ Iesus. Amen.

Psalme 147.

It exhorts to praise God, for encreasing & building his Church, *typyfied by* Ierusalem; *for many particuler mercies to his people, & for overthrowing the proud &c.* The vse is apparant.

OH glorify the Lord;
For, of God's praise to sing,

V With

With juftice doth accord :
Yea, 'tis a pleafant thing.
Ierufalem,
Hee will erect, and recollect
His Flock to him.
2 The Contrite hart, hee heales,
Hee cures their bruifes, all.
The Starrs, he, alfo, tells ;
And, them by Name cann call.
This Lord of our,
In wife forefight, is infinite,
And great in powre.
3 The Lord, the Meek doth raife,
The proud, he brings to ground.
Oh therfor, fing his praife,
Let Harps, his praife refound.
He, Clouds doth bring,
And, fhewres diftills, which on the hills,
Makes graffe to fpring.
4 Ev'n Beafts, & Ravens yonge,
He feedeth when they call :
In horfe, or footmen ftrong,
He ioyeth nought at all :
God loves all them ;
Who in his grace, their hopes doe place,
And honor him.
5 *Syon*, & *Salem*, bleffe
The Lord your God, (in fong)
Who doth your feed encreafe,
And, hath your Gates made ftrong.
His Peace hath, yet,
Your bounds vphild ; &, you he fild,
With flowre of wheat.
6 Through earth, his Mandates goe,

His

His word, with ſwiſtnes flies,
Like wooll, he giveth ſnowe;
His froſt; like Aſhes lies:
And, then (beſide)
He forth doth ſlice, cold flakes of Ice,
Which who cann bide?
7 He ſpeakes, & ſtreight it thawes:
He breaths, & water flowes.
His, Statutes, & his Lawes,
He, to his people ſhowes:
No nation els,
His Iudgments know, & therſore, ſoe
With none he deals. *Haleluiah.*

Moſt mercifull God, who buildeſt vp thy heavenly Ieruſalem, *by the gathering together of all the Faithfull; Not only taking notiſe of them, who have ſtarr-like perfections; but even of vs alſo, whoe are of thoſe* Blind *and* Lame, *whome thou haſt cauſed to be called to thy banquet: Nay; though wee are as brute Beaſts, or vncleane Birds, thou art ready to extend thy Mercy, whenſoever wee ſeek thee. Oh make vs thanckfull for thy great Bounty. Send out thy word to compell us by* Stormes, *or to allure by* Calmes, *accordingas it shal findevs diſpoſed: & let the graces of thy* Spirit, *ſo thawe our congealed harts, that the teares of true penitence may flow from vs, & produce all ſuch other effects, as may cauſe vs to know thy Iudgments; & to be of thoſe people, whome thou loveſt in* Ieſus Chriſt. *Amen.*

Pſa. 148.

Halelujah. *All Creatures are here, in a* Poetical *manner exhorted to glorify their* Creator. Wee ſhould vſe it to remember vs, that God requireth all his Creatures (*& vs eſpecially*) to praiſe him according to their natures.

THe Lord of heav'n, confesse;
On high, his glories raise:
Him, let all Angells blesse;
And, all his Armies praise.
Him, glorifie
Sunn, moone & starrs; yee higher Spheares,
And, Cloudie skie.
2 From God, your Beeings are;
Him, therefore, famous make:
You, all, Created were
When he the word, but, spake.
And, from that place,
Where fixt you be by his Decree,
You cannot passe.
3 Praise God, from Earth belowe,
Yee Dragons, & yee Deeps;
Fire, haile, Clouds, winde, & snowe,
Whome, in Command, he keeps.
Praise yee his Name
Hills, great & small; Trees, low & tall;
Beasts, wilde & tame.
4 All things, that creep or flye,
Yee Kings, yee vulger Throng,
All Princes, meane or hye,
Both men, & Virgines yonge:
Ev'n yong & old,
Exalt his Name; For, much his fame,
Should be extold.
5 Oh let God's Name be praisd
Above both earth & skye:
For, he his Saints hath raisd,
And, sett their horne on hye:
Yea, they that are
Of *Isr'els* race, are in his grace

And

And, ever dear. *Haleluiah.*

Almightie God *(worthie to be praiſed of all Creatures both in heaven & earth) vouchſafe, that thy whole* Creation, *may ioyne in aſcribing to thee, that glorie for which it was ordained: And let vs (whome thou haſt exalted above the reſt of thy workmanship) advance the higheſt Trophies to thy glorie. At leſt, grant this, that, wee who have dishonored thee in all thy Creatures, may ſome way (& in ſome degree) magnify thee, alſo, in every thing which thou haſt made: That ſo, wee may be, yet, more exalted; & continue to be of thoſe people whome thou haſt elected, & loveſt eternally, in* Chriſt Ieſus. Amen.

Pſa. 149.

Halelujah. *This* Pſalme *exhorts to praiſe God, in the* New ſongs *of the* Goſpell; *& declares the powre, which shall be given thereby both to convince the Conſciences of heathen* Idolators; *& to chaine vp our imperious* Affections *&c.* Wee ſhould vſe it, to provoke vs to praiſe God, for the many priveledges, given vnto his Saints. &c.

IN ſongs-newe made, your voice employ,
God's praiſe among his Saints to ſing:
Let *Iſr'el* in his maker ioye,
And, *Syon* tryvmph in her king.
The praiſes of his Name, advance;
With Harpe & Tymbrell, in the dance.
2 The Lord, his people doth reſpect;
And, with his healp, the meek arayes.
Then, let the Saints his praiſe affect,
And, on their bedds, gladd Voices raiſe.
Let in their mouths, his praiſe remaine;
And, two-edg'd blades, their hands retaine.
3 Vpon the heathen people, then,

V 3 They

They fhall inflict avenging paines,
And, binde their kings, & noblemen,
In yron Fetters, & in Chaines.
For, to fulfill the written doome;
The *Saints*, thus honor'd fhall become. *Haleluiah.*

Grant Almighty God, *that wee may fing vnto thy* Glorie, *the* New-fongs *of the* Gofpell, *to the* tenn-ftringed Inftrument *of thy* Lawe; *& by thy grace, attaine that meeknes; & that holines which becommeth fuch, as are thy* Saints, *by their* Vifible Callinge. *Replenish our harts with ioyes of the* holy ghoft; *fill our mouthes with fongs of thy* praife; *Strengthē our handes to execute* Iuftice *without partialitie; give vs powre to chaine vp thofe heathenish* Affections, *& thofe noble-feeming* Paffions, *which had the* Soveraigntie *over vs heretofore; & fo enable vs to fullfill all Righteoufnes which thou haft commanded in thy word: that, wee may enioy all the Priveledges, & honours, pertaining to thy* Saints, *in* Chrift Iefus Amen.

Pfa. 150.

Halelujah. *It exhorts all Creatures to praife God, & shewes in what manner wee fhould praife him; mistically expreffing the fame by Inftruments of Mufick.* Wee fhould vfe it, to ftirr vs vp to glorify God, with every facultie which he hath beftowed on vs.

COme praife the Lord, come praife him,
With in his holy-feat:
In all his glories, praife him,
And his great Acts repeat.
As he excelleth, praife him,
With Trumpet, and with Flute;
With Harp & Pfaltry, praife him,
With Viol, & with Lute.
2 Vpon the Tymbrel praife him,
In Song, his praife advance:

Vpon

Vpon the Organs praiſe him,
  And, praiſe him in the Dance.
On tingling Cimballs praiſe him,
  On Cymballs loud that ſound ;
And, let all Creatures praiſe him,
  In whome, life-breath is found. *Haleluiah.*

Oh bleſſed God; thou beſtoweſt all things neceſſary, & requireſt nothing backagaine, but thanckfulnes. Grant therfor, wee pray thee, that our ſoul, & every faculty thereof; our body & every member of the ſame; our ſighs, our teares, our grones, our ioyes, our paines, our proſperities, our Adverſities, our Virtues which wee have by thy grace; our very ſinns (which wee have committed by our owne corruption) our lives; our deaths, our ſalvations; the condemnations of the vnrepentant (& all other things which in vs, & in thy whole Creation, have either Beinge, *or poſſibility to* bee, *or to be thought vpon; may altogether (& ſeverally) both in their Diſcordes & Agreemēts; make vp a pleaſant harmony, to the glorifieng of thy Maieſty, for ever & ever* Amen.

FINIS.

A concluding HYMNE.

YEt, *among thoſe many Creatures,*
  Which for living-breath *are debters,*
  (Though vnworthy) I am one.
But, not many weekes are paſſed,
Since, the Blaſt *that's now poſſeſſed,*
  Was in danger to be gone.
2 They, *that prayd for my Salvation,*
(Far beyond their expectation)
  My deſired preſence have:
And, I ſing, among Livinge,

V 4 Songs

Songs of Thancks, *&* praiſes-givinge,
VVhome they look'd for, in my Grave.
3 *Hee,* (oh Freinds) *for whome yee mourned,*
From thee Pitt, *is back returned:*
Ioie, with him, in God, *therefore.*
Hee (my Foes) *whome you oppreſſed,*
Lives; *& praies you may be bleſſed:*
VVish him evill, now, no more.
4 *Come*; *imagine, I were lieng*
In my Grave; *& let envieng,*
(Spight, & evill Cenſures) goe:
VVee shall all (e're long) *come thither*;
And, be quiet, there, togither:
Let us, whil'ſt wee live, *be ſoe.*
5 *Or, though* God *hath ſo permitted,*
That wee muſt, for him, be fitted,
By each others wounding blowes:
Naitheles, his praiſe, *endeavour*;
And, Aſſent in what ſoever,
(Any way) his glorie *showes.*
6 *VVhen I ſawe* life's *Taper waſting,*
(And, my end by ſicknes haſting)
Many things, to minde it brought:
And, among my Meditations
Muſings, *&* Expoſtulations,
Theſe, were often in my thought.
7 Lord, *are all thoſe hopes bereaved,*
VVhich I formerly conceaved,
That I should have here enioy'd?
Shall, as well my good intentions,
As my vaine *&* fond Inventions,
Now, be fruſtrate, & deſtroi'd?
8 *I haved looked, everie Morrowe,*
For an ending of may ſorrowe.

And,

And, once thought, an end I had.
But, perceaving newe Afflictions
God, (ſayd I) *whoe gives* Corrections,
May, yet, one day make mee glad.
2 *He hath ſeene ſuch* Follies *in mee,*
That his Mercies *cannot winn mee;*
Therefor, he his Rodd *extends:*
But, when that hath purer made me,
Peradventure he will glad mee,
And, declare that wee are freinds.
10 *Thus, from tyme to tyme, I eaſed*
My nigh fainting hart, & pleaſed
My Deſires, *which did rebell:*
And I ſtrongly, Lord, beleived
I, ſome Good *should have received;*
Till this deadlie Arrow *fell.*
11 *But, I finde, my great* Corruption
Hath bene ſuch an Interruption
To my Earthlie hopes *in mee;*
That, ther's now no expectation
Save, the hope of that Salvation
VVhich my Soul *in heav'n shall ſee.*
12 *VVhen my* Sicknes *mee tormented*
Thus I muſ'd; & was contented,
In my Soul, *it should be thus.*
And, I praiſed God in Spirit,
For the lot shee should inherit;
But, ther's Fleſh & bloud *in vs.*
13 *Twas enough this* Grace *was showne me:*
But, my Fleſhlie-part, *was on me,*
VVhich was loth, her works to loſe.
I, (Said shee) *have watch'd, & cared,*
Holy Hymns *to have prepared:*
VVhat shall now become of thoſe?

14 A

14 *All my* Youth *I have consumed,*
(VVhere as els, it is presumed:
VVealth or ease, I might have wonn)
Pyous Laies *to have composed,*
To restraine men ill-disposed,
From those Paths *in which they runn.*
15 *Had I* Honour *sought, or* Treasure ;
I had witt in equall Measure,
To the most that walk those waies :
But, another Path I prized,
VVherein, Death *hath mee surprised*
Iust at Noonetide *of my daies.*
16 *And I see, & see it plainely,*
That I spent my time as vainely
As the most whome I condemn'd:
They, had Fruits *of their* Endeavor ;
Mine, *to me, is lost for ever ;*
And, of others, is contemn'd.
17 *Many things that I intended,*
Are begunn, & almost ended ;
VVherein, I my paines have lost.
VVhat, on David's Hymns *I mused,*
Lies vnperfect, vnpervsed ;
And, (of all) that, greeves me most.
18 *Suchlike* Thinckings, *partly holie,*
(Guilt with Good, *& mixt with* Follie*)*
Did possesse my wasting braine.
God, had promis'd Isack *to mee,*
(And, the Blessing he did show me)
Yet, of Ism'el *I was faine.*
19 *On the* Handmaid *of Perfection*
(By her Mistresse's *direction)*
I begot the Birth *you see ;*
And, when Life *was halfe expired,*

In

In my hart, I much desired,
That the Fruite *might spared be.*
20 *which, behold, my* God *hath granted;*
And, some hopes I have not wanted
That I shall precave the Same
Glad my hart, (that hath bene sory)
And, be sung vnto the glory,
And the honor of his Name.
21 *Be it so, as* God *hath willed:*
Though this hope, be not fulfilled,
I have Hopes *that shall remaine.*
Nay; those Hopings *which have failed*
Are not lost: but, much prevailed
My cheef Longings, *to attaine.*
22 *For which* Grace, *Almighty maker,*
And, for that I am partaker
Of the Common-life, *this day;*
I do offer, as Oblations,
These my harty Meditations:
Them, & mee, *accept I pray.*
23 *All my former sinns forgivinge,*
Grant, that (since among the living,
I obtaine a second Breath)
I, in manners, & Affection,
May beginn that Resurrection,
VVhich prevents the Second-death.
24 *Here, let these my* Meditations
Yeald mee, still, sweet Consolations,
VVhilst thy Grace *this life prolongs.*
And, at last, advance me thither,
VVhere all Blessed Saints, *togither,*
Sing to thee, eternall Songs. Amen.

A Table

A Table directing to what Tunes, heretofore in vse; every Psalme in this Translation, may be sung.

TO *the* Tune *of the first* Psalme *in the olde* Translation *& to* 30. *other Tunes there vsed, sing these*; 3. 4. 5. 7. 10. 11. 13. 15. 18. 22. 23. 24. 26. 29. 31. 35. 37. 42. 43. 44. 46. 47. 50. 53. 59. 61. 62. 64. 65. 70. 73. 75. 76. 77. 85. 86. 88. 92. 95. 102. 110. 111. 116. 119. 120. 128. 130. 131. 134. 135. 142. 145.

To the Tunes *of the* 51. Psalme *& of the* 100. *Psalme heretofore vsed*; *& to the* Tunes *of the X* commandements. *Of the* Lamentation *imprinted at the end of the old* Psalmbooke, *& to the* Tune *of the* Songe, *beginning thus.* From Turke & Pope *&c. Being five severall Tunes, may these* Psalmes *be sung.* 1. 2. 6. 14. 16. 19. 20. 21. 27. 28. 30. 32. 34. 38. 41. 45. 49. 51. 52. 54. 56. 63. 66. 69. 72. 79. 81. 83. 84. 89. 90. 91. 96. 98. 99. 100. 101. 103. 109. 112. 114. 117. 121. 136. 139.

To the Tune *of the* Pater noster *at end of the old* Psalmebooke, *may be sung these. Psal.* 5. 9. 17. 33. 39. 40. 48. 57. 87. 94. 118. 105. 122. 123. 233. 137. 149.

To the Tune *of the* 25. Psalme *heretofore: sing these.* 25. 36. 67. 82. 115. 126.

To the Tune *of the* 50. Psalme *heretofore: sing these* 16. 68. 78. 104. 106. 107. 132. 140. 141. 143. 144.

To the Tune *of the* 113. Psalme *heretofore, sing these.* 12. 58. 60. 80. 108. 113.

To the Tune *of the* 122. Psalme *heretofore: sing these.* 13. 55.

To the Tune *of the* 124. Psa. *heretofore: sing these* 71. 74. 91. 124. 129. 138.

To the Tune *of the* 130. Psalme *heretofore:* sing *these,* 39. 100. 127. 150.

To the Tune *of the* 148 *heretofore: sing these.* 113. 146. 147. 148.

The Psalmes *that are* Aphabeticall *are doubly translated, & some few other: One of which* translations *is to be sung to* French Tunes.

www.ingramcontent.com/pod-product-compliance
Lightning Source LLC
Chambersburg PA
CBHW021212270326
41929CB00010B/1101